EXPLORE THE BOOK

THE BOOKS OF J. SIDLOW BAXTER

AWAKE, MY HEART
Daily devotional meditations for the entire year. These readings are "beautifully simple and simply beautiful, profoundly simple and simply profound." — *Evangelical Christian*

GOING DEEPER
A deeply spiritual study on the theme of knowing, loving and serving our Lord Jesus Christ.

HIS PART AND OURS
Enriching exposition and devotional studies in the reciprocal union of Christ and His people. "A truly great book."
— *Moody Monthly*

GOD SO LOVED
A captivating new presentation of John 3:16. Theological, devotional, practical. In two parts — (1) The New Testament Truth, (2) The Old Testament Type.

STUDIES IN PROBLEM TEXTS
Informing, elucidatory and applicatory expositions of certain Scripture passages which have occasioned perplexity.

MARK THESE MEN
Arresting studies in striking aspects of Bible characters with special relevances for our own times and the days ahead.

EXPLORE THE BOOK
A notable work on the Bible; in six handsome volumes of approximately 300 pages each; uniform in size and style with this present volume.

EXPLORE THE BOOK

A Basic and Broadly Interpretative Course
of Bible Study from Genesis to Revelation

J. SIDLOW BAXTER

In Six Volumes

VOLUME TWO
JUDGES TO ESTHER

ZONDERVAN PUBLISHING HOUSE
GRAND RAPIDS, MICHIGAN

This printing — 1962

Printed in the United States of America

CONTENTS OF VOLUME TWO

THE BOOK OF JUDGES (1)

Lesson Number 24

NOTE.—For this study read the whole book of Judges, preferably at one sitting.

The Bible is the chart of history. It affords a panoramic view of the whole course of events from the creation and the fall of man, to the final judgment, and the inauguration of the new heaven and the new earth. It gives us, not events only, but their moral character, tracing the motives of the various actors in the drama, as well as the results of their actions. Events are shown in relation to their causes and effects, and the judgment of God as to their character is revealed. Without the Bible, history would be a spectacle of unknown rivers flowing from unknown sources to unknown seas; but under its guidance we can trace the complex currents to their springs, and see the end from the beginning.

—*Dr. H. Gratton Guinness.*

THE BOOK OF JUDGES (1)

WOULD that we might erase from the tablets of Israel's history the many dark doings and sad happenings which make up the bulk of this seventh book of the canon! But alas, the sin of Israel is written "with a pen of iron and with the point of a diamond." Though Israel wash herself "with nitre" and take "much soap," yet is her iniquity here marked for all time and for all to see. Says Jehovah, long afterwards, through His prophet Jeremiah: "I brought you into a plentiful country, to eat the fruit thereof; but when ye entered ye defiled My land, and made My heritage an abomination" (Jer. ii. 7). As we cannot obliterate the tragic record, let us be quick to learn from it; for although it is such a pathetic anticlimax to the book of Joshua, it is nevertheless one of the richest books of Scripture in the salutary lessons and examples which it contains.

Its Name

The book of Judges obviously takes its name from its contents, which are devoted to the period of Israel's so-called "Judges," and to certain of the Judges themselves. We may say that it covers roughly the first three hundred and fifty years of Israel's history in Canaan. This is the period of the Theocratic regime, in which Jehovah Himself is Israel's "King Invisible."

The four-hundred-year periods of Israel's history are worthy of note just here.

From the Birth of Abram to the Death of
    Joseph in Egypt (the family period)   about 400 years.

From the Death of Joseph to the Exodus
    from Egypt (the tribal period)   .   about 400 years.

From the Exodus to Saul, the first of the
    kings (the Theocracy period).   .   about 400 years.

From Saul to Zedekiah and the Exile (the
    monarchy period)   .   .   .   about 400 years.

The period of the Judges falls in the third of these four-hundred-year periods, that is, the Theocratic. The Theocracy was a glorious experiment with superlative possibilities; and Israel's failure is therefore the more tragic.

Of the Judges as a class Dr. Joseph Angus says: "The Judges (*shophetim*) here described were not a regular succession of governors, but occasional deliverers raised up by God, to rescue Israel from oppression, and to administer justice. Without assuming the state of royal authority, they acted for the time as vicegerents of Jehovah, the invisible King. Their power seems to have been not unlike that of the *Suffetes* of Carthage and Tyre, or of the *Archons* of Athens. The government of the people may be described as a republican confederacy, the elders and princes having authority in their respective tribes."

Nature and Authorship

The records preserved for us in this book of the Judges are, of course, historically *true*; yet manifestly they do not intend to constitute a scientific *history* of the period with which they deal; for the first characteristic of a scientific history is a careful attention to chronology—a characteristic which is markedly missing from the book of Judges. The emphasis here is on the spiritual significance of selected events, not on mere chronological continuity. What we have is a collection of narratives selected because of their bearing on the main design of the book; and it is this purposeful selectivity which explains why such space is devoted to the episodes connected with Deborah, Gideon, Abimelech, and the shameful lapse of Benjamin, while long stretches are passed over in silence. It is this which explains, also, the otherwise strange non-mention of the High Priests in the body of the book, and certain other of its peculiarities. In a word, this book of Judges is not so much concerned with forging a historical chain as with driving home a vital lesson—which we will mention presently.

The authorship of this book is not known, though Jewish tradition attributes it to Samuel. "It seems scarcely open to doubt that the mass of the book consists of the original contemporary annals of the different tribes. The minute and graphic details of the narratives, Deborah's song, Jotham's fable, Jephtha's message to the king of Ammon, the exact description of the great

Parliament at Mizpeh, and many other like portions of the book, must be contemporary documents." Yet at the same time it is equally clear that these original documents were edited and compiled later. It is clear from chapter xviii. 31 and xx. 27, that the compilation took place after the Ark was removed from Shiloh. From the repeated clause: "In those days there was no king in Israel" (xvii. 6; xviii. 1; xix. 1; xxi. 25), we gather that it was made after the commencement of the reign of Saul, the first of the kings. Yet the mention of the Jebusites (i. 21), as dwelling in Jerusalem "unto this day," makes it equally plain that it was before the accession of David (who dispossessed the Jebusites from their stronghold—1 Chron. xi. 5). What could be more probable, then, than that Samuel, who links the two periods of the Judges and the Kings, should have had a large hand in the work as it has come down to us?

The reference, in chapter xviii. 30, to a "captivity of the land," has caused some to argue that the book was not compiled until the deportation of the ten tribes, hundreds of years later; but the other time-data in the book combine against this. The words obviously point to one of the earlier servitudes, in the time of the Judges, and still fresh in the memory of the people.

The original documents of the book, then, are practically contemporaneous with the events recorded; and their compilation into the present form dates somewhere in the reign of King Saul, being effected—as likely as not—by that great Israelite, Samuel; for, as Dr. Ellicott remarks, "The subordination of all the incidents of the history to the inculcation of definite lessons shows that the book, in its present form, was arranged by one person."

Its Picture of Israel

"The moral character of the Israelites, as described in this book, seems to have greatly deteriorated," writes Dr. Angus. "The generation who were contemporaries with Joshua were both courageous and faithful, and free in a great measure from the weakness and obstinacy which had dishonoured their fathers (Judges ii. 7). Their first ardour, however, had now somewhat cooled, and more than once they fell into a state of indifference which Joshua found it needful to rebuke. As each tribe received its portion, they became so engrossed in cultivating it, or so much fonder of ease than of war, that they grew unwilling to help the rest. Another generation arose. Living among idolaters, the Israelites copied their example, intermarried with them, and became contaminated with their abominations (ii. 13; iii. 6). The old inhabitants of the land, left alone, gathered strength to make head against the chosen race: surrounding nations and tribes, as the Syrians, Philistines, Moabites, and Midianites, took advantage of their degeneracy to attack them; while the licentiousness, ease, and idolatry, to which the Hebrews were giving way, impaired their powers of defence."

Its General Significance

The Judges whom God raised up were living object-lessons by which God sought to preserve in Israel the understanding that faith in Jehovah, the only true God, was the one way of victory and well-being. But the people only responded so far as served the selfish end of the moment—the saving of their necks from bondage, and the grabbing of fleshly advantages. They did not *love* Jehovah one whit more for His painstaking patience; nor did they even take the lower level of serving Him from a sense of *duty*. Speaking generally, the God of their fathers was simply a convenient resort in time of extremity. When things were tolerably comfortable, barefaced betrayal of Jehovah was the order of the day. The people chafed under the disciplinary requirements of God's high calling to Israel through Abraham and Moses. They neglected the book of the Covenant, and "turned quickly out of the way" to indulge in the unclean and forbidden.

From time to time, out of sheer pity for His humiliated and groaning people, God raised up these men, the Judges, whose exploits of deliverance—despite vulgarities and crudities in the character and behaviour of the Judges themselves—were so manifestly miraculous interventions of Jehovah, in response to faith in Himself, that Israel was thereby forced to recognise Jehovah again as the one true God, and was thus encouraged to return to the first faith and the first love. Yet these gracious interventions had no durable effect; and Israel's early obstinacy developed into incurable obduracy. So much, alas, for Israel's first three hundred and fifty years in Canaan! It is a pathetic anti-climax to the Book of Joshua.

Its Central Lesson

And *why* this tragic landslide? It is the answering of this question which forms the controlling purpose of this book of Judges. Its intent is to expose the cause and course of Israel's ruining downgrade in such a way as to sting the national conscience into repentant return to Jehovah: and we can well imagine how that great-souled patriot, Samuel, could compile this book with such an end in view. The plan of the book, which we mention below, leaves us in no doubt as to its central lesson. It is—

FAILURE THROUGH COMPROMISE

Every page of the book contributes to the driving home of this central truth. Of course, the exploits of the Judges teach the lesson that a return to the true faith brings renewed victory; yet in their very teaching of this they but accentuate the main, stark reality, that all the failure is due to *compromise.*

How did it all begin? Well, in the opening chapter, we are told that the nine and a half tribes which settled in Canaan did not destroy or even drive out the Canaanite nations, as God had commanded. They suffered them to remain. The other two and a half tribes—Reuben, Gad, and half the tribe of Manasseh, had already sadly compromised in choosing to settle in Gilead, on the eastern side of the Jordan. The first chapter of Judges gives us a list of eight incomplete conquests—by Judah, Benjamin, Manasseh, Ephraim, Zebulun, Asher, Naphtali, and Dan. The other two tribes, Issachar and Simeon, are not mentioned, but the presumption is that their behaviour was like that of the others. Incomplete mastery of an evil at the outset always means constant trouble from it afterwards, and often defeat by it in the end. So was it with Israel. So has it been with others. Let us beware for ourselves! It is no use taking hold of a nettle with a tender hand. It is ruinous folly to try half-measures against sin! The Divine command to Israel was austere, but necessary. Israel allowed quarter to the foe, and lived to rue it.

Next, in the second and third chapters, we find the successive steps of further compromise. Having only partially mastered the Canaanites, Israel now makes leagues with them (ii. 2)—a thing which God has prohibited. Then, having made league with

them, Israel intermarries with them (iii. 6)—another thing God
has prohibited. Then, having mixed blood in marriage, Israel
descends to their ways, bows to their idols, forsakes Jehovah,
and serves Baal and Ashtaroth (ii. 13; iii. 6). Mark well these
stages—incomplete mastery, military leagues, intermarriage,
idolatry and complete apostasy—followed by humiliating captivity (ii. 14, etc.). The Judges who were mercifully raised up to
recall and deliver Israel, stopped the rot for the moment, but it
set in again worse than before as soon as the grave silenced each
Judge's voice; for in chapter ii. 18, 19, we read: "And when
the Lord raised them up Judges, then the Lord was with the
Judge, and delivered them out of the hand of their enemies all
the days of the Judge; for it repented the Lord because of their
groanings by reason of them that oppressed them and vexed
them. And it came to pass when the Judge was dead that they
returned and corrupted themselves *more than their fathers,* in
following other gods to serve them, and to bow down unto them.
They ceased not from their own doings, nor from their stubborn
way."

Yes, this is the tragic story of this book of Judges—*failure
through compromise.* Let the words burn into the mind, and burn
out any easy-going toleration of the unholy or questionable thing.
We can never enjoy God's promised rest for long if we tolerate
only partially crushed sins to continue with us. If we make
league with questionable things because they seem harmless, we
shall soon find ourselves wedded to the desires of the flesh again,
and down from the heights to which God had lifted us.

Failure through compromise! Oh that Israel had heeded the
message of this book! Oh that a compromising Church today
never disregard it! God's word to His people of today is still
that of 2 Corinthians vi. 17, 18—

"WHEREFORE COME OUT FROM AMONG THEM, AND
BE YE SEPARATE, SAITH THE LORD, AND TOUCH NOT THE
UNCLEAN THING, AND I WILL RECEIVE YOU, AND WILL
BE A FATHER UNTO YOU, AND YE SHALL BE MY SONS
AND DAUGHTERS, SAITH THE LORD ALMIGHTY."

THE BOOK OF JUDGES (2)

Lesson Number 25

NOTE.—For this study read the whole book of Judges through again, marking in the main part of the book (chapters iii. to xvi.) the six servitudes beginning with the words, "And the children of Israel did evil in the sight of the Lord."

This, then, is the ground-plan of Judges:

THE BOOK OF JUDGES

THE BOOK OF DECLENSION

FAILURE THROUGH COMPROMISE		
Explanatory Prologue—i.–ii. Main Narrative—iii.–xvi.		
Apostasy	*Servitude*	*Deliverer*
iii. 5–8	To King of Mesopotamia, 8 years.	Othniel (iii. 9–11).
iii. 12–14	To King of Moab, 18 years.	Ehud (iii. 15–30) (also Shamgar, 31).
iv. 1–3	To King of Canaan, 20 years.	Deborah (iv. 4–v. 31) (and Barak).
vi. 1–10	To Midianites, 7 years.	Gideon (vi. 11–viii. 35).
x. 6–18	To Philistines, etc., 18 years.	Jephthah (xi. 1; xii. 7).
xiii. 1	To Philistines, 40 years.	Samson (xiii. 2; xvi. 31).
Illustrative Epilogue—xvii.–xxi.		

THE BOOK OF JUDGES (2)

The Arrangement

THE orderly scheme of this book is in itself such as to argue pretty conclusively its compilation by one person rather than several. The actual records of the Judges run from chapter iii. to chapter xvi.; and it is these chapters which form the body of the book. The other chapters consist of a prologue (i.–ii.), and an epilogue (xvii.–xxi.). The prologue is by way of *explanation*. The epilogue is by way of *illustration*. The prologue explains how the unhappy conditions of the period came about. The epilogue illustrates the conditions themselves. Thus:

> Explanatory Prologue (i.–ii.).
>
> Main Body of Book (iii.–xvi.).
>
> Illustrative Epilogue (xvii.–xxi.).

As for the main body of the book (iii.–xvi.), there can be no mistaking its arrangement. Twelve Judges are successively spoken of—Othniel, Ehud, Shamgar, Deborah (with Barak), Gideon, Tola, Jair, Jephthah, Ibzan, Elon, Abdon, Samson. Of these *six* stand out pre-eminently—because the whole story gathers round six successive apostasies and servitudes of Israel, and these six deliverers, or judges, who wrought deliverance. The six are: Othniel, Ehud, Deborah, Gideon, Jephthah, and Samson. The six major apostasies are signalised, in each case, by the words: *"And the children of Israel did evil in the sight of the Lord."* Just the six times do these words occur in the body of this book; and in each case judgment falls, and servitude ensues.

It is a striking fact that all these six servitudes of Israel are said to have been brought about *by Jehovah Himself*. First—"The anger of the Lord was hot against Israel, and *HE* sold them into the hand of Chushan-rishathaim, King of Mesopotamia" (iii. 8). Second—"The *LORD* strengthened Eglon, King of Moab, against Israel" (iii. 12). Third—"The *LORD* sold them into the

Jabin, King of Canaan" (iv. 2). Four—"The LORD
them into the hand of Midian seven years" (vi. 1).
he anger of the Lord was hot against Israel, and HE
into the hands of the Philistines" (x. 7). Six—"The
LORD delivered them into the hands of the Philistines forty
years" (xiii. 1).

Israel's servitudes were not just accidents. They were punish-
ments. This is a point for serious consideration. God may confer
special privileges on certain persons and nations, but He is no
respecter of persons in any sense of indulgence to favourites.
Those who sin against extra privilege bear heavier responsibility
and incur heavier penalty. God may give many privileges, but
He never gives the privilege to *sin*. Let us beware lest a sense
of privilege should beguile our own hearts into the sin of presumption.

As we read this book of Judges we may well feel amazed that
such low living could go with such high calling. Yes—high
calling and low living! A convention chairman once said: "It
is possible to be moral without being spiritual: and it is even
possible to be spiritual without being moral!" Paradoxical?
Impossible? Yet have we not come across persons knowing the
deeper and higher truths of the Christian life, able to converse
freely in a most spiritual vein, and who, nevertheless, could stoop
to behaviour that the average non-Christian would shrink from
in disgust? It is only too easy for familiarity to engender callousness, and then for callousness to be hypocritically covered with
an outer garment of seeming spirituality. We must watch and
pray, lest we ourselves enter into this temptation.

A Strikingly Sustained Emphasis

The main narrative of Judges is remarkable for a striking fourfold emphasis which it sustains throughout. The six apostasies,
servitudes, and deliverances are each set out in this quadruple
order:

SINNING.

SUFFERING.

SUPPLICATION.

SALVATION.

This will be seen with ease and clearness if we set out the six episodes in parallel columns, in the actual words and the actual order of the Scripture narrative.

It is worth while for us to get the fourfold sequence vividly in our minds, for it has living applications to our own times. It may be that so far as Israel is concerned, the long period of sinning and suffering is now forever drawing to a close, and the prophesied age-end supplication and salvation drawing near.

The Six Episodes

	First iii. 7–11.	*Second* iii. 12–30.	*Third* iv. 1–v. 31.
Sin . . .	" And the children of Israel did evil in the sight of the Lord, and forgat the Lord their God, and served Baalim and the groves . . ."	" And the children of Israel did evil again in the sight of the Lord . . ."	" And the children of Israel again did evil in the sight of the Lord when Ehud was dead . . ."
Suffering .	" Therefore the anger of the Lord was hot against Israel, and He sold them into the hand of Cushan-risha-thaim, King of Mesopotamia ; and the children of Israel served Cushan-rishathaim eight years . . ."	" And the Lord strengthened Eglon the King of Moab against · Israel, because they had done evil in the sight of the Lord ; and he gathered unto him the children of Ammon and Amalek, and went and smote Israel, and possessed the city of palm trees. So the children of Israel served Eglon the King of Moab eighteen years . . ."	" And the Lord sold them into the hand of Jabin, King of Canaan, that reigned in Hazor ; the captain of whose host was Sisera, which dwelt in Harosheth of the Gentiles . . ."
Supplication	" And when the children of Israel cried unto the Lord . . ."	" But when the children of Israel cried unto the Lord . . ."	" And the children of Israel cried unto the Lord ; for he had nine hundred chariots of iron ; and twenty years he mightily oppressed the children of Israel . . ."
Salvation .	" The Lord raised up a deliverer to the children of Israel, who delivered them, even Othniel the son of Kenaz, Caleb's younger brother," etc.	" The Lord raised them up a deliverer, Ehud the son of Gera, a Benjamite, a man left-handed," etc.	" And Deborah, a prophetess, she judged Israel at that time, . . . and she sent and called Barak, the son of Abinoam," etc.

	Fourth vi. 1–viii. 35.	*Fifth* x. 6–xii. 7.	*Sixth* xiii. 1–xvi. 31.
Sin . . .	" And the children of Israel did evil in the sight of the Lord . : ."	" And the children of Israel did evil again in the sight of the Lord, and served Baalim and Ashtaroth and the gods of Syria, and the gods of Zidon, and the gods of Moab, and the gods of the children of Ammon, and the gods of the Philistines, and forsook the Lord, and served not Him . . ."	" And the children of Israel did evil again in the sight of the Lord, . . ."
Suffering .	" And the Lord delivered them into the hand of Midian seven years . . ."	" And the anger of the Lord was hot against Israel, and He sold them into the hands of the Philistines, and into the hands of the children of Ammon . . ."	" And the Lord delivered them into the hand of the Philistines forty years . . ."
Supplication	" And the children of Israel cried unto the Lord: And it came to pass when the children of Israel cried unto the Lord because of the Midianites . . ."	" And the children of Israel cried unto the Lord, saying: We have sinned against Thee, both because we have forsaken our God, and also served Baalim ; . . . Deliver us only, we pray Thee, this day . . ."	No supplication recorded, — evidently because they had said, in their last extremity : " Deliver us *only*, we pray Thee, *this* day " (see former column).
Salvation .	" And there came an angel of the Lord, and sat under an oak which was in Ophrah that pertained unto Joash the Abiezrite ; and his son Gideon threshed wheat by the winepress, to hide it from the Midianites . . . the Spirit of the Lord came upon Gideon," etc.	" Then the Spirit of the Lord came upon Jephthah, and he passed over Gilead, and Manasseh, and passed over Mizpeh of Gilead . . . thus the children of Ammon were subdued before the children of Israel," etc.	" The angel of the Lord appeared and said . . . he (Samson) shall begin to deliver Israel out of the hand of the Philistines." (Here follows the account of Samson and his exploits.)

This recurrent emphasis is meant to do its own work in the reader's mind. Let us read, mark, learn, and inwardly digest. There are things in the moral realm which are indissolubly wedded. Sin and suffering always go together. They cannot be divorced. Oh that human hearts might be persuaded of this! It is also true that supplication and salvation are similarly joined. God will be entreated by a true supplication in which there is a putting away of the evil thing; and then He will show His salvation.

GIDEON—AND HOW HE STILL SPEAKS

Some of the characters depicted in this book of Judges are worthy of careful study. We pick out Gideon for brief mention here, to show how these characters speak to us today.

Gideon, the fifth Judge of Israel, is rightly counted as one of the outstanding heroes in Israel's early history. Yet we need to realise at the outset that his heroism was not a product of his natural make-up, but the outcome of a transforming spiritual experience. It is this which gives him a living significance to ourselves today.

When first we see Gideon he cuts a pathetic figure of unbelief (vi. 11–23). He is a furtive, nervous young man secretly threshing wheat in the winepress, to hide it from the marauding Midianites. What pathetic exclamations of unbelief escape his lips when the Lord suddenly appears as a Mighty One of valour!—for undoubtedly the reading of verse 12 as "The Lord is with thee, even the Lord mighty in valour" is the correct one, and not that which makes Gideon the mighty one of valour instead of the Lord (as does our English version). Mark unconverted Gideon's reactions. He gasps—"Oh, my Lord, if Jehovah be with us, why then is all this befallen us? And where be all His miracles which our fathers told us of, saying: Did not Jehovah bring us up out of Egypt? But now Jehovah hath forsaken us . . ." A rather dismal reception this!—"Oh! . . . if . . . why? . . . where? . . . but . . ." Verse 14 continues, "And Jehovah looked upon him and said: Go in this thy might, and thou shalt save Israel from the hand of the Midianites: have not *I* sent thee?" These were strong and reassuring words, but Gideon can only moan, "Oh, my Lord, wherewith shall *I* save Israel . . .?" The Lord replies still further, "*Surely* I will be with thee, and thou shalt smite the Midianites as one man." Yet even this only evokes another stammering "if"—"If now I have found grace in Thy sight, then *show me a sign.*" To be sure, in these replies of Gideon we have a fair sample of the vocabulary of unbelief. In his successive exclamations and lamentations we have the sceptical *surprise* of unbelief, then its *uncertainty* and its *questioning* and its *complaining* and its *false humility* and its *resourcelessness* and its *persistent dubiety* and its *seeking for signs.* Unconverted Gideon presents a sorry picture of the paralysis which always accompanies unbelief.

Gideon's Transformation

But now look at Gideon's transforming experience. In the first place he became *converted.* We use the word thoughtfully. By the time that the "Angel of the Lord" had completed his visit to him he had become quite convinced regarding the true God of Israel. Note verse 24, "Then Gideon built an altar there unto the Lord, and called it *Jehovah-Shalom.*" There is vital significance about that altar. The altar is ever the place where God and man meet. It is the outward symbol of an inward transaction between the human soul and God. When Gideon built that altar to Jehovah he turned his back on false gods and became a worshipper of the one true God. Moreover he gave that altar a significant name—*Jehovah-Shalom,* which means, "Jehovah my peace." For the first time in his life this young Hebrew came into a sense of peace. That is always a first product of true conversion.

But Gideon went further. He became *consecrated.* He yielded his own will to the will of God. Read verses 25–7. We only need to think our way back into the circumstances a little, to appreciate what an acute challenge to Gideon's new faith and obedience this test was. The command that he should "throw down the altar of Baal" reminds us at once that Gideon lived in a time of widespread religious apostasy. Israel's religious leaders were "modernists," and had caused the people to err. To wreck Baal's altar was to run counter to the popular will, and to invite death. But Gideon did it. And how remarkable was the result! Read again verses 28–32. Gideon's father became converted too! Maybe the old man had secretly sighed for the "good old ways" and had longed for some brave champion of the old-time faith to arise and call his fellow-countrymen back to Jehovah; and now, when his son stood up for the old-time faith Joash was immediately by his side. We may apply this to ourselves. In nine cases out of ten, the reason we have so little influence for Christ among our own kith and kin is that we ourselves are not prepared to go the length of full consecration to the will of God.

Finally, Gideon became *controlled*, by which we mean that he became controlled by the Spirit of God. See verse 34, "The Spirit of the Lord came upon Gideon; and he blew a trumpet, and Abi-ezer was gathered after him." He became at once a leader and a saviour of his people. The people recognised the transforming power of God in him, and flocked to him when he sounded his clarion. The story which follows in the Scripture account tells of Gideon's marvellous victory over Midian, and his freeing of Israel from the alien yoke.

What a transformation had now taken place in Gideon! The man who had first been converted and had then become consecrated had now become controlled by the Holy Spirit. That thirty-fourth verse is noteworthy. A near translation would be: "The Spirit of Jehovah *clothed Himself* with Gideon." Gideon's personality became, so to speak, a garment in which God moved among men. What a sermon, then, is this man to us! Like Abel, "he being dead, yet speaketh." This soul-saving, life-changing, character-transforming experience through which he passed may be known by ourselves—not in its outward accidentals, of course, but in its inward essentials. *We* may become truly converted to God, truly consecrated to His will, and really controlled by the Holy Spirit. And we may be taken up and used by God as definitely as Gideon was. Converted, consecrated, Spirit-controlled!—God grant that it may be true of ourselves! We must get our eyes away from doubt-provoking circumstances, and fix them on the word of God Himself. "Faithful is He that calleth you, who also will do it" (I Thess. v. 24).

> Doubt sees the obstacles,
>   Faith sees the way.
> Doubt sees the darksome night,
>   Faith sees the day.
> Doubt dreads to take the step,
>   Faith soars on high.
> Doubt whispers, "Who believes?"
>   Faith answers—"I."

THE BOOK OF RUTH (1)

Lesson Number 26

NOTE.—For this study read the book of Ruth right through at one
sitting.

This is one of the richest rewards of truly knowing the Scriptures.
No other book proves such an exhaustless mine of precious treasures
to those who are content to delve deep into it. It is a field for endless
study and ceaseless discovery; and the humblest believer may find hid
treasure never before dug up by any other, and therefore peculiarly
his own. No more unanswerable proof of the Divine origin of the Bible
can be found than this capacity to reveal to every devout reader something absolutely new.

—*Arthur T. Pierson, D.D.*

THE BOOK OF RUTH (i)

PRICELESS gems have often been found in unlikely places. Many a choice flower has been found blooming in a rocky crevice. Rainbow artistries have suddenly lit up the drabbest skies. Beauty spots have charmed the traveller at surprise turns on the least-promising road. It is even so with this superbly beautiful little idyl, the book of Ruth.

It opens with the words: "Now it came to pass in the days when the judges ruled . . ."; so that its story clearly belongs to the period covered by the book of Judges—a tragic period indeed, as we have seen. Yet so touchingly beautiful is this episode, centring in Naomi and Ruth and Boaz, that it comes as a kind of redeeming contrast after our painful reading in the book of Judges. Such a lovely story we should least expect in such a setting.

The book of Judges leaves us with the all-too-well-founded conviction that the general condition was one of moral deterioration: but the book of Ruth turns a new sidelight on the scene, and shows us that amid the general degeneracy there were instances of noble love and godly chivalry and high ideal. Truly, the story is a silver star in an inky sky, a glorious rose blooming amid desert aridness, a pure gem flashing amid foul debris, a breath of fragrance amid surrounding sterility.

But it is still more. If this one instance of godly chivalry was picked out by the anonymous author, and committed to written form (maybe because of its special connection with David and the throne), may we not reasonably suppose that it represents many other such instances amid the surrounding decline, which were never recorded, and of which we know nothing? There is truth in Alexander Maclaren's word that "the blackest times were not so dismal in reality as they look in history."

This little biographical episode is given in the form of a *story*. It is a series of pastoral idyls, or pen-and-ink sketches with a rural background, showing the noble devotion of a young Moabitish

widow for her widowed Hebrew mother-in-law, and the
providential reward by which her self-sacrificing devotion was
afterward crowned.

It is a *true* story. Its transparent simplicity bespeaks its
honesty. It tells of actual happenings, and of real persons whose
names figure in real genealogical records. Dr. James Morison
says: "The material of the story is of such a nature that its
unreality, if it had not been honest, would at once have been
detected and exposed. The stuff out of which the story is woven
consisted, so to speak, of very sensitive filaments. It had to do
with the genealogy of the royal family. The principal personages
in the story were ancestors of king David. That there was a
Moabitish link in the chain of his genealogy must have been well
known to the king himself, and to all his household, and to a
large proportion of the people of Israel in general. It must likewise have been well known that this Moabitish link did not lie
far back in the line. The existence of such a link was too great
a peculiarity to be treated with indifference. We cannot doubt
that the whole history of the case would be a frequent topic
of narration, conversation, and comment at once within and
around the royal court. The probability, therefore, is that the
writer would be careful to do no violence to the facts of the case.
Any alloy of fiction or romance on such a subject would have
been at once resented, alike by the royal family, and by the
great body of the people, the devoted admirers of the king."

Its Unique Features

This is one of the only two books in Scripture which bear the
names of women. Those two are Ruth and Esther; and they
stand in marked contrast. Ruth is a young Gentile woman who
is brought to live among Hebrews and marries a Hebrew husband
in the line of royal David. Esther is a young Hebrew woman who
is brought to live among Gentiles and marries a Gentile husband
on the throne of a great empire. Both Ruth and Esther were
great and good women. The book of Ruth, however, is quite
alone in this, that it is the only instance in the Bible in which
a whole book is devoted to a woman.

The book of Ruth is a *love* story; and no doubt one of its purposes is to extol virtuous love, and to show how it can overcome

all alienations and prejudices. But the remarkable thing is that it is not the story of a romantic love between a young man and a young woman; it is—as Dr. Samuel Cox says—"the story of a woman's love for a woman; and, strangely as it would sound in the ears of our modern wits, it is the story of a young wife's passionate and devoted love for her mother-in-law!"

Another striking feature about this book is its *catholicity of outlook*. The three pivotal figures in the book are Naomi, Ruth, and Boaz. All three are lovely characters; yet, somehow, without in the least detracting from the other two, Ruth excels, and with each new turn of the story the author deftly emphasises that Ruth is the heroine here, despite the fact that, unlike the other two, she is not of Israel. When we think of the jealous exclusiveness of the old-time Jews, it is remarkable to find this ungrudging portrayal of Moabitess Ruth as the focus of admiration. She is seen to excel even Israel's daughters; yet this occasions not the slightest resentment, but the admiration which it merits. That the grace and virtue of Moab's sweet-spirited daughter should have had such frank recognition speaks well for the author himself. The whole story is written in a spirit of charity and catholicity. "It is fair, and even generous, in the tone it takes toward those who were outside the Hebrew pale. It has no word of blame for Elimelech, although he left the land of his fathers to sojourn among the heathen; nor for Orpah, although she turned back from Naomi; on the contrary it records her kindness and self-devotion in at least intending to remain with her 'mother' till Naomi herself dissuaded her; while for Ruth it has no praise too high. It bases itself on the truth which Christ has made the common property of the race, that in every nation a pure and unselfish love is acceptable to God. So far from asserting the exclusive privilege of the chosen people, it rather invites other races to come and put their trust under the wings of Jehovah, by showing that as soon as they trust in Him the privilege and blessings of Israel become theirs."

Again, it is striking that this young Moabitess, Ruth, should not only have married so honourably in Israel, but have actually become the great-grandmother of David (as the closing verses show) and one of the mothers in the line from which the Messiah should eventually come. Ruth is one of the four women who are mentioned in the Messianic line. The other three—Tamar,

Rahab, and Bath-sheba, recall unworthy conduct; but virtuous Ruth redeems them.

A careful examination of the line from Adam down to the birth of Jesus shows that there were some sixty generations, and that these sixty seem to go in six tens, with the tenth man in each case being singularly representative of some great truth concerning the coming Messiah. Take the first group of ten:

Adam,	Jared,
Seth,	Enoch,
Enos,	Methuselah,
Cainan,	Lamech,
Mahalaleel,	*NOAH.*

Noah is the tenth man. As Satan had tried to cut off the Messianic hope at the very gateway of human history, by the murder of Abel, so now in Noah's day, behind the utter corruption of the race generally, he seeks to thwart it; but amid the corruption there is one man who walks with God and is clean in his generations (Gen. vi. 9); and when the whole race is destroyed there is the exception of this one man and his family; and this man is the very one in whom the Messianic line runs. All the power of Satan, and all the sin of men, cannot frustrate the purpose of the Lord God. Now take the second ten:

Shem,	Reu,
Arphaxad,	Serug,
Salah,	Nahor,
Eber,	Terah,
Peleg,	*ABRAHAM.*

Abraham is the tenth man here. Abraham is the one picked out to become the father of the chosen people from whom the Messiah should come. To him God specially reveals Himself, and gives unconditional promises which He later confirms with an oath. Now take the third ten:

Isaac,	Ram,
Jacob,	Amminadab,
Judah,	Nahshon,
Pharez,	Salma,
Hezron,	*BOAZ.*

Boaz is the tenth man here. And what of Boaz? Well, that is
what our priceless little book of Ruth tells us (and may we not
now be touching one of the deeper significances in the writing of
the book of Ruth?). It was Boaz who took Gentile Ruth into the
Davidic ancestry and the Messianic line; and as Ruth passes
into that line she representatively takes all the Gentiles with her,
so that now both Jews and Gentiles share common hope in the
coming of Him who was to be "a Light to lighten the Gentiles,
and the Glory of His people Israel." (The other "tenth" men
will be mentioned later). Yes, Ruth belongs to us all, as, even
more, does that wonderful Saviour who came, in the fulness of
time, of that lineage in which Ruth shines like a gentle star.

> What star of Messianic truth
> More beautiful than Gentile Ruth?
> In her the Gentiles find a place
> To share the hope of Judah's race;
> Now see from royal David's line
> One hope for Jew and Gentile shine!

When it was Written

Most probably this little book was written during the reign of
David—as the following considerations suggest. (1) The opening
verse says: "Now it came to pass in the days when the Judges
ruled. . . ." This indicates that the book was written *after* the
days of the Judges, for the writer is plainly looking back on a
time that had gone. (2) In chapter iv. 7, the writer speaks of a
custom which prevailed in Israel "in former time"; so that the
book, besides having been written after the time of the Judges,
must have been written long enough after the time it writes of
to allow this little custom to drop into disuse—for the fact that
the writer stays to explain the custom shows that it *had* fallen
into disuse. (3) The genealogy at the end of the last chapter is
carried down to David, and stops there (see iv. 17–22). But *why*
should it stop there if written *later* than David's time? and how
could it even *mention* David if written *before* David's time?
(4) The time of David's reign would be about *long enough* afterward to allow for the little custom in the earlier or mid period of
the Judges to fall out of use (say 100 to 150 years), which is made
clear by the fact that David, the seventh son of Jesse, was great-
grandson of Boaz, and reigned, therefore, between 100 and 150

years after the happenings described in the book of Ruth; while on the other hand the time of David's reign would not be *too* long afterward to be out of keeping with the intimacy of detail shown in the book concerning persons and incidents which would have faded from memory in times *later* than that of David. (5) The Davidic reign was a literary epoch in Hebrew history. The king himself was a man of letters, and would draw literary men around him. David was also a man of deep human sympathies, and would be much interested in the recent Moabite connection with his ancestry. Moreover, he was too free from Jewish narrowness to be ashamed of his Moabitish link (especially in view of I Samuel xxii. 3–4); rather, indeed, would not David's chivalrous soul be proud of a link with such an one as Ruth? We conclude that as the book of Judges was probably written in David's time, so this choice little addition, which concerns the same period, was written then too.

And now, in anticipation of our next lesson, here is a simple outline of the book of Ruth.

THE BOOK OF RUTH

The love that suffers reigns at last
Chapter i. LOVE'S RESOLVE: (*Ruth's noble choice*). RUTH THE FAITHFUL DAUGHTER—cleaves to Naomi in her sorrow.
,,   ii. LOVE'S RESPONSE: (*Ruth's lowly service*). RUTH THE MOABITESS GLEANER—responds to Naomi's pressing need.
,,   iii. LOVE'S REQUEST: (*Ruth's tender appeal*). RUTH THE VIRTUOUS SUPPLIANT—appeals to the chivalrous kinsman.
,,   iv. LOVE'S REWARD: (*Ruth's marital joys*). RUTH THE BELOVED WIFE AND MOTHER—joys in the blissful consummation.

THE BOOK OF RUTH (2)

Lesson Number 27

NOTE.—For this further study in the book of Ruth read the entire story again twice through, checking off the analysis which we have given at the end of the preceding study.

When the last day is ended,
 And the nights are through;
When the last sun is buried
 In its grave of blue;
When the stars are quenched as candles,
 And the seas no longer fret;
When the winds unlearn their cunning,
 And the storms forget;
When the last lip is palsied,
 And the last prayer said,
Love shall reign immortal
 While the worlds lie dead.
 —*Anon.*

THE BOOK OF RUTH (2)

The Story

Chapter i.

SOMEWHERE in the period of the Judges a famine befell Canaan, and was felt even in such fertile districts as that around Bethlehem. Under its stress, Elimelech, a Hebrew with an inheritance in the Bethlehem locality, sought temporary refuge in the land of Moab, taking with him his wife, Naomi, and their two sons, Mahlon and Chilion. We gather that they were a godly family; and no doubt it would cost them painful cogitation before they decided to go and seek sustenance among the idolatrous Moabites. Yet they went; and without doubt they did wrong in abandoning the covenant land of Israel and their place among the elect people. Israel knew that famine was only inflicted for default (Lev. xxvi., etc.).

They reached Moab, but fared ill; for in seeking a livelihood they forfeited life itself. They sought bread but found graves. First Elimelech died; then his fatherless sons married Moabite women (another forbidden thing—Deut. vii. 3, etc.); and soon afterwards these sons themselves were laid beneath the soil of Moab, leaving their two young widows with the already widowed mother, Naomi.

Ten years have now slipped away. Naomi hears of bounty in the old home-country, and resolves to return. Her two daughters-in-law have grown to love her, and wish to go with her. They have learned of the true God in Naomi's household. The love is mutual. They set off with Naomi, but under her kindly dissuasion the one, Orpah, decides to retrace her steps to Moab. Ruth, however, has grown so to love Naomi that she is prepared to forgo everything for widowed Naomi's sake; and, in one of the purest gems of noble utterance, assures her beloved mother-in-law of her own resolve so to cleave unto her that nought but death itself should part them:—

"Intreat me not to leave thee, nor to return from following after thee: for whither thou goest I will go, and where thou lodgest I

35

*will lodge; thy people shall be my people, and thy God my God.
Where thou diest will I die, and there will I be buried. The
Lord do so to me, and more also, if ought but death part thee
and me."* √ 16

To appreciate the meaning of Ruth's self-sacrificing love here,
we need to perceive the significance in Naomi's urging the two
younger women to return to the shelter of their own parents'
homes. See verses 8 and 9—"Go, return each to her mother's
house. The Lord deal kindly with you, as ye have dealt with
the dead, and with me. The Lord grant you that ye may find
rest, each of you in the house of her husband."

Note that word "rest"—"The Lord grant you that ye may
find *REST*, each of you in the house of her husband." The
Hebrew word so translated is *menuchah*. It signifies rest, not so
much in the ordinary sense, as rather in the sense of *a safe shelter*.
This is the word by which the Hebrews used to speak of a husband's house. It was a woman's *menuchah*, or safe resort. In
the ancient Orient the position of unmarried women and young
widows was perilous. The one place where they could find safety
and respect was in the house of a husband. This alone was a
woman's safe shelter from servitude, neglect, or licence.

Now it was this fact that Naomi had in mind when she urged
the return of Orpah and Ruth to seek safety, respect, and honour,
in their parents' homes, and then in "the house of a husband."
Naomi has no more sons who can husband Orpah and Ruth, as
she sadly tells them. If they accompany her back to Israel, there
is utterly no prospect for them, nor is there even the guarantee
of safety. If they stay in Moab there is good prospect of their
finding a husband's shelter; but there is no such prospect if they
travel to Canaan, for the Hebrew sons are forbidden by the law
to marry aliens. Certainly we need feel no censure toward Orpah
in her eventually deciding to remain in Moab.

But see the glorious love of Ruth. Knowing the cost full well,
she will gladly give up all, and suffer all, for Naomi!

And so Naomi returns home—with Moabitess Ruth; and "all
the city was moved about them, and they said: Is this Naomi?"
Thus ends the first chapter, and the first scene.

Chapter ii.

With chapter ii. comes *scene* 2, and it is touchingly beautiful. Naomi is so destitute that she must allow Ruth to go even as a poverty-stricken gleaner among the roughish reapers, to fetch home at least some little for food. With beautiful self-forgetfulness Ruth goes to the fields, only too willing to make this somewhat humiliating yet honest effort after sustenance. She is providentially guided to a field of Boaz, a wealthy kinsman of Naomi. Every recorded word and act of Boaz reveal his manly piety and kindliness. He is impressed by the charm and modesty of the graceful gleaner, and, after enquiring about her, is only too glad to extend special privileges and protection to her for the full duration of the harvest, so that she may eat and drink with his reapers, and glean a goodly portion, being safeguarded the while from any improper freedom on the part of the young men. Ruth returns with the first day's welcome load to Noami, who at once perceives the hand of God in what has happened. So Ruth continues her gleaning, throughout the barley and wheat harvests, in the fields of Boaz.

Chapter iii.

Chapter iii. gives the crisis. It reads strangely to westerners, and should be carefully understood. Harvesting is ended. The daily interviews with Boaz are over. An attachment has developed between Boaz and Ruth, yet the wealthy kinsman has not taken any practical step about it. Naomi detects the sadness that creeps over Ruth's tender spirit, and contrives a plan to find out what the intention of Boaz is, so as to bring things to a head. The expedient was in full accord with old-time Hebrew custom and the teaching of the Mosaic Law. There is not the faintest touch of impurity about it. The Mosaic statute ran—"If brethren dwell together, and one of them die, and have no child, the wife of the dead shall not marry without unto a stranger; her husband's brother shall take her to him to wife, and perform the duty of an husband's brother unto her. And it shall be that the firstborn which she beareth shall succeed in the name of his brother which is dead, that his name be not put out of Israel" (Deut. xxv. 5, 6).

Now when Naomi sent Ruth to Boaz, as described in this chapter, she was really appealing to him to honour this Israelite law, and thus, at the same time, give a husband's shelter to Ruth, and honour the name of Mahlon, her deceased Hebrew husband. Boaz clearly understood this, as his noble words shew (iii. 10-13).

Notice how both Ruth and Boaz use that word "*kinsman.*" Ruth says: "Thou art a near kinsman." Boaz replies: "It is true that I am thy near kinsman: howbeit, there is a kinsman nearer than I." This word "kinsman," in the Hebrew, is *goel*; and the Hebrew law of the *goel*, or next-of-kin, is of great interest. This law is laid down in Leviticus xxv.; Numbers xxxv.; Deuteronomy xix. and xxv. There were three obligations devolving upon the *goel*:

(1) He was to redeem his brother and his brother's inheritance, according to ability, if poverty had compelled his brother to go into slavery, or to dispose of his land.

(2) He was to be the avenger of any fatal violence against his brother.

(3) He was to raise up a successor to his brother, if his brother had died without leaving a son.

The obvious purpose behind all this was the saving of Israelitish families, as such, from extinction. The *goel's* qualification was that he must be the *next* of kin, or a *near* kinsman. Each near kinsman was *one* of the "goelim"; but he who was actually the *next* of kin was distinctively *the* "goel."

Coming back, now, to this third chapter of Ruth, with this law of the *goel* in mind, we should also observe understandingly how far removed from our modern western ideas are the simple, rustic ways and surroundings in which this scene is set. As Dr. Samuel Cox truly says—"An age in which the wealthy owner of a large and fertile estate would himself winnow barley and would sleep among the heaps of winnowed corn in an open threshing floor (verse 7), is obviously an age as different from this as it is remote from it. Moreover, Ruth, in creeping softly to the resting-place of Boaz, and nestling under the corner of his long robe (verse 7), was simply making a legal claim in the approved manner of the time." When Ruth said, "spread thy skirt over thine handmaid," Boaz fully understood the appeal of widowed

Ruth for protection, as the casting of the outward garment over the bride's head was a customary ceremony at old-time eastern marriages, in token of the husbandly protection thenceforward given to the bride.

This then is what happens: Boaz wakes and finds Ruth present. For a moment he is taken aback, but, on hearing Ruth's words, sympathetically appreciates the situation. His gracious reply (verses 10–13), reveals both his own honourableness and that of Ruth. And now the two reasons are disclosed why he had not proposed wedlock to Ruth—(1) his considerable seniority in years; (2) his not being the *nearest* kinsman. It may be also that a third reason had been in the mind of Boaz, namely, that Naomi, the wife of Ruth's deceased father-in-law, really had the prior claim on him; though now, by this very act of sending Ruth, Naomi had waived her claim in Ruth's favour, The "six measures of barley" which Ruth took home next morning told Naomi that the honourable Boaz would lose no time in taking the appropriate steps.

Chapter iv.

Chapter iv. crowns the story. Boaz, without delay, contracts with the nearer kinsman, in the presence of elders and witnesses, and, according to custom, at the city gate. This anonymous kinsman admits his obligation, and is willing to buy the land which was Elimelech's, but declines when he learns that in so doing he must also take a *Moabitess* to be his wife, his objection being—"lest I mar mine own inheritance." His view would be that Mahlon and Chilion had broken the law in marrying alien women, and that the calamities which had befallen them and Naomi were due to this, and would come to himself if he married one of these widowed women. So he handed over his right to Boaz, publicly acknowledging this by the old-time custom of plucking off his shoe, and handing it to Boaz—a custom which originated in the fact that men took legal possession of landed property by planting their foot, or shoe, on the soil. The elders and witnesses in the gate then cried, "We are witnesses."

To Boaz, Ruth was far more precious than the land. She became his wife, and by him became the mother of a son who in turn became the father of Jesse, who in turn became the father of David, Israel's greatest king. As for Naomi, her joy was brimful. She became the babe's nurse—and never did babe have tenderer nurse or sweeter mother; while the women of the place said to Naomi: "Thy daughter-in-law, which loveth thee, is better to thee than seven sons."

Thus, this story which begins with famine, death, and mourning, ends with fulness, new life, and rejoicing. Weeping has endured for a night, but joy has come with the morning. The sad beginning has given place to a sweet and beautiful ending. With a voice of gentle reassurance this precious little book of Ruth calls to us from the bygone, telling us that *the love which "suffereth long and is kind" never fails of its reward in the end.*

Typical Aspects

A careful reading through this book of Ruth seems to show that there is a latent typical meaning hidden in it, which develops as the story itself develops. The very names which occur in the story put us on the track of this; and once we get on the track we can easily follow it right through.

The story opens at Bethlehem, the name of which means "House of Bread" (*Beyth* = house; *lechem* = bread). The first-mentioned figure is *Elimelech*, whose name means "My God is King," or "My God is my King" (*Eli* = my God; *melech* = king). This Israelite, along with his wife *Naomi*, whose name means "pleasantness," or "favour," leaves Bethlehem in the land of Israel, because of famine, and seeks succour in the alien land of Moab. The names of their two sons, whom they take with them are *Mahlon* (joy, or song) and *Chilion* (ornament, or perfectness). Under testing they forsake the place of covenant standing, and resort to an expedient involving compromise. In Moab, Elimelech (my God is my King) dies; so do Mahlon (song) and Chilion (perfectness). After ten tragic years Naomi, the pathetic remnant, returns; but instead of being Naomi (pleasantness, sweetness, favour), she is, by her own testimony, *Mara* (bitterness).

Now if this is not a striking type-picture of Israel we are much deceived. Israel as originally constituted in Canaan was a Theocracy. God was Israel's King. Israel was Elimelech—and could say "My God is my King." Israel was married, as it were, to Naomi—pleasantness, favour, and blessing; and Israel's offspring were Mahlon and Chilion—song and perfectness. But, under testing, Israel compromised and went astray, leaving the early allegiance to Jehovah. Elimelech died. No longer could Israel say with a perfect heart before the Lord—"My God is my King." Mahlon and Chilion passed away too—the "song" of praise and the "ornament" of devout godliness died off; while eventually Naomi, the once "favoured" and "pleasant" returns, a sorry remnant, "empty" and "bitter," as in the days when the remnant returned, under Ezra and Nehemiah.

But from the point of Naomi's return, Ruth ("comeliness") takes the prominent place; and Ruth is a type of the *Church*. The type-picture is made up of three scenes—(1) Ruth in the harvest field, (2) Ruth in the threshing floor, (3) Ruth in the home of Boaz.

First we see the Ruth who gleans in the harvest field, the alien, poor and destitute; having no part or lot in Israel, or in the covenant of promise, yet seeking refuge under the wing of Jehovah, God of Israel, and begging kindness at the hand of the gracious, wealthy Boaz. The name, Boaz, means "In him is strength"; and surely Boaz, the strong, the wealthy, the noble, the gracious, is here a type of Christ, as he looks on the Gentile Ruth with generous favour and with tender love toward her.

Second, we see the Ruth who, having no hope in anyone other than Boaz, goes to the threshing floor, risking everything, believing in his kindness, staking her all on his honour and grace and his power to redeem; coming to him poor and friendless, yet loving him because he had first loved her; lying at his feet, praying the shelter of his name, asking the protection of his arm, seeking the provision which only his love could give; and finding in him more than hope had dared to expect.

Third, we see the Ruth who, having been graciously received by redeemer-Boaz, becomes united to him as his wife, shares with him his life, his home, and all his wealth and joys.

We think it does not require any very acute insight to perceive in all this a beautiful consistency of type-teaching concerning Christ and the Church. Perhaps the emphasis is slightly more on the Ruth aspect of things; yet the type parallels are quite definitely there in the case of Boaz. In acting as redeemer, Boaz must exhibit the three main and indispensable qualifications: that is, he must have the *right* to redeem; he must have the *power* to redeem; and he must have the *will* to redeem. Christ, as *our* "Goel," or Kinsman-Redeemer, has the right as our true Kinsman, and the power as the Son of God, and the gracious willingness. Nor has our heavenly Boaz merely redeemed for us the forfeited estate of Elimelech—an earthly possession; He has made us His bride, to share for ever with Him His life, His home, His wealth, and His eternal joys. In Him we boast more blessings than our father Adam lost for us!

But who is that *unnamed kinsman* who would *not* redeem (iv. 6)? I think the answer may be suggested to us if we read over again those words which occur in the book of Deuteronomy xxxiii. 3: "An Ammonite or Moabite shall not enter into the congregation of the Lord; even to their tenth generation shall they not enter into the congregation of the Lord for ever." That unnamed and unwilling kinsman, in Ruth iv. 6, is the LAW. The Law, in itself, is just, but it has no smile, no place, no welcome, for alien Ruth. The unnamed kinsman would have paid the price for the *estate* of Elimelech if that had been all there was to think of (iv. 4); but as soon as he heard that Moabitess Ruth was involved he refused. And the *Law* can do nothing for *us* as sinners and spiritual aliens to God. It cannot forgive. It cannot cleanse. It cannot renew us or empower us. It can only condemn us. Thank God, the Moabite who is shut out by law is admitted by grace! And those very sinners against whom Mount Sinai thunders, "The soul that sinneth, it shall die," may hear the gracious words from Mount Calvary, "He that believeth on Me hath everlasting life, and shall not come into the judgment, but is passed from death unto life!"

> O all-embracing mercy,
>   Thou ever-open door,
> How could I do without thee
>   Now heart and eyes run o'er?
> Tho' all things seem against me,
>   To drive me to despair,
> I know one gate is open,
>   One ear will hear my prayer.

THE FIRST BOOK OF SAMUEL (1)

Lesson Number 28

NOTE.—For this study read the First Book of Samuel right through, and the first seven chapters through at least twice.

What, then, shall we think about the Bible? I will tell you very plainly what I think we ought to think. I hold that the Biblical writers, after having been prepared for their task by the providential ordering of their entire lives, received, in addition to all that, a blessed and wonderful and supernatural guidance and impulsion by the Spirit of God, so that they were preserved from the errors that appear in other books and thus the resulting book, the Bible, is in all its parts the very Word of God, completely true in what it says regarding matters of fact, and completely authoritative in its commands.

—*J. Gresham Machen.*

THE FIRST BOOK OF SAMUEL (1)

WE HAVE said adieu to gentle Ruth, and have turned over another page of our Bible. The "First Book of Samuel" lies before us, introducing us to one of the most venerable figures in Israel's history, and opening up a stirring new chapter in the fascinating story of God's earthly people. This "First Book of Samuel" heads what have been called the three "double books" of the Old Testament—1 and 2 Samuel, 1 and 2 Kings, 1 and 2 Chronicles. These three double books together form a complete section. They record *the rise and fall of the Israelite monarchy.*

Samuel and Kings

In the Hebrew manuscripts, 1 and 2 Samuel form but one book, as also do 1 and 2 Kings and 1 and 2 Chronicles. Their division into two books each, as we now have them, originates with the so-called Septuagint translation of the Hebrew Scriptures into Greek, said to have been made in the third century B.C. In the Septuagint, 1 and 2 Samuel and 1 and 2 Kings are called, respectively, the First, Second, Third and Fourth Books of the Kingdoms (the plural word "Kingdoms" meaning the two kingdoms, Judah and Israel). The Latin Vulgate—Jerome's famous translation of the entire Bible into Latin, in the fourth century A.D.—continues the Septuagint division of Samuel and Kings into two books each, but calls them the First, Second, Third and Fourth Books of the Kings (not Kingdoms). It is from this that there came the sub-titles to these four books in our Authorised Version. As will have been noticed, under the title: "The First Book of Samuel," it says, *"Otherwise called the First Book of the Kings."* 2 Samuel and 1 and 2 Kings are similarly sub-titled. In the Revised Version, however, these sub-titles are dropped.

The present division into 1 and 2 Samuel has been decried by some scholars; yet undoubtedly it has much merit. *Second Samuel* is distinctively the book of David's forty years' reign; and it is well that such an epochal reign should be marked off, and given

45

a book to itself. As for this _First_ Book of Samuel, it equally clearly marks off a definite period, running from the birth of Samuel, the last of the Judges, to the death of Saul, the first of the Kings. It covers a period of about one hundred and fifteen years. ⟋

For sheer interest, 1 Samuel is unsurpassed. Not only does it recount eventful history; it is eventful history interwoven with the biographies of three colourful personalities—Samuel, Saul, David: and it is around these three that the chapters are grouped; thus—

> Chapters   i. to vii.   —SAMUEL. _1 ~ 7_
> ,,   viii. to xv.   —SAUL. _8 – 15_
> ,,   xvi. to xxxi. —DAVID. _16 ~ 31_

Of course, the three accounts overlap. Samuel lives well on into the reign of Saul, and also sees David rise to prominence; while Saul continues his reign until David is thirty years old. Yet it is none the less true that 1 Samuel is grouped as we have just indicated. In the first seven chapters Samuel is the prominent figure. In the next eight chapters all focusses on Saul, and Samuel is in the background. In the remaining chapters, although Saul is still reigning, there is no mistaking that the main attention is now on David.

Central Feature and Message

In the case of 1 Samuel there is really no need to burden ourselves with a detailed analysis. Fix it well in the mind—and the memory will easily retain it—that 1 Samuel is the book of _the transition from the theocracy to the monarchy_; and the book of the three remarkable men—Samuel, the _last_ of the Judges, Saul, the _first_ of the Kings, and David, the _greatest_ of the kings.

If we remember this, we cannot easily forget the central _spiritual_ message of the book. God had called Israel into a unique relationship with Himself; and God Himself was Israel's King invisible. Through disobedience the people had brought chastisement upon themselves from time to time, but were willing to attribute much of this, later, to the fact that they had no _human_ and _visible_ king, such as the surrounding nations had: and now, at length, as Samuel ages, and his sons prove perverse, the people make it the occasion to press for a human king. The fateful choice is recorded in chapter viii. which should be read carefully. It

monarchy = the sovereinty of a single person.
theocracy = the government of the state by the immediate direction of God
heos - God + kratein - to rule

THE FIRST BOOK OF SAMUEL (I)   47

was a retrograde step, dictated merely by seeming expediency. It was the way of human wisdom, not of faith in God. It was taking the lower level. It was a refusing of God's *best*, for the *second* best—and there is much difference between the two.

The people thought it would solve their many problems, and make things wonderfully easier, if only they could have a human and visible king such as the neighbouring peoples had; but, alas, they were quickly to learn how self-deceived they were in thinking so, for new troubles were now to break upon them through the very king they had demanded: and herein lies the central message of I Samuel to us, namely: Troubles increased through choosing the seemingly easier but lower way of human wisdom, in preference to God's way—*by choosing less than God's best.*

> God has His best things for the few
> Who dare to stand the test;
> God has His second choice for those
> Who will not take His best.
>
> It is not always open ill
> That risks the promised rest;
> The better often is the foe
> That keeps us from the best.
>
> And others make the highest choice,
> But when by trials pressed,
> They shrink, they yield, they shun the cross,
> And so they lose the best.

Let us now look briefly at the three outstanding men around whom the story is woven. First of these is Samuel.

Samuel (i—vii)

As a character study Samuel has few peers; and as a factor in the early growth of his nation he is equalled only by Moses. The ministry of Samuel marks the institution of the monarchy. From now onwards we are to see Israel under the kings.

Besides this, the appearance of Samuel marks the institution of the prophetic office. There were those in Israel, even before Samuel's time, on whom the mantle of prophecy had fallen (Num. xi. 25; Judges vi. 8). Moses himself is called a prophet (Deut. xviii. 18). But there was no organised prophetic office.

Samuel founded the *schools* of the prophets, and originated the prophetic *order*. In a very real sense, therefore, he is "the first of the prophets"; and this distinction is recognised in the New Testament, as the following verses shew:

> "Yea, and all the prophets from Samuel and those that follow after, as many as have spoken, have likewise foretold of these days"—(Acts iii. 24).

> "And, after that, He (God) gave unto them Judges about the space of four hundred and fifty years, until Samuel the prophet"—(Acts xiii. 20).

> "And what shall I more say?—for the time would fail me to tell of Gideon . . . and Samuel and the prophets"—(Heb. xi. 32).

Samuel, then, is a significant figure. He ends the period of the Judges; he heads the order of the prophets; he originates the first great educational movement in the nation; he places Israel's first king on the throne, and later anoints David, the greatest of all Israel's kings. There is a fine article about Samuel in the Pulpit Commentary, of which the following remarks are somewhat of a précis.

His Timely Appearing.

Israel's training had been remarkable. The tribes had grown up amid that mental culture in which Egypt had outstripped the world. Then, under the educated leadership of Moses, there had been the endowment of the Law, which although merely preparatory in certain civil and administrative aspects, contained a summary of the fundamental principles of morality which has never been surpassed. But great as was the impress of Moses upon Israel, we must not think that the bulk of the people had risen to the level on which he himself stood. Scarcely had Moses and his generation passed before the people reverted to barbarism; and instead of realising the grand ideal which their lawgiver had sketched for them, they sank lower and lower (as seen in Judges), until the nation seemed at the point of breaking up. The Philistines, strengthened by a constant influx of immigrants and the importation of arms from Greece, were fast reducing Israel to a subject race. Thus Judah's neglect to conquer the sea coast in the earlier days (Judges i. 18, 19), was now imperilling the nation's independence. But just when it seemed that Israel must be crushed out, Samuel came. Never did times seem more hopeless; yet Samuel arrested the nation's decay, built it up into an orderly and progressive kingdom, and planted it on the path which led it, though by an uphill and tangled route, to its high destiny as teacher of the true God to mankind.

His Educational Work.

Samuel set himself to give the nation mental culture and orderly government. These were the urgent needs. The foundation of all his reforms was the restoring of the moral and religious life of the people. One must always begin there. Moreover, Samuel was too wise to trust merely to his personal influence. Many a man who has wielded great influence in his lifetime has left nothing lasting. If Israel was to be saved it must be by institutions which would exercise continual pressure, and push the people upward to a higher level. The means he employed for this internal growth of the nation was the founding of schools. These, besides raising Israel to a higher mental level, fostered the worship of Jehovah by teaching true ideas of the Divine nature. Samuel must often have found that the chief obstacle to his work as Israel's Judge was the low mental state of the people. Nowhere in Israel were educated men to be found to bear office or administer justice. The pathetic failure of the highly gifted king Saul shews this, and proves that Samuel was right in his hesitation about creating a king. Schools were the urgent need, through which the whole mental state of Israel should be raised, and men trained for educated leadership. Up and down the land these schools were planted, where young men learned reading and writing, and gained knowledge. From these came a David, and most of David's leaders. A system of national education grew up. Other results followed, of which the whole world reaps the benefit even today. Apart from it, that series of inspired men who have given us the Scriptures would have been impossible. Isaiah and his compeers were educated men, speaking to an educated people. Both Old and New Testaments are largely the fruit of Samuel's schools.

Samuel's other great labour was the shaping of the constitutional monarchy. In this again he was ahead of his age. To a degree he was unwilling, for he saw that the time was not ripe. A limited monarchy is only possible among an educated people. Samuel's Book of the Kingdom (1 Sam. x. 25) could have little influence on a Saul who could neither read nor write: and Saul became only too like what Samuel had feared. The government which Samuel sought to establish was that of kingly power in the hands of a layman, but acting in obedience to the written law of God, and to His will as declared from time to time by the living voice of prophecy which should appeal to the king's moral sense. Not till Samuel had trained David was there a Jewish Alfred ready for the throne. Despite his private faults, David, unlike Saul, never attempted to set himself above God's law, or even to pervert it to his own use. He kept strictly within the understood limits.

We begin to see what a great figure Samuel is. He initiated the first movement toward national education, and shaped the constitutional monarchy of the nation. Samuel is indeed a great man.

THE FIRST BOOK OF SAMUEL

TRANSITION FROM THEOCRACY TO MONARCHY

SAMUEL: THE LAST OF THE JUDGES (i.–vii.).

HIS BIRTH AND HIS YOUTH (i., ii.).
HIS CALL AND HIS OFFICE (iii.).
HIS TIMES AND HIS ACTS (iv.–vii.).
Summary—vii. 15–17.

SAUL: THE FIRST OF THE KINGS (vii.–xv.).

HIS APPOINTMENT AS KING (viii.–x.).
HIS PROMISING BEGINNING (xi.–xii.).
HIS LATER FOLLY AND SIN (xii.–xv.).
Rejection—xv. 23, 28, 35.

DAVID: THE ANOINTED SUCCESSOR (xvi.–xxxi.).

HIS ANOINTING BY SAMUEL (xvi. 1–13).
HIS SERVICE BEFORE SAUL (xvi. 14–xx.).
HIS YEARS AS A FUGITIVE (xxi.–xxx.).
Death of Saul—xxxi.

THE FIRST BOOK OF SAMUEL (2)

Lesson Number 29

NOTE.—For this further study in the First Book of Samuel read again chapters eight to the end.

When for a moment, a man is off-guard, in all probability you will know more truth about him than in all his attempts either to reveal himself or to hide himself. The ever-present consciousness, habitually hidden, flashes forth. Later, he may apologise, and say he did not mean what he said. The fact is that he was surprised into saying what he was constantly thinking. In all probability Saul had never said that before, and would never say it again; but he had been thinking it for a long time—"I have played the fool." There is no escape for any man, so long as reason continues, from the naked truth about himself. He may practise the art of deceit so skilfully as not only to hide himself from his fellow-men, but in his unutterable folly to imagine that he has hidden himself from God; but he has never hidden himself from himself. In some moment of stress and strain, he says what he has been thinking all the time.

Saul had slept deeply that night, for the record tells us that "a deep sleep from the Lord was fallen" upon him. He was awakened from his slumber by the voice of David calling to him from the opposite mountain. Waking, he became keen, acute, neither dulled by food nor drugged by wine; everything was clear and sharp about him, as it so often is in the waking moment. Ere he knew it, he had said, "Behold, I have played the fool." That is the whole story of the man.

—*G. Campbell Morgan.*

THE FIRST BOOK OF SAMUEL (2)

As WE have said, this first book of Samuel is the book of *the transition from the Theocracy to the Monarchy*; and it will be well for us to remember it fixedly by this as we seek to get a broad hold on the books of the Bible. We have seen, also, that this book gathers round three men—Samuel, Saul, David. Already we have considered Samuel, the last of the Judges, and now we turn our thoughts to Saul, the first of the Kings: but we ought to note carefully beforehand how the change-over from the Judges to the Kings came about.

TRANSITION FROM JUDGES TO KINGS

The Request.

The change-over came about through the insistence of the people themselves. This we find in chapter viii., which marks the turning-point. Verses 4 and 5 say: "Then all the elders of Israel gathered themselves together and came to Samuel at Ramah, and said unto him: Behold, thou art old, and thy sons walk not in thy ways: now make us a king to judge us like all the nations." Now as Dr. Kitto says, "The demand was not the outcry of an ignorant and deluded rabble, but the grave and deliberate application of the *elders* of Israel—of those whose years or high standing in the nation gave to them the utmost weight and influence. It was not made from the mere impulse of the moment, but was the result of previous deliberation and conference; for the elders repaired to Ramah *for the purpose* of proposing the matter to the prophet; and beyond all doubt they had met together and considered the matter well before they took a step so decided."

Their approach to Samuel was marked by considerateness. They had no dissatisfaction with Samuel personally; but in view of his advanced years and the unsatisfactory behaviour of his sons they must urge that the government be put on the new basis of kingship while Samuel is yet with them, and by the sanction of Samuel's authority. Yes, they were deliberate and considerate; but they were wrong. Their eyes were away from God again. Such a request had never been born in prayer. They had held a committee meeting instead of a prayer meeting!— and now they were determined on taking a retrograde step instead of going on with God. How often is unbelief thus dressed up as the corporate wisdom of committees!

The Response.

Samuel's reaction to the request is given in verse 6: "But the thing displeased Samuel when they said: Give us a king to judge us. And Samuel prayed unto the Lord." The Divine answer is: "Hearken unto the voice of the people in all that they say unto thee; for they have not rejected thee, but they have rejected Me, that I should not reign over them. . . . Now therefore hearken unto their voice: howbeit yet protest solemnly unto them, and show them the manner of the king that shall reign over them." Samuel thereupon makes disuasive protest to them (10–18), but without avail; for verse 19 says: "Nevertheless, the people refused to obey the voice of Samuel; and said: Nay, but we will have a king over us, that we also may be like all the nations, and that our king may judge us, and go out before us to fight our battles." The request has now become a demand: and God's further word to Samuel is: "Hearken unto their voice, and make them a king" (verse 22).

Three things, therefore, we ought to note about this demand for a king. First the outer *reason* for it was the degeneracy of Samuel's sons. Second the inner *motive* was that the people might become like the other nations. Third, the deeper *meaning* was that Israel had now rejected the theocracy, which was the most serious thing of all; and this is emphasized in the Divine response— "They have not rejected thee, but they have rejected *ME*, that *I* should not reign over them." Alas, how many once bright Christians have been spoiled through wanting to be like the people of the world around, even as did Israel in demanding a human king! And how insidious is the temptation to lean on that which is seen and human instead of resting in the invisible God! It is a temptation to which we are all prone; but to yield to it invites a harvest of regrets.

The Result.

So then, the people claimed and exercised what in these days is called "the right of self-determination." The change-over from theocracy to monarchy was of themselves. God gave them a king and constituted a kingship. The fact would seem to be that Israel had wearied of a theocratic form of government which made their wellbeing dependent on their right conduct. Perhaps they vaguely supposed that a government under a human king would relieve them somewhat of this responsibility, inasmuch as their wellbeing would rest more with the character of the government and the qualities of the king himself.

But in giving them a king, God safeguarded the moral interests of the nation by constituting a kingship which preserved as far as possible the principles of theocratic government. The king is made directly responsible to God, and the people are no less responsible to Him through their king. Israel's king was not to be an autocratic king, but a theocratic king. The prophet and the priest, in their *official* capacity, were coördinate with, rather than subordinate to, the king, being themselves directly dependent on God; though, of course, as men and citizens they were subject to the king, like all others. As we have already said, the government was to be that of kingly power in the hands of a layman, but acting in obedience to the written law of God, and to His will as declared from time to time by the living voice of prophecy. Therefore, when we speak of the change-over from theocracy to monarchy we do not mean that all the principles of theocratic government were then waived. Theocratic responsibility still persisted through the monarchy: but absolute theocracy had ceased to be.

Observations.

We can understand the *feelings* of Israel's leaders in pressing for a human king. There were signs of trouble coming, so it would seem, from the Philistines, ever planning war, on the west, and from the Ammonites on the east (xii. 12); and it was an understandable anxiety that in Israel there was no man marked out, either by preëminent fitness or station, to be their leader in such conflicts as were likely to come. We can understand, too, the craving for outward dignity of state such as the surrounding nations had, for the Oriental mind is pervadingly regal; and maybe it was a stigma on Israel that there was no royal head of the nation. Yet in view of the theocratic privileges and high calling of Israel, this peremptory demand for a human king was gravely wrong.

The people's asking for a king had been *anticipated* in the word of God through Moses. See Deuteronomy xvii. 14–20. Maybe the elders of Israel inferred from this that it was the ultimate Divine intent to establish a monarchical government among, them—and perhaps rightly so; yet even so, the least they could have done was to seek the counsel of their Divine King about this. Note further that instead of being gratefully anxious to preserve the liberties and public rights which were theirs under the theocracy, they insisted on being ruled as the surrounding peoples were ruled. In other words, they insisted on surrendering their present mild government for the overlordship of a despotic human royalty. Samuel solemnly warns them against what they were intending to bring upon themselves. See chapter viii. 11–20. Such a king would take their sons and daughters to wait on him and work for him and war for him. He would take their fields and vineyards, and the tenth of their seed and produce and flocks and other possessions; and he would do much more, so that they should cry out because of him. And without doubt, Samuel's words accurately depicted the monarchical governments which then existed round about Israel. Yet still undeterred, Israel's leaders pressed to surrender their precious immunities! The fact that the monarchy which was thereupon constituted in Israel was *not* despotic, like those around, is due, as Dr. Kitto says, to "the sagacious care and forethought of Samuel, acting under Divine direction, in securing from utter destruction at the outset, the liberties which the people so wilfully cast into the fire."

Saul : Israel's First King

Saul, the first king of Israel, is one of the most striking and tragic figures in the Old Testament. If we are at all sensitive as to the supreme values and vital issues of human life, the story of Saul will challenge us. In some ways he is very big; in others very little. In some ways he is commandingly handsome; in others definitely ugly. He began so reassuringly, but declined so disappointingly, and ended so wretchedly, that the downgrade process which ruined him becomes monumental to all who will give heed. We note the three main phases of his career—(1) his early promise, (2) his later decline, (3) his final failure.

His early promise (ix.–xii.).

Never did a young man give fairer promise or find brighter possibilities greeting his young manhood. To begin with, he was distinguished by *a striking physical superiority*. He is described as "a choice young man, and a goodly: there was not among the children of Israel a goodlier person than he; from his shoulders and upward he was higher than any of the people" (ix. 2). He had health and height and handsomeness; and while the physical is not the more important part of a man, such splendid physique as Saul had was a wonderful possession. It gave him the initial advantage of being immediately prepossessing.

Second; young Saul showed certain *highly commendable qualities of disposition*. We note his *modesty* (ix. 21; x. 22). We note his *discreetness* (x. 27). We mark his *generous spirit* (xi. 13). And there were other fine qualities too—his considerateness of his father (ix. 5), his dash and courage (xi. 6, 11), his capacity for strong love (xvi. 21), his energetic antagonism to such evils as spiritism (xxviii. 3), and his evident moral purity in social relationships.

Third, there were *special equipments* which God gave him when he became king. We read, "God gave him another heart" so that he became "another man" (x. 6, 9). Again, "the Spirit of God came upon him" so that he "prophesied" (x. 10). Such expressions cannot mean less than that Saul became inwardly renewed, and was under the special guidance of the Holy Spirit. Nor is this all: he was given a "*band* of men whose hearts God had touched" (x. 26). He also had that trusty counsellor, the inspired Samuel, at his side. To crown all this, God signalised the beginning of Saul's reign by granting a spectacular military victory which set the new king high in the confidence of the people (xi. 12).

This was the young Saul of fair promise. Extraordinarily rich in natural endowments, and specially equipped by supernatural conferments, the future seemed bright indeed. His call to the kingship was an opportunity in a million, coming to a man in a

million. He was called to kingship, and he was constitutionally
kingly. He was called to *theocratic* kingship, and God supernaturally equipped him for that. What scope for glorious co-
operation with God! What opportunity to bless men! He
betrayed none of the symptoms of vain-glory which others, less
gifted than himself, have betrayed when suddenly elevated.
His accession to Israel's throne was indeed a morning of fair
promise.

His later decline.

Alas, Saul's early promise is a morning sky soon overcast with
sullen clouds. Defection, declension, degeneration, disaster—
that is the dismal downgrade which now sets in, until this giant-
hero drops as a haggard suicide into ignominious death.

The first defection occurred early. See chapter xiii. It was an
act of *irreverent presumption.* The Philistines were arrayed against
Israel. Saul was bidden to wait for Samuel at Gilgal. When
Samuel did not seem to be coming before the appointed time
expired, Saul, in wilful impatience, violated the priest's pre-
rogative, and foolishly presumed to offer up with his own hand the
pre-arranged sacrifices to the Lord. We can allow for Saul's
anxiety. Yet he violated that obedience to the voice of God
through the prophet which was a basic condition of theocratic
kingship. Samuel's rebuke was, "Saul, thou hast done foolishly:
thou hast not kept the commandment of Jehovah."

The next default follows quickly. See chapter xiv. It is an
act of *rash wilfulness.* Using Jonathan as his instrument, God
spreads confusion among the Philistines. Israel's watchmen
report what they see. Saul calls the priest, to ask God guidance,
but with stupid impatience cuts short the enquiry and rushes his
men off without guidance. He also rashly imposes death-sentence
on any man who should eat food that day (verse 24), with the
result that his men are too weak to follow up the victory (verse
30), and that his hunger-smitten men sin by eating flesh with the
blood (verse 32), and that Jonathan comes under the death-
sentence through ignorance, and is only rescued by the intervention of the people (verses 27, 45).

But in chapter xv. comes still graver failure. It is a blend of
disobedience and deceit. Saul is told to destroy utterly the vile

Amalekites; but he spares the king and the best live-stock. Then he equivocates to Samuel. He slips blame for the booty on to the people. He even pretends the booty is for sacrifice to Jehovah. Samuel's rebuke begins, "When thou was little in thine own sight. . . ." Alas, humility had now given place to arrogance. Samuel sees right through the sham to the real—"Wherefore didst thou not obey?" "Thou hast rejected the word of Jehovah."

From this point the decline is steep. "The Spirit of the Lord departed from Saul" (xvi. 14) and "an evil spirit" troubled him. He gives way to a petty jealousy until it becomes a fiendish malice—against David. Thrice he tries to kill him. Then he hunts him for months on end, like "a partridge in the mountains." He gives way to the basest in himself. Twice David spares Saul's life, and twice Saul promises to leave off his blood-thirsty hunt. He knows that in seeking to slay David he is actually fighting against God. He admits, "I know well that thou shalt surely be king" (xxiv. 20); yet, even after this, he resumes his dastardly pursuit. Well does Saul say of himself, "*I have played the fool!*" (xxvi. 21).

His final failure.

The last tragic act in the mournful drama of this man is depicted in chapters xxviii. to xxxi. His downgrade course at length brings him to the witch of Endor, as an embittered and desolate-hearted fugitive from doom. This giant wreck of a man who once enjoyed direct counsel from heaven now traffics with the under-world. We need not dilate on the nocturnal consultation, nor on Saul's battlefield suicide the following day. There is no need here to pick on details. It is enough to know the stark fact, the final plunge—witchcraft and suicide! Saul is no more. He lies a corpse, with lovely Jonathan. How are the mighty fallen! How is this son of the morning brought to shame! Yes, Saul—Saul of early promise, but of later decline and final ruin, you have "played the fool"!

And as we see this man Saul come from such heights to such depths, do we not ask what it was which lay behind his fearful self-frustration? It was *self-will*. Saul's two besetting sins were presumption and disobedience to God; and behind both these was impulsive, unsubdued *self-will*. We may trace the four progressive stages of this ruinous self-ism in Saul: first, self-sensitiveness, then, self-assertiveness, then self-centredness, increasingly issuing in self-destructiveness.

"He being dead yet speaketh."

In sad and awesome tones the voice of Saul still speaks, and we do well to heed. First, he preaches to us that *the one vital condition for the true fulfilment of life is obedience to the will of God.* Let us mark this well—Saul was called to *theocratic* kingship; so is each one of us. Every human personality is meant to be a theocratic kingship. Saul was never meant to have a kingship of *absolute* power. It was never intended that the last word should be with *him.* He was anointed of God to be the executor of a will higher than his own. He was to be the human and visible vice-regent of Israel's Divine and invisible King, Jehovah. He could only truly rule the subjects beneath him to the extent in which he obeyed the supreme King above him. So is it with ourselves. We are not the independent proprietors of our own beings. We are God's property. He has made us kings and queens over our own personalities with their gifts and powers and possibilities; but our rule is meant to be theocratic, not an independent, self-directed monarchy. We are meant to rule for *God,* so that our lives and personalities may fulfil His will and accomplish His purpose. When we obstinately rule independently of God our true kingship breaks down; we lose the true meaning and purpose of life. In greater or lesser degree we "play the fool."

But Saul teaches this further and kindred truth, that *to let "self" get the upper hand in our life is to miss the best and court the worst.* The Philistines were not Saul's worst enemies. His worst foe was himself. Every man who lets "self" fill his vision till it blinds his inner eye to what is really true and Divine is "playing the fool." All of us who live for self in preference to the will of God are "playing the fool." The downgrade process in our life may not be as outwardly observable as it was with Saul, simply because we do not occupy as conspicuous a position, but we are just as really playing the fool, and our ultimate corruption is just as certain.

There are many other lessons, of a more incidental kind. We see that advantages are not in themselves the guarantee of success. Saul had many, yet he failed ingloriously. We dare not lean on them. We see also that wonderful opportunities do not in themselves crown men. Nor even do special spiritual equipments immunise us from the possibility of getting out of the will of God, and "playing the fool." Again, a man plays the fool when he neglects his best friends, as Saul neglected Samuel; or when he goes on enterprises for God before God sends him, as Saul did; or when he disobeys God in small matters, as Saul at first did and then went on to worse disobedience; or when he tries to cover up disobedience by a religious excuse, as Saul did, or when he allows jealousy and hate to master and enslave him, as Saul did. Oh what warnings this man utters to us! God help us each to say, and really to mean it,

> Take my will, and make it Thine;
> It shall be no longer mine.
> Take my intellect, and use
> Every power as Thou shalt choose!

THE SECOND BOOK OF SAMUEL (I)

Lesson Number 30

NOTE.—For this study read through the whole of Second Samuel and the first six chapters twice.

So pervaded are the narratives of scripture with the didactic and ethical element, that all its biographical and historical parts seem dignified by a moral purpose, teaching truth by example. The prophetic and historic are therefore so close of kin that the history seems another form of prophecy, imparting instruction at the time present and typically forecasting the time to come. The Bible becomes a picture and portrait gallery, where lessons are so taught as to impress even those dullest of comprehension. And every line and lineament is full of meaning.

—A. T. Pierson, D.D.

THE SECOND BOOK OF SAMUEL

THE BOOK OF DAVID'S REIGN

SECOND Samuel is distinctively *the book of David's reign*. It opens
with David's accession over Judah, immediately after Saul's
death, and closes just before David's death, when he is "old and
stricken in years." The book therefore covers a period of some
forty years; for that was the duration of David's reign. Chapter
v. 4 and 5, says: "David was thirty years old when he began to
reign, and he reigned forty years. In Hebron he reigned over
Judah seven years and six months; and in Jerusalem he reigned
thirty and three years over all Israel and Judah." It will be help-
ful, then, if we always remember Second Samuel by this—that it
is the book of David's forty years' reign.

Composite Authorship

The authorship of Second Samuel is far from certain, though
the likeliest indications still favour the older view that while
Samuel himself is responsible for the first twenty-four chapters
of the *first* of these two books which bear his name, the remaining chapters, to the end of Second Samuel, are the work of
the two prophets, Nathan and Gad. See 1 Chronicles xxix.
29–30.

As already mentioned, 1 and 2 Samuel were originally one book,
the present division being handed down from the Septuagint.
Despite those who complain that the separation of the one book
into two is "without reason or necessity," there is this definite
advantage, that it marks off the epochal reign of David, and
presents it as a subject of outstanding prominence, deserving our
special study. As David was the real founder of the monarchy,
the reorganiser of Israel's religious worship, the pre-eminent hero,
ruler, and poet of his people, and as his dynasty continued on
the throne of Judah right up to the Captivity, and as the promised
Messiah was to come of the Davidic line, it is not surprising that
so much prominence should be given to him.

The Tragic Divide

This second book of Samuel, as Matthew Henry is quick to observe, falls into two main parts. Alas, there is no mistaking it. David's great sin, recorded in chapter xi., marks the sad divide, right in the middle of the book and right in the middle of David's forty years' reign, for it falls about the end of the first twenty years. Up to this point all goes triumphantly for David; but after this there are ugly knots and tangles, grievous blows and tragic trials. In the first part, we sing David's triumphs. In the second part, we mourn David's troubles.

Mark it well that the Second Book of Samuel is cut exactly in half, with twelve chapters in each part. Chapters xi. and xii., which record David's sin and repentance, must be included in the first part, as rightly belonging there. It was through the very prosperity which had come to him by his widespread conquests that David had become exposed to the temptation of unguardedness and indulgence. At the end of that twelfth chapter there is the account of the conquest of Rabbah, the royal city of Ammon. That marks the end of any such recorded triumphs in this book. Here, then, is the outlay of the book:

THE SECOND BOOK OF SAMUEL

THE BOOK OF DAVID'S FORTY YEARS' REIGN

TRIUMPHS TURNED TO TROUBLES THROUGH SIN

I. DAVID'S TRIUMPHS (i.–xii.).

i.–iv.—KING OVER JUDAH ONLY, AT HEBRON
  (*Civil War Period—7 years*).

v.–xii.—KING OF ALL ISRAEL AT JERUSALEM
  (*Conquest Period—13 years*).

II. DAVID'S TROUBLES (xiii.–xxiv.).

xiii.–xviii.—DAVID'S TROUBLES IN HIS FAMILY
  (*Amnon Sin to Absolom Revolt*).

xix.–xxiv.—DAVID'S TROUBLES IN THE NATION
  (*Sheba Revolt to Pestilence*).

Central Spiritual Message

The central spiritual message of this book, therefore, stands out clearly, namely: *TRIUMPHS TURNED TO TROUBLES THROUGH SIN*. Or we may put it that in the two parts of the book, respectively, we have triumph through faith, and trouble through sin. Second Samuel emphasises that all sin, whether in king or commoner, whether in high or low, whether in the godly or the godless, certainly brings its bitter fruitage. Sin is the destroyer of prosperity. However full and fair the tree may look, if rot is eating its way within the trunk, the tree will surely break and fall, or else become a leafless skeleton. There is no sinning without suffering. Especially is all this true about the lust of the eye, and sexual sin, which was the point of David's breakdown. We should flee it as we would a viper. See, too, how David's sin led on to the even greater sin of murder. More often than not, one sin leads on to another of a worse kind. Let us, like Job, "make a covenant with our eyes" not to look on that which is seductive, lest, weaker than we suppose ourselves to be, we should give way to sin, and thereby heap sharp thorns into our bosom.

Key Facts to Note

There is no need for us to accompany the student chapter by chapter through this Second Book of Samuel; but we would call attention to certain key facts and events which should be carefully noted.

David at Hebron.

David reigned at Hebron for seven years and six months, over Judah only, because the other tribes would not accept him as Saul's successor. At the instigation of Abner, captain of Saul's army, Ishbosheth, a son of the deceased Saul, was proclaimed king, in opposition to David; and to Ishbosheth the tribes other than Judah gathered—a fact undoubtedly due to the pressure of the said Abner, who was a leader of much influence and renown.

Yet this repudiation of David was a grave wrong, and Israel was seriously at fault. Hereditary succession to the throne was not a principle in the constitution of the Hebrew monarchy; and even had it been so, Saul's true heir was Mephibosheth, the son of Jonathan—and Jonathan had renounced all claims for himself and his house, in favour of David.

But the guilt of Abner and Israel is the greater because in their hearts they knew well enough that David was Jehovah's appointed successor to Saul. Hear Abner's words as he quarrels with Ishbosheth—"So do God to Abner, and more also, except *as the Lord hath sworn to David,* even so I do to him; to translate the kingdom from the house of Saul, and to set up the throne of David over Israel and over Judah, from Dan even to Beersheba" (iii. 9, 10). A little later Abner says to the elders of the tribes: "Ye sought for David in times past to be king over you. Now then, do it; for *the Lord hath spoken of David,* saying: By the hand of My servant David I will save My people out of the hand of the Philistines and out of the hand of all their enemies" (iii. 17, 18). A little later still, the tribes acknowledged to David: "*The Lord said unto thee:* Thou shalt feed My people Israel and thou shalt be captain over Israel" (v. 2). Abner and Israel's leaders thus stand convicted by their own words.

Do we ask *why* Abner and Israel refused David at first? One reason may have been a jealous fear in Abner's mind that he could not hope to retain his position of supreme leadership under such a king as David, who already had his own "mighty men" of renown around him.

But there may have been another reason for Israel's refusal, namely, that the tribes had felt their faith in David shaken because of his recent sojourn among Israel's chief enemies, the Philistines, to escape Saul.

David's behaviour in the delicate situation created by Israel's refusal is commendable. He did not try to force himself to the throne by his armed power. He knew that he had been appointed of God to the throne; and his experience of God during the discipline of the preceding few years had taught him to bide God's time. Nor did God fail him. David would not act without Divine guidance (ii. 1). He was guided to Hebron. Judah welcomed him; and David reigned in Hebron, which ancient city of Abraham was Judah's capital. In the months that followed, "David waxed stronger and stronger; and the house of Saul waxed weaker and weaker" (iii. 1). The people of Israel could not but see, with self-rebuke, the contrast between the feeble

character of Ishbosheth and the brilliant qualities of David, with
his firm and beneficent government, the success which crowned
all his projects, his victories in any clashes between Israel and
Judah (ii. 12–32), and the attachment of his people to him.

Chapter v. is of outstanding importance. David is here, at last,
acclaimed king of all Israel, and he transfers the seat of his government to Jerusalem. The words of Israel's leaders as they offer
David the kingship are both touching and arresting. "Then
came all the tribes of Israel to David, unto Hebron, and spake,
saying: Behold we are thy bone and thy flesh. Also in time past,
when Saul was king over us, thou wast he that leddest out and
broughtest in Israel: and the Lord said to thee: Thou shalt feed
My people Israel, and thou shalt be captain over Israel." Thus
we see that the acknowledgment of David's right to the kingship rested on a threefold basis:

1. His human kinship—"*We are thy bone and thy flesh.*"
2. His proven merit—"*Thou leddest out and broughtest in Israel.*"
3. His Divine warrant—"*The Lord said unto thee: Thou shalt
   be captain over Israel.*"

Is not this a sermon in itself, speaking of *Christ's* right of kingship over *our* lives? He is our kinsman—"bone of our bone and
flesh of our flesh." He is our Saviour of proven merit, who
espoused our cause and fought our foe, and brought us deliverance from the guilt and tyranny of sin. And He is king by Divine
warrant, the prince and Lord of His people, the One to whom
is committed all administrative authority in heaven and on earth.
"The government shall be upon His shoulders." Can we each
say: "The government of my life *is* upon His shoulders"?

The New Centre.

Upon becoming king of a united Israel, David transferred the
seat of his government to Jerusalem. Hebron, although a quite
suitable capital while David's kingdom was confined to Judah,
was too far south to become a metropolis for a kingdom uniting
all the tribes. Jerusalem itself was about as southerly as an
Israelite capital city dare be; and perhaps David's choice of it
was partly dictated by a reluctance on his part to remove too
far north from the tribe on which he could most surely rely,

that is, the tribe of Judah, of which tribe David himself was a member.

Jerusalem at that time was called Jebus (1 Chron. xi. 4). It was a naturally strong position, which fact was also in David's mind, no doubt, when he chose to settle there. It was called Jebus after the Jebusites who still retained possession of it, or at least of that upper and fortified part of it which we know as Mount Zion. Probably in the lower part of Jebus, that is, in the *town* as distinguished from the *citadel*, Jebusites and Benjamites lived intermingled.

The Jebusites defied David to take Mount Zion. This fortress was so formidable and had so long been retained by the Jebusites, that it was regarded as impregnable. The Jebusite garrison derisively challenged David—"Except thou take away the blind and the lame, thou shalt not come in hither." It is added that they spake thus thinking: "David cannot come in hither." But David took the citadel. We are told that he said: "Whosoever getteth up to the gutter, and smiteth the Jebusites, and the lame and the blind that are hated of David's soul, he shall be chief, and captain." And to this it is added that the Jebusites therefore said: "The blind and the lame shall not come into the house." And who *were* these lame and blind who were hated of David's soul? They were not lame and blind *persons*, for David had no such hate of the lame and blind as such. He was far too generous-hearted for that. Besides, what a strange thing it would be to have had a fortress garrisoned by cripples and blind people! The blind and the lame here mentioned were the Jebusite gods. The meaning of the Jebusites in their challenge that David should not enter Zion unless he took away their gods was that David would *never* be able to take away their gods, and therefore he would never enter Zion. Probably the Jebusites brought out their gods—their idols of brass—and placed them on the fortress walls, which would explain their saying: "They shall not come into the house."

It was Joab who cleaved a way into the fortress, as 1 Chronicles xi. 6 tells us. Thenceforward Zion became "The City of David." Thus Jerusalem became the centre-city of Israel, and entered upon that historic career which has made it the most sacred and wonderful city of the world, a city, moreover, with a future even more wonderful than all its glorious and tragic past!

THE SECOND BOOK OF SAMUEL (2)

Lesson Number 31

NOTE.—For this further study in Second Samuel read chapters vii. to the end again, with special attention to chapters vii. and xi. and xii.

The reigns of David and Solomon constitute the golden period of the Jewish state. From the first, David showed the utmost anxiety that every step he took towards the possession of the kingdom should be directed by Jehovah (1 Sam. xxiii. 2, 4; 2 Sam. ii. 1.) He acted ever as "His servant"; and when established in his kingdom, his first concern was to promote the Divine honour and the religious welfare of his people (2 Sam. vi. 1–5, vii. 1, 2). As a king he sought the prosperity of the state, and as the visible representative of Jehovah he strictly conformed to the spirit of the theocracy. It was due to this character of his administration, probably, rather than to his private virtues, that he is designated as "a man after God's own heart" (1 Sam. xiii. 14; see also Acts xiii. 22), who was to "execute all His will." It is, indeed, impossible to vindicate all his acts, or to regard him as a perfect character. And yet when we look at the piety of his youth, the depth of his contrition, the strength of his faith, the fervour of his devotion, the loftiness and variety of his genius, the largeness and warmth of his heart, his eminent valour in an age of warriors, his justice and wisdom as a ruler, and his adherence to the worship and will of God, we may well regard him as a model of kingly authority and spiritual obedience.

—*Angus, Bible Handbook.*

THE SECOND BOOK OF SAMUEL (2)

The Davidic Covenant

WE MUST now turn to chapter vii., the chapter in which the Davidic covenant is made known. On no account should we fail to weigh duly the fact and the terms of this covenant; for, besides largely affecting all that follows in the Scriptures, it determinatively affects the whole history of mankind, especially that part which is yet future. It is one of the supremely great passages of the Bible, and one of the principal keys to the Divine plan of history. From the time when this covenant was announced, the Jews have always believed that the Messiah must come of David's line. They believed it in the time of our Lord, and they believe it now. That the Messiah should indeed be of David's line was later affirmed by the prophets, in such passages as Isaiah xi. 1; Jeremiah xxiii. 5; Ezekiel xxxvii. 25; and in accord with such prophecies the angel Gabriel announced to Mary, concerning Jesus: "He shall be great, and shall be called the Son of the Highest; and the Lord God shall give unto Him the throne of His father, David; and He shall reign over the house of Jacob for ever, and of His Kingdom there shall be no end."

The Davidic covenant is uttered in the following words:

"Also the Lord telleth thee that He will make thee an house; and when thy days be fulfilled, and thou shalt sleep with thy fathers, I will set up thy seed after thee, and I will establish his kingdom. He shall build an house for my name; and I will stablish the throne of his kingdom for ever. I will be his Father, and he shall be my Son. If he commit iniquity, I will chasten him with the rod of men, and with the stripes of the children of men; but My mercy shall not depart away from him as I took it from Saul, whom I put away before thee. And thine house and thy kingdom shall be established for ever before thee: thy throne shall be established for ever" (2 Sam. vii. 11–16).

The first important significance of these words is that here we have *the Divine confirmation of the throne in Israel*. Hitherto, as

73

we have seen, the throne of Israel was a man-appointed throne (see I Sam. viii.). It had been conceded at the clamouring of the people. Saul, the first king, was the man of the people's choice; for although he was Divinely selected and anointed and presented to the people, the choice was finally left with the people. Hitherto, also, the throne of David had rested upon the choice of the people—first of the men of Judah, and then of the other tribes. But now the throne of David is confirmed by *Divine appointment*. It now becomes statedly incorporated into God's plan for Israel, and, through Israel, for the race, from that time forth to the end of the ages.

The second important fact here is *the predicted perpetuity of the Davidic dynasty*. Three things are made sure to David—(i) a "house," or posterity; (ii) a "throne," or royal authority; (iii) a "kingdom," or sphere of rule; and then in verse 16 all three are secured to him "for ever." "Thine *house* and thy *kingdom* shall be established for ever before thee; thy *throne* shall be established *for ever*." This is emphatic language. That thrice-occurring expression, "for ever," is not just to be taken in a popular sense as meaning that Solomon's descendants should hold undisputed possession of the kingdom for many centuries. To take the expression in this popular way is ruled out by other Scriptures where we find references or allusions to this passage, notably Psalm lxxxix., which is both a confirmation and an exposition of the Davidic covenant. See verse 29: "His seed also will I make to endure for ever, and his throne *as the days of heaven*." And see verses 36 and 37: "His seed shall endure for ever, and his throne *as the sun* before Me. It shall be established for ever *as the moon*." There is no mistaking words like these. To crown the solemn emphasis, the covenant is sealed with an oath. See Psalm lxxxix. 35: "*Once have I sworn* in my holiness that I will not lie unto David." See also Acts ii. 30. This covenant, let it be most definitely understood, has to do with a literal posterity, and a literal throne, and a literal kingdom. To start "spiritualising" it into meaning a heavenly posterity and a spiritual kingdom synonymous with the Christian Church is to violate the very first drinciple of Scripture interpretation, namely, the principle that plainly spoken words should at least be accepted as meaning what they say.

The third great fact to grasp concerning this Davidic covenant is *its Messianic implication*. The emphatic threefold repetition of the promise to establish the kingdom of David *for ever* could only be fulfilled in the coming Messiah; and it has always been understood, therefore, as finding its final fulfilment in Him. In the words spoken to David, no doubt, Solomon is first in view; but the promise looks on through the long succession of human kings, and on through the present long dispersion, to find its culmination in Him who, having already been to earth as Prophet, and having now ministered in the heavenly sanctuary as Priest, shall yet return in glory as David's greater Son, the King of kings and Lord of lords, of whose kingdom "there shall be no end, upon the throne of David, to order it and to establish it with judgment and with justice from henceforth even for ever " (Isa. ix. 7).

It is because this Davidic Covenant finally envisages Christ that it is *unconditional*. Certainly, inside the covenant there is a provision made against possible sin and failure by David's reigning sons, in the words of verse 14: "If he commit iniquity I will chasten him with the rod of men and with the stripes of the children of men"; but this is not a *condition* on which the fulfilment of the covenant depends, for the next verse immediately goes on to say: "But my mercy shall not depart away from him, as I took it from Saul whom I put away before thee." That clause is put into the covenant to cover Solomon and his erring human descendants until the true and perfect King should come. As in the Abrahamic covenant the promised "seed" was Isaac, in the immediate sense, and Christ in the ultimate sense (Gal. iii. 16), so, in the Davidic covenant the promised "son" is Solomon, in the immediate sense, and Christ in the ultimate sense. Now it is noticeable that both the Abrahamic and the Davidic covenants are unconditional; and their being so is due to this fact that they both find their final fulfilment in Christ, for there can be no failure on Christ's part.

And again, this Davidic covenant marks *a fourth major development in Messianic prophecy*. The first great prophecy was made to Adam, in Genesis iii. 15, where we are told that *the seed of the woman* should bruise the head of the serpent. The second was made to Abraham, in Genesis xxii. 18, "*In thy seed* shall all the nations of the earth be blessed." The third was made through Jacob, in Genesis xlix. 10—"The sceptre shall not depart *from*

Judah . . . until Shiloh come." The fourth is now made to David in 2 Samuel vii. See the development then. First, in the case of Adam, the promise is to the *race* in general. Then, in the case of Abraham, it is to one *nation* in the race—the nation Israel. Then, in the case of Jacob, it is to one *tribe* in that nation —the tribe of Judah. Then, in the case of David, it is to one *family* in that tribe—the family of David. Thus are we prepared for that completing word which Isaiah adds still later, namely, that the coming Seed of the woman, Son of Abraham, Lion of Judah, and Heir of David, should be *born of a virgin*.

Notice that in the covenant God says of David's son: "He shall build an house for my Name." David, being a man of *war*, could not really typify Christ as Melchisedek, who is King of Peace: this glory was reserved for Solomon. David established the kingdom over which Solomon reigned. But Christ will be both David and Solomon. As David, He will conquer all foes and set up the kingdom on earth; and, as Solomon, He will reign in everlasting peace. Even so, may He soon come!

David's Full Establishment

In chapters viii. to x. we see David's reign at its zenith. Wherever he turns he is a victorious warrior, while at home he is an upright and constructive administrator. Never before has Israel been such a power among the nations. In chapter viii. 12, 14 we find a list of the seven surrounding powers which were subdued by David—the Philistines on the west, the Syrians and Hadadezer in the north, the Ammonites and Moabites on the east, the Edomites and Amalekites in the south. The secret behind David's successive conquests is found in verse 14—"And *the Lord* preserved David whithersoever he went"; while the reason for Israel's internal consolidation is given in verse 15, namely, that "David executed judgment and *justice* unto all his people." Thus Israel becomes the central and supreme power among the peoples.

We only need to glance through these chapters to see that David was a skilful general and a virtuous ruler. Chapter viii. begins by telling us that "David smote the Philistines, and *subdued* them." Remember, David came to the throne immediately after Saul's crushing defeat by the Philistines, when almost the whole land was under their heel. His subjugating of the Philistines, therefore, is the more remarkable.

Next, we are told that "he smote Moab, and measured them with a line, casting them down to the ground: even with two lines measured he to put to death, and with one full line to keep alive." There have been many criticisms of the barbarity of David's procedure here; but actually it is meant to be the evidence of generosity. The usual procedure in those days was to slay *all* prisoners of war, often without regard either to age or sex. Here, however, is a touch of leniency. A third are to be spared, with the added clemency that of the three lines used for measuring the two-thirds to be slain and the one-third to be spared, the line to mark off the third to be spared was a "full line," which indicates that it was longer than the other two. We agree that even so the procedure was brutal; but so has war always been, and never more so than today, despite all our boasted civilisation. Is there in all past wars anything more dastardly than the modern air-bombing of innocent women and children, and the deliberate machine-gunning of drowning men and women at sea? Has there ever been any torture worse than that of the German and Russian concentration camps? Moreover, before we criticise David and the old-time Israelites overmuch, we must realise that unless they were to wage war at a great disadvantage, and with bound hands, it was unavoidable that they should wage it on the principles recognised by the peoples with whom they were brought into conflict. Let us do David the justice of at least recognising that here, in his sparing a considerable percentage of the Moabites, he was taking a forward step of humanitarianism foreign to the warfare of his time. Had he spared the whole, those foes whom he was seeking to subdue would immediately have presumed upon his leniency, and perhaps with disastrous results.

Next, we read how David smote the King of Zobah, and took from him his chariots and horsemen. The defeat which David inflicted, with infantry only, upon an army equipped with so powerful a force of chariots and cavalry (verses 3–6) indicates his military skill; and the *capture* of them shows even more clearly his clever generalship.

And so we might go on; but we must forbear. The chapters should be read through with the help of good commentaries.

They are full of interest and information. Think of the broken condition of Israel at David's accession and then remember that at his death he transmitted to Solomon a united empire extending from "the river of Egypt" to the Euphrates, and from the Red Sea to Lebanon. What an achievement this was! Besides this, the religious development of Israel received a quickening impulse from the piety of their beloved king and the influence of his sacred poetry. In the Sanctuary the services became systematically arranged, and sacred song was given prominent recognition. It has been truly said that "never was there a more earnest effort to conduct the affairs of the nation on religious principles." David's reign was truly a noble epoch in Hebrew history.

David's Great Sin

As we have said, David's great sin, recorded in chapter xi., marks a sorrowful turning-point. It is well to emphasise certain considerations which should be borne in mind whenever we think of it. Critics have seized upon it as being the evidence of the moral corruptness of one whom the Bible holds up as a hero. "There!" they exclaim—"there is your great Bible hero! What a fine specimen he is!" It has been repeatedly asked, also, how we can reconcile this shameful fall of David with the Bible statement that God Himself declared David to be "a man after Mine own heart" (1 Sam. xiii. 14; Acts xiii. 22).

Now the answer to such criticism and questioning is that in all honesty and fairness we must take into account the full facts of the case.

1. *We must view David's life as a whole.* It is not fair or honest so to emphasise this blot on David's record as to make it appear the biggest thing in his life. Critics should remember that were it not for the strict honesty of the Bible itself, this black episode could easily have been withheld from us, and we would have known nothing about it. Therefore, we must in fairness judge David by the *whole* of the Biblical account. We must see his faith and obedience toward God through many years, his general uprightness and generous-heartedness, the high-principled conduct and ardent spiritual aspirings which largely characterise him throughout his career.

2. *We must take David's repentance into account.* Never was a man more stricken and abased by self-condemnation and godly contrition than was David after this sin "Beyond all question," says Ellicott,

"Psalm li. is the expression of his penitence after the visit of Nathan" to rebuke him. Who, then, can read that Psalm of sobs without realising that David's sin was the *exception to*, and not the *expression of*, his habitual aim and desire? The sin was committed in a spasm of weakness. The repentance shows the true attitude of the man to such sin— and it is *God's* attitude.

3. *We must judge David's character in the light of his own times.* The Christian Gospel and the New Testament ethic were not at that time given to men. Judged by the moral standards of his own day, David rises head and shoulders above his fellows. Especially when we compare him with the *kings* of that age does he excel. The extravagant sensual indulgence of ancient eastern kings is notorious. Their power over the life and property of their subjects was often absolute. They appropriated women-folk at will, with little regard to crimes which lay in the way of such appropriation. Compare David with such kings, and the comparison reveals the contrast.

4. *We must see David's inner life, as revealed in the Davidic psalms.* In the books of Samuel and the Chronicles we see David's life *outwardly*. In the Davidic psalms we see his life as it was *inwardly*. Here the man's very heart is laid bare; and, as we see it thus, we can only come to one honest conclusion. Many of those who have criticised David and the Bible would be glad if their own hearts could be laid bare in such goodly terms. These psalms, so moving in their evident sincerity, furnish proof positive that David was a good man—that he was, indeed, as the Scripture says, a man after God's own heart. In warfare, a general may lose a battle and yet win a campaign. Although one or several battles may be lost, and lost badly, the result of the whole campaign may be victory. This is true of men in a *moral* sense; and, in the case of David, the full account of his life, supported by the noble testimony of his psalms, shows decisively that though there were defeats, and one outstandingly grievous fall, the final result is such as to justify the pronouncement that he was a man after God's own heart.

In our own judgment, any one of the foregoing considerations is enough to justify the Bible estimate of David; and when taken together they become conclusive. But see also the note about David at the beginning of this present study. Should critics *still* object, however, we may fall back on the fact that when David was declared to be a man after God's own heart he was then merely in his early twenties. Surely, however, no honest appraisal of David could require us to limit the words to his youth: and, as for ourselves, we will not do so. With the full facts before us, we gladly subscribe to the verdict that in David we have one of the godliest men of all the pre-Christian era. As

Augustine said, David's fall should put upon their guard all who have *not* fallen, and save from despair all those who *have* fallen.

Salient Lessons.

And now mark some of the salient lessons connected with David's sin. First, note *the honesty and faithfulness of the Scriptures* in recording such a dark incident. Had the writing of the Bible been left merely in human hands, it would have contained no such chapter. David's guilt is here exposed without the slightest effort to extenuate it, much less excuse it. There is a severe truthfulness about the way in which the Bible deals with human characters. Dr. Edersheim says: "It need scarcely be pointed out how this truthful account of the sins of Biblical heroes evinces the authenticity and credibility of the Scriptural narratives. Far different are the legendary accounts which seek to palliate the sins of Biblical personages, or even to deny their guilt. Thus the *Talmud* denies the adultery of David on the ground that every warrior had, before going to the field, to give his wife a divorce; so that Bathsheba was free."

Note, too, that *David's fall occurred when he was in prosperous ease.* All his foes were crushed. The pressure of dangers that had kept him prayerful was now removed. He had not thought it worth troubling himself to go personally with his armies to reduce the last citadel of the Ammonites, but had sent Joab at their head (see xi. 1). We little realise what we owe to those seemingly hard circumstances from which we long to get free, but which are God's means of keeping us prayerful. Prosperity and ease are always perilous; and we are never so exposed to temptation as when we are idle.

Note further that David's sin was the culmination of a process. As a rule, falls so violent as that of David do not occur without being preceded by a weakening process. David had given way to the flesh in accumulating many wives (2 Sam. v. 13), a thing expressly forbidden to Israel's kings, in Deuteronomy xvii. 17. David, by nature a man of strong passions, had indulged the flesh; and now the tragic culmination is reached. How we need to guard against the *beginnings* of sin! See James i. 14, 15.

Again, see how *David's sin led on to even worse sin.* He vainly endeavoured to hide his crime. Uriah, the wronged husband of

Bathsheba, was intoxicated so that under its influence he might become irresponsible enough for it afterwards to be said that the child born to Bathsheba was his son (II Sam. xi.) ; but this shameful trick failed through the valorous behaviour of Uriah, who, besides being one of David's "mighty men" (2. Sam. xxiii. 39), was one of David's most upright and loyal supporters. Thereupon David—who had been shocked when Joab slew Abner—made Joab his accomplice in sin, and brought about the death of Uriah! Oh, the ugly chain that one sin can forge! If we *do* fall into sin, the one safe measure is confession and restitution.

Once again, note that *David's sin resulted in years of suffering*. Incest, fratricide, rebellion, civil war, intrigue, revolt—all these are traceable to David's sin. What a sorry harvest sin brings! David's wrong was forgiven, but its consequences were not thereby obliterated: and the Divine sentence upon David, in chapter xii. 11, "Behold, I will raise up evil against thee out of thine own house," furnishes the key to David's following history, which was as troubled and adverse as his earlier reign had been happy and successful.

We must now leave the student to make independent study of the remaining chapters in 2 Samuel. In the main they are sad, but are not without touches of beauty and cheer here and there: and they are full of profitable lessons.

As we think of David's awful sin, his prostrating remorse, his heart-breaking penitence which brought him absolution from the guilt of his sin but could not obliterate its consequences, we are reminded of words written, years ago now, by that remarkable British padre of the First World War, the late Studdart Kennedy. In an article on the sin of Judas, he writes:

" Why did I do it? How could I have done it? These can be the bitterest and most tragic questions men and women ask themselves. Something done that cannot be undone, something final and irrevocable, and a man looks at it, and cannot recognise it as his own act, cannot see himself in it, and yet he knows that it is his, and must be his for ever.

> " So Judas must have looked on Christ,
> As from the Judgment hall He went
> In bonds, the blood still wet upon
> His back. Why did I do it? How

Could I have done it? I loved Him,
Yet I sold Him. How can that be?
Which am I—traitor—lover—friend
Or fiend incarnate? Am I mad?
Aye mad—stark mad—my reason rocks.
These coins are bloody—Jesus help!
I did not mean to do it. Bloody—
Wet and bloody—and they burn—hot.
Hot as hell. I cannot bear it.
I am not I. I am some damned
And dreadful thing spewed out of hell.
I am—and I must kill it—now.
I cannot live—it must go back
To hell—I must—and never see
Him—never—Jesus Mercy! Death—
I must find death.

" Remorse and repentance are human facts, peculiarly human facts. Of no other creature could that scene be true, but only of a man. It might be true of you or me. Quite ordinary people can feel like that, and do. I have seen them, sat with them, tried to comfort them. I have heard them muttering over and over again: How could I have done it? How could I have done it?

" A man cannot be really free unless he surrenders himself utterly and without reserve to the service of the highest. The real tyrants which cramp and cabin man are his own undisciplined and unorganised desires. He cannot be free except through the inner union of his passions, without that the only freedom he possesses is freedom to hang himself. However much rope you give him that is what he must use it for in the end, unless he has some great aim and purpose which gives meaning and unity to his life. If he has that aim and purpose, and his desires are organised and disciplined about it, then when he acts against that aim and purpose, when he forgets it, and follows some wayward and rebellious passion, there comes to him the sense of sin. He knows that there is something awful, something deadly, about the word or deed. It is not merely a piece of folly, a mistake, a sin against himself or his neighbour, it is a denial of the whole meaning of the world. It is a sin against his God."

THE FIRST BOOK OF KINGS (I)

Lesson Number 32

NOTE.—For this study read right through this First Book of Kings, and the first eight chapters twice.

As we have already mentioned, the two books of the Kings were originally one (see our introduction to 1 Sam.). They were first divided into two by the Septuagint translators in the third century B.C.; and this division has been followed in all subsequent versions. They open with the accession of Solomon, and close with the destruction of Jerusalem. At the beginning we see the temple built. At the end we see the temple burnt. The two books together cover a period of about four hundred years. As to their authorship, scholars are in no doubt that "the language of the two books" and their "unity of purpose" point to "a single writer." Who then was the writer? Jewish tradition says he was Jeremiah the prophet. This tradition cannot be accepted as conclusive, yet neither can it be easily refuted. Indeed there is much in its favour. Of course, Jeremiah would make use of documents already existing (1 Kings xi. 41; xiv. 29, etc.); and after him redactors would make minor contributions to the eventual completeness of the work: but substantially the work is that of one writer, and that writer was probably the aged Jeremiah. We turn now to the *first* of these two books of the Kings.—*J.S.B.*

THE FIRST BOOK OF KINGS (1)

WHAT HEIGHT of glory and depth of tragedy lie in the history which stretches before us in the books of the Kings! What deep spiritual truths and prophetic foreshadowings, also, lie in these records! The splendours of Solomon's reign and the building of the temple forepicture the glory and the worship of Christ's coming kingdom upon the earth. The ministries of Elijah and Elisha are rich with spiritual meanings and latent typical significances. It would be easy to write at great length on such fertile themes; but our purpose here is simply to give the scope and gist of these records, as the basis for further study.

The Book of the Disruption

In getting a mental hold on the books of the Bible, it is a help if we remember each book by its distinctive feature. It will help us, therefore, if we always remember this First Book of Kings as being *the book of the Disruption*, by which we mean, of course, that it is the book which records the division of the one united kingdom, over which Saul and David and Solomon reigned, into *two* kingdoms—the two kingdoms henceforth being known respectively as *Israel* and *Judah*. The kingdom of Israel, comprising ten of the tribes, becomes the *northern* kingdom, while the kingdom of Judah, comprising Judah and Benjamin, becomes the *southern* kingdom. In the northern kingdom (Israel) *Samaria* becomes the capital. In the southern kingdom (Judah) *Jerusalem* remains the capital. This, then, is the central feature of First Kings—the one kingdom is divided into two; which event is usually called the Disruption.

This First Book of Kings falls into two main parts which are almost too obvious to need pointing out. There are twenty-two chapters in the book. The first eleven are devoted to Solomon and his wonderful reign of forty years. The remaining eleven chapters cover approximately the first eighty years of the separate kingdoms of Israel and Judah. The closing verses of chapter xi. record Solomon's death, thus marking off the two equal divisions of the book. In the first eleven chapters we have the united kingdom. Then comes the disruption; and in the ensuing eleven chapters we follow the fortunes of the *two* lines of kings.

The central spiritual message of 1 Kings is unmistakable, namely, *DISCONTINUANCE THROUGH DISOBEDIENCE.* This is seen in chapter xi. 11, which marks the tragic turning point, and foretells the coming disruption, thus becoming the key to the whole story: "Wherefore the Lord said unto Solomon: Forasmuch as this is done of thee, and *thou hast not kept my covenant and my statutes, which I have commanded thee*, I will surely rend the kingdom from thee, and will give it to thy servant. Notwithstanding in thy days I will not do it for David thy father's sake; but I will rend it out of the hand of thy son. Howbeit I will not rend away all the kingdom, but will give one tribe to thy son for David my servant's sake, and for Jerusalem's sake which I have chosen" (xi. 11-13).

THE FIRST BOOK OF KINGS
THE BOOK OF THE DISRUPTION

DISCONTINUANCE THROUGH DISOBEDIENCE

I. THE GREAT FORTY YEARS' REIGN OF KING SOLOMON (i.–xi.)

SOLOMON'S ACCESSION AND EARLY ACTS (i.–iv.)
SOLOMON'S TEMPLE AND PALACE BUILT (v.–viii.)
SOLOMON'S MERIDIAN FAME AND GLORY (ix.–x.)
SOLOMON'S DECLENSION AND DECEASE (xi. 1–43)

II. THE FIRST EIGHTY YEARS OF THE TWO KINGDOMS (xii.–xxii.)

ACCESSION OF REHOBOAM: THE DISRUPTION (xii. 1–33)
JUDAH KINGS—REHOBOAM TO JEHOSHAPHAT (xiii.–xxii.)
ISRAEL KINGS—JEROBOAM TO AHAZIAH (xiii.–xxii.)
MINISTRY OF PROPHET ELIJAH TO ISRAEL (xvii.–xxii.)

King Solomon

Solomon is a figure of striking interest in three ways—historically, personally, and typically.

Viewed *historically*, his special interest lies in the fact that he represents the peak period of Israel's prosperity as a kingdom. His reign marks the most splendid and affluent period of Hebrew history. No doubt can be left in our minds; even by a superficial reading of chapters ix. and x., that Solomon's riches and Israel's abundance at that time were such as to become a marvel both then and now. "Solomon in all his glory" has become, indeed, the classic figure of royal opulence. But besides this, Solomon is of historical interest as being the *last* of the kings to reign over a united Hebrew kingdom. It was through Solomon's own disobedience that the disruption took place, as we have seen; and there never will be a king reigning over a united Hebrew kingdom again until Christ Himself returns as David's Son and Lord.

Considered *personally*, Solomon is without doubt a remarkable figure; though it is not easy to reach a true estimate of his character. His super-normal wisdom made him a wonder to all the surrounding peoples. His prayer at the dedication of the temple reveals lofty spiritual capacity. His successful governmental administration bespeaks his more than ordinary mental power. Yet somehow, as to personal godliness there is a certain lack of decisiveness about him. There is a want of moral vigour. We miss that dash of fine passion which characterised the piety of David. While, on the one hand, Solomon never indulged such impetuous and presuming disobedience as that of Saul, yet, on the other hand, he never displayed such energetic devotion to God as that of David. If he partly escapes Saul's *condemnation*, he quite fails of David's *commendation*.

But the historical and personal interest attaching to Solomon is eclipsed by his significance *typically*. Like David, he is one of the greatest Old Testament types of Christ; and, like David, he typifies Christ in His yet future reign on earth. There are those who see an interesting difference in the way that David and Solomon respectively typify the coming reign of Christ. David is the type of Christ's *millennial* reign, that is, His reign on the earth for one thousand years, as David's greater Son, over the restored and regathered house of Israel. Solomon is the type of Christ's *post*-millennial reign, which Paul calls "the dispensation of the fulness of times," when Christ shall reign in that "new Jerusalem" which cometh down "from God, out of heaven." We shall not attempt to go into that matter here (but see further our note preceding the next lesson).

The Temple (v.–viii.)

We have shown that this first book of Kings is in two parts, the first eleven chapters wholly relating to the forty years' reign of Solomon, and the remaining eleven chapters covering the first eighty years of the two kingdoms. We would now point out that each of these two periods is made memorable by an outstanding phenomenon. In the first there is the building of the wonderful temple at Jerusalem. In the second there is the remarkable ministry of the prophet Elijah to the northern kingdom. Let us here note certain matters concerning the temple.

Chapter v.

In chapter v. we have the *preparations* for the temple. Solomon applies to Hiram, king of Tyre, for cedars from Lebanon. Israel's native timber wood was the sycamore (x. 27), which, although serviceable, was coarse, and much inferior to Lebanon cedar, which was hard, and close-grained. Hiram, king of Tyre, years before this, had sent cedars to David (2 Chron. ii. 3) to build him a royal dwelling; and it was characteristic of David that he should feel compunction about living in "an house of cedar" while the ark of God still remained in a mere tent (2 Sam. vii. 2). The superiority of Lebanon cedar, coupled with the expense of bringing it from so far away, made it a kind of luxury in Israel; and those houses which were made of it were looked upon as Israel's "quality" dwellings.

The communication between Solomon and Hiram is given more fully in 2 Chronicles ii., and with additional details of much interest. Solomon "*sent*" his message to Hiram, whereas Hiram "answered *in writing*." On both sides this was the courteous thing. Solomon, who is the one making request, sends a special envoy to deliver the message orally; and to such a request Hiram must needs send a written reply, sealed with the royal seal, and presumably returned by Solomon's own appointed envoy. Incidentally, also, here is an instance of communication by writing, in those long gone times.

Solomon's message to Hiram is striking in the testimony it bears to Jehovah. We have to remember that Hiram was an idolater, and that Solomon might easily have considered, therefore, that it was the more becoming to omit references to his own God, and simply mention the commercial details of his requirements. But see his glorious words in 2 Chronicles ii. 4-6 "Behold, I build an house to Jehovah my God . . . and the house which I build is great; for great is our God above all gods. But who is able to build Him an house, seeing the heaven and heaven of heavens cannot contain Him?" Here is noble testimony to the supremacy and infinity of Jehovah such as leaves no room for other supposed deities; yet the message is one of real courtesy. Still more remarkable is the reply of Hiram, who, far from being offended, acknowledged Jehovah in these words—"Blessed be Jehovah, God of Israel, *that made heaven and earth*, who hath given to David the king a wise son, endued with prudence and understanding, that might build an house for Jehovah, and an house for his kingdom" (2 Chron. ii. 12).

These were Solomon's full requirements from Hiram—"Send me now, therefore, a man cunning to work in gold and in silver and in brass and in iron, and in purple and in crimson and in blue, and that can skill to grave with the cunning men that are with me in Judah and in Jerusalem, whom David my father did provide. Send me also cedar trees, fir trees, and algum trees, out of Lebanon: for I know that thy servants can skill to cut timber in Lebanon; and, behold, my servants shall be with thy servants" (2 Chron. ii. 7, 8). Solomon, then, required a specialist in architecture and design, skilled hewers and cutters, and large supplies in several kinds of wood. His payment was to be in terms of agricultural produce described in 2 Chronicles ii. 10.

All this agrees with what we know about Phœnicia and Israel in those times. The country of the Phœnicians, among whom Hiram reigned, ran along the coast of the Mediterranean, and the Phœnicians themselves were a nation of merchantmen, with little time for agriculture, and a limited territory which was inadequate to supple the needs of their large and populous cities. Solomon's inland kingdom, on the other hand, was rich in various fruits and cereals, and could well supply peoples outside of itself.

The later verses of chapter v. tell us that Solomon raised a levy of thirty thousand men, and employed them in shifts of ten thousand per month at Lebanon, so that each man did four months out of the twelve, with a break of two months at home between each shift—a very considerate ratio. Besides these, Solomon had seventy thousand carriers, and eighty thousand hewers in the mountains. These mere menial workers were not Israelites, but Canaanites (see 2 Chron. ii. 17, 18), and there were three thousand three hundred superiors over them. These figures make a vast total of over *one hundred and eighty-three thousand*! We begin to see the magnitude of the undertaking.

Chapter v. closes with the words: "And the king commanded, and they brought *great stones, costly stones, and hewed stones*, to lay the foundation of the house. . . ." These great foundation stones remain to this day, now known as "Haram-esh-Sheref"; and upon them there stands the Mosque of Omar. Some of these "great stones" are from seventeen to nineteen feet in length; others are over twenty-four feet in length, eight feet in width and three or four feet thick. One stone is no less than *thirty-eight feet nine inches long*! A recent report says: "This great stone is one of the most interesting stones of the world, for it is the chief corner stone of the temple's massive wall. Fixed in its abiding position three thousand years ago, it still stands sure and steadfast." There can be no doubt that these huge blocks date back to Solomon. Decipherers have recently verified that the masons' signs on them are those of the *Phœnicians*—from whom, as the Scripture tells us, Solomon asked and received such material for the temple. When we consider the size and weight of these "great stones," and reflect that they would be transported all the way to Jerusalem by means of ox-drawn low-wheeled trucks, we cannot but marvel.

Chapters vi.–viii.

In chapter vi. we have the dimensions, materials, and construction of the temple. The data here given to us, while exact and detailed concerning each part described, have not enabled scholars to agree as to the contour and external architecture of the building. The ground-plan, however, is quite clear, its measurements throughout being exactly double those of the tabernacle. It was sixty cubits long, by twenty cubits wide. The length was divided into two parts, the one being the Holy Place, which was forty cubits, the other being the Holy of Holies, which was twenty cubits. Then, in front of the building, there was a porch which was as wide as the building itself (twenty cubits), and was ten cubits in depth. This porch, therefore, brought the length of the temple up to seventy cubits (excluding the thickness of the walls). Then, around the two sides and rear of the temple, there were small rooms built against the walls, from the outside, for the use of the priests. These ran round the walls in three stories, one room above another: and so that the flooring joists of these rooms should not need to be inserted into the walls of the sacred building, the temple walls were made with ledges on which these joists, or floor beams, could rest. The width of these rooms, plus the thickness of the walls, adds ten cubits to each side of the temple, and to the rear; so that the full length is now *eighty* cubits, and the breadth *forty* cubits.

Thus we see that the temple of Solomon was not a large building. The cubit is about one foot six inches: so that a building eighty cubits long by forty cubits wide is in English measurement 120 feet by 60 feet. This means that Solomon's temple was a very small building compared with some of our own churches; and this may at first seem surprising, if not disappointing, to us. But we must remember that, in view of the purpose and object of the temple, it was never intended to be of an imposing size. Unlike our modern *churches*, which are made to accommodate congregations, the temple was *not* made for assemblies of the people. The congregation never met *within* it, but offered worship *towards* it, as being the residence of the Deity. It was a place for the Divine presence, and for the priests who ministered before it; and for no others. In this, it was like the ancient Egyptian temples, and other temples of antiquity; and viewed in this light, any surprise at its seeming smallness disappears. As Dr. Kitto says, "The importance of the temple of Solomon, which we have been led to regard as one of the wonders of the ancient world, consisted not in its size, but in the elaborate, costly, and highly decorative character of its whole interior and furniture, and also in the number, extent, grandeur, and substantial masonry of its surrounding courts, chambers, walls, and towers. Indeed, it is not too much to presume that these outer constructions, forming the massive ring in which the costly gem of the temple was set, cost as much as the sacred building itself, immense as was the quantity of gold bestowed upon it."

We cannot here speak about the exquisite ornamentation of the interior, but must simply draw attention to the outstanding fact that the whole interior was "*overlaid with pure gold*" (verse 21). This was not mere gilding, but actual gold *overlaying*, of which art there are ample specimens preserved to us from olden times. The decorative carving was first done on cedar wood; and this formed the *base* of the enchasement which appeared on the gold surface. The amount of gold expended on the interior and furniture of the temple must have been very great. It is well, however, to remember that gold, in Solomon's day, was not *money*. It was not a medium of exchange, a standard of value, as it is today. Silver was the standard of value: and it is quite probable that Solomon bought gold with silver. We should clearly understand that gold was then valued for ornamental workings, but not as money, and that, therefore, as has been truly observed, the gold which is said to have been used in Solomon's temple does not represent the monetary *cost* involved, but the actual amount of the metal used.

We cannot here speak about the two wonderful golden cherubim, each fifteen feet tall, of the two great pillars of brass, each twenty-seven feet high, in the porch at the front (which porch, be it noted, was higher than the rest of the building), of the molten sea, the lavers and candelabra and tables and vessels, and of other interesting appurtenances of the temple. These should be read up carefully with the aid of a good commentary. But there are three points we ought to mention.

First, we are told that Solomon made narrow *windows* for the temple (vi. 4); and it may be that the question arises in some mind as to how there could be such windows if there were three stories of rooms built against the exterior of the temple walls. The answer is that these three stories together were only *fifteen* cubits high (vi. 10), whereas the temple was *thirty* cubits high (vi. 2). So that, even allowing for the flooring and roofing of the three stories of rooms, there was ample space above for the windows. These windows, of course, would not be glazed, but probably filled with ornate lattice work, which was then the common way of filling such windows.

Second, the opening verse of chapter vii. says: "But Solomon was building his own house *thirteen* years." Since the temple only took *seven* years, it might seem to suggest selfishness on Solomon's part that he should take six years longer than this over the building of his own house; but we wrong Solomon if we think thus. The "But" with which chapter vii. commences should be "And" (as in the Revised Version). There is no thought of *contrast* between the last words of chapter vi. (which say that Solomon took seven years to build the temple) and the first words of chapter vii. The *palace* buildings were much larger, and the undertaking a more extensive one; nor had there been any such preparation of materials for these buildings as there had been for the temple; and probably less workmen were engaged. It speaks well for Solomon that before ever he commenced his own house he completed the house for the Lord.

Third; we should not overlook *David's* part in the temple. Although he was not permitted to be its builder, and although he knew that he must die before ever it was built, yet with characteristic generosity he set about preparing for it. He seems to have thrown himself into this with as much zest as if he himself had been going to be its builder. In 1 Chronicles xxii. 2-5 we read: "And David commanded to gather together the strangers that were in the land of Israel; and he set masons to hew wrought stones to build the house of God. And David prepared iron in abundance for the nails for the doors of the gates, and for the joinings; and brass in abundance without weight; also cedar trees in abundance; for the Zidonians and they of Tyre brought much cedar wood to David. And David said: Solomon my son is young and tender, and the house that is to be builded for the Lord must be exceeding magnifical, of fame and of glory throughout all countries: I will therefore now make preparation for it. So David prepared abundantly before his death." How characteristic of David is this generous language and behaviour! In verse 14 of the same chapter we are told that he also left for the temple "an hundred thousand talents of gold, and a thousand thousand talents of silver, and of brass and iron without weight."

Moreover, in a remarkable passage (1 Chron. xxviii. 10-19) we find that David also left for Solomon *plans* and *patterns* for the temple, which he claimed to have received from God (verses 12 and 19). And he also left for Solomon good *friends* who gave ready help. Such an one was Hiram, King of Tyre, who, we read, "was ever a lover of David" (1 Kings v. 1), and who helped Solomon for David his father's sake.

There is something noble and touching, as well as pathetic, in David's enthusiastic provision for the temple which he himself would never see. May we have a like unselfishness toward those who are to follow us! God help us to leave our children the *moral* materials for the building of their lives as living temples! May we leave our children patterns which we have received from God; and may we leave them godly friends who will be wise and willing helpers of them when we ourselves have passed beyond!

THE FIRST BOOK OF KINGS (2)

Lesson Number 33

NOTE.—For this further study in the First Book of Kings, read again chapters i.-iv. and ix.-xi.

Homer has been translated into about twenty different languages. Shakespeare has been translated into about forty different languages. Leaving out all others, there are two books, so far as I know, that have gone out into over one hundred translations. Those are John Bunyan's *Pilgrim's Progress* and *The Imitation of Christ*, by Thomas à Kempis. The only two which have reached the three figures are those dependent upon the Bible. They are the offspring of the Bible . . . The Bible in its entirety, or parts of it, has been translated into just over *one thousand* languages of human speech.

—*G. Campbell Morgan.*

THE FIRST BOOK OF KINGS (2)

SOLOMON: HIS RISE, WISDOM, GLORY, AND FAILURE

The Accession of Solomon (i.-ii.)

SOLOMON was very young when he came to the throne. His own word is that he was "but a little child" (iii. 7). Eusebius says he was twelve. Josephus says he was fifteen. We may safely say he was not more than twenty. His early accession was precipitated by a conspiracy of Adonijah, David's eldest surviving son, who aspired to the throne. Adonijah apparently judged that he could bring off his *coup d'état* on the threefold ground of David's enfeeblement through old age, Solomon's disqualification through immaturity, and his own eminent suitability as being a favourite son of David, and a very attractive person (i. 6). He was backed up by Joab, the head of the army, and Abiathar, head of the priesthood, both of whom presumably sought their own interests—Joab to retain his leadership as under David, and Abiathar to oust his rival, Zadok.

But the stratagem proved abortive owing to the quick counter move of Nathan the prophet, who procured and then proclaimed the aged David's solemn oath that Solomon was the appointed successor. Adonijah's guilt is seen in his own confession, shortly afterward, that he had known the kingdom to be Solomon's *"from the Lord"* (ii. 15).

See chapter ii. Here is David's death-bed charge to Solomon. While the first part of it is sound and noble enough, the latter part contains certain grim touches which seem strange to a modern reader. David's word about Joab is: "Let not his hoar head go down to the grave in peace." His word about Shimei is: "His hoar head bring thou down to the grave with blood." But if these words of dying David are thought to express a revengeful spirit they are quite misunderstood. David's *personal* attitude to Joab and Shimei had been shown already. He had generously tolerated Joab through the years, and had pardoned the cursing of Shimei. His death-bed words about them are uttered from the standpoint of public duty, not of private vengeance.

See what Israel's Law enjoins—"Ye shall take no satisfaction for the life of a murderer which is guilty of death: but he shall surely be put to death. . . . *So ye shall not pollute the land wherein ye are; for blood it defileth the land: and the land cannot be cleansed of the blood that is shed therein, but by the blood of him that shed it*" (Num. xxxv. 31-3). "Thine eye shall not pity him; but thou shalt put away the guilt of innocent blood from Israel, *that it may go well with thee*" (Deut. xix. 13). Now Joab had cold-bloodedly murdered both Abner and Amasa; and he was therefore under a double guilt. It was now over thirty years since he had slain Abner, but at that very time David had evidently been thinking of the words of Israel's Divine law when he said: "I and my kingdom are guiltless before the Lord for ever from the blood of Abner the Son of Ner. Let it rest on the head of Joab, and on all his father's house" (2 Sam. iii. 28, 29). As a theocratic king, David is responsible for the maintenance of the Divine law; and it is this which lies behind his charge to Solomon. As the late Dr. J. L. Porter has said: "At the close of his life, David was roused to a sense of his neglect of this imperious duty. The kingdom was in peril. Divine vengeance was impending over it. He was then too weak to carry out the law. He was at the point of death; but, as the representative of the Divine Law-giver and Judge, he pronounced sentence upon the criminals, and charged his heir and successor to carry it out. In this there was no 'cold-blooded revenge.' There was strict, though somewhat tardy, justice."

The far sadder thing about David's charge concerning Joab is that Joab was called *so late* to pay for the blood of Abner, and that he should be punished after so long an interval *by those whom he had served so loyally and successfully*. Saddest of all was the fact that David himself had used this very man Joab as his accomplice in the murder of Uriah! It is greatly to be regretted that David should have gone down to the grave with such matters on his conscience.

In the case of Shimei there had been *treason* coupled with *blasphemy*—his cursing of "the Lord's Anointed." Solomon was not to regard him as altogether expurgated from that double crime. Shimei was a dangerous person, and not above suspicion. David had the safety of his son's kingdom at heart in his word about Shimei. Moreover, his word should be read in the light of what subsequently happened between Solomon and Shimei. In strict justice Shimei should have been put to death years before-hand; and David's clemency to him ought to have evoked a loyalty which seems to have been lacking.

The Wisdom of Solomon (iii.-iv.)

Solomon's prayer for wisdom, in preference to wealth, power, and length of days, is a beautiful passage (iii. 5-15). It reveals that the young king *already possessed* a marked degree of wisdom; for that he should *ask* wisdom above all else was above all else a *mark* of wisdom. In nothing is his early wisdom seen more clearly than that he should ask for *more* wisdom. Yet without lessening our appreciation of the noble choice here made by Solomon, it is right that we should clearly understand the *kind* of wisdom which he here besought, and with which he thereafter became supernaturally gifted; for unless we *do* understand this we shall find it puzzling to reconcile his wisdom with that later foolishness which appeared alongside of it.

Solomon's own words indicate that in asking for wisdom he did not mean *spiritual* wisdom—that insight in Divine things which comes only of regeneration and sanctification and a close fellowship with God, that wisdom of which Paul speaks in the New Testament. No; in *that* kind of wisdom Solomon falls considerably behind his father, David. The wisdom Solomon sought —and with which he became supernaturally endowed—was administrative discernment, sagacious judgment, intellectual grasp, aptitude for the acquisition of knowledge, a practical wisdom in the directing of affairs. In *this* kind of wisdom he excelled even the renowned philosophers of his day; as we read, in chapter iv. 29-34:

"*And God gave Solomon wisdom, and understanding exceeding much, and largeness of heart, even as the sand that is on the sea shore.*

"*And Solomon's wisdom excelled the wisdom of all the children of the east country, and all the wisdom of Egypt.*

"For he was wiser than all men; than Ethan the Ezrahite, and Heman, and Chalcol, and Darda, the sons of Mahol: and his fame was in all nations round about.

"And he spake three thousand proverbs: and his songs were a thousand and five.

"And he spake of trees, from the cedar tree that is in Lebanon even unto the hyssop that springeth out of the wall: he spake also of beasts, and of fowl, and of creeping things, and of fishes.

"And there came of all people to hear the wisdom of Solomon, from all kings of the earth, which had heard of his wisdom."

To the people at large, the first evidence of the young king's penetrating insight came with his decision in the case of the two young mothers who came as rival claimants to the same babe (iii. 16–28). Solomon's handling of this case is indeed striking. Any misgivings hitherto entertained on account of his immaturity were thereby removed. The people recognised a wisdom in him which was far beyond his tender years. This was indeed the wisdom of God in him. Thenceforth, Solomon held the confidence and veneration of all his people.

The Glory of Solomon (ix.–x.)

The completion of the temple and the palace mark off the first twenty years of Solomon's reign (see ix. 10). The remaining twenty are briefly dealt with in chapters ix. to xi. The two chapters ix. and x. mark the peak period. Their eloquent description needs almost no comment here. They leave us in no doubt as to the material splendour of that time. The account of Solomon's revenue and splendour (x. 14–29) is an astonishing paragraph; and when we read that Solomon made silver to be as common as stones in Jerusalem, it is well to remember that silver, not gold, was the *money* of that day!

The visit of the Queen of Sheba (x. 1–13) has an interest all its own; and Solomon's generosity to her becomes a beautiful illustration of the *heavenly* King's bounty to ourselves. In chapter x. 13 we read: "And king Solomon gave unto the queen of Sheba all her desire, whatsoever she asked, beside that which Solomon gave her of his royal bounty." The wondering-eyed Queen was fairly overcome by all the much-to-be-coveted treasures which she saw. With womanly appreciation, she simply could not resist asking for this and that and the other thing, until eventually she found herself in the quandary of seeing much more that she desired, without being able to commit the rudeness of asking still further! Solomon, however, read her heart, and gave her not only all that she *asked*, but all that she *thought*; and then, even to that, he added his "royal bounty." See, then, the three measures of Solomon's generosity which we have here—(1) All that she *ASKED*; (2) All that she *THOUGHT*; (3) Solomon's royal *BOUNTY*.

With this in mind, turn to Ephesians iii. 20—"Now unto Him that is able to do exceeding abundantly above all that we ask or think, according to the power that worketh in us." Here is the same three-fold measure of giving—(1) "all that we *ask*"; (2) "all that we *think*"; and (3) "*exceeding abundantly above.*" God grant us faith to ask for big things, and to have large desires toward Him!—for giving does not impoverish Him, and withholding does not enrich Him.

It is interesting to note that in the verse above-quoted, where Solomon is said to have given the Queen of Sheba "of his royal bounty," the Hebrew reads, literally, "*according to the hand of King Solomon.*" Think what that "according to" meant. Solomon was the richest king in all the earth, and his giving was such as *corresponded* with that! What lavish bounty, then, is in that "according to"! It reminds us of Philippians iv. 19—"My God shall supply all your need *according to* HIS riches in glory by Christ Jesus." May the Holy Spirit teach us the meaning of that "according to," and enrich our lives with that royal bounty which comes from Him who said, "A greater than Solomon is here."

The Failure of Solomon (xi.)

Alas, the glory of the Solomonic period was short-lived. Soon were Israel's sons to lament, "How is the gold become dim!" The fault was Solomon's alone. The following sentences, picked from chapter xi., tell the story of his failure. "But king Solomon loved many strange women." "Solomon clave unto these in love." "His wives turned away his heart after other gods." "Solomon did evil in the sight of the Lord." "The Lord was angry with Solomon." "The Lord said: I will surely rend the kingdom from thee." It was this infidelity of Solomon which precipitated the disruption into the two kingdoms. The sun of Solomon's glory set in dark clouds. Not all the gorgeous apparel of his costly wardrobe could hide the ugly blot on his character. Not only had Solomon abused marriage; he had filled his great harem with women from those nations against which Israel had repeatedly received Divine interdict—Moab, Ammon, Edom, and others, and had even built "high places" for their abominable deities. The *king's* behaviour being such, what more likely than that the *people* would quickly sink, too? Solomon had forfeited further Divine favour. The wisest of all men had become the greatest of all fools, for he had sinned against light and privilege and promise such as had been given to no other man in all the earth. The kingdom should be rent from his family, except that Judah should be retained for David's sake. Chapter xi. closes with the death of Solomon, and thus ends the first part of the book. Truly, in Solomon we see how inferior is the greatest human wisdom to true piety. If, as the psalmist says, "the fear of the Lord is the *beginning* of wisdom," then surely the highest of all wisdom is to obey the Lord in all things, and thus to walk before Him with a perfect heart.

The following quotation gives a fair criticism of Solomon: "In estimating him, we must remember his privileges and opportunities. He did not, as his father, inherit a wrecked kingdom and a demoralised army, but a kingdom established in righteousness, and an army all-victorious. Then he had the experience of the two previous kings to guide him. Peacefulness, as his name indicates, certainly characterised his reign; but how far he merited his other name, Jedidiah, 'Beloved of the Lord, may be questioned. Abraham was the 'friend of God,' and David the man 'after God's own heart'; but Solomon did not walk in their ways. His record has its bright features, as is seen in his early humility, his wise choice of a gift, his building of the temple, and his wonderful prayer at its dedication (1 Kings iii. 7 and 9; viii. 22–53). Were these removed from the record, what would be left to the credit of his memory? He was a man of extraordinary ability, a botanist, zoologist, architect, poet, and moral philosopher; and yet a man who strangely lacked in strength of character. Moses had said that Israel's future kings should not multiply wealth, horses, or wives (Deut. xvii. 14–20), but Solomon did all three. He who was beloved of his God, not so much, one would think, for his own sake as for David's, was made to sin by 'outlandish women' (Neh. xiii. 26), after the Lord had appeared to him twice. He took to himself seven hundred wives, and from amongst those very nations against which Israel had been warned (1 Kings xi. 1, 2). This led to the introduction of false gods and false worship, for which the judgment of the Lord was pronounced against him. If any man could ever have been satisfied by getting all his heart's desire, that man was Solomon; yet he has put it on record (Eccles.) that everything under the sun is vanity and vexation of spirit. Solomon's is the self-life having its full fling, and at the end turning away sad and sick of it all."

So much, then, for king Solomon—his accession, his wisdom, his glory, and his failure. Is there anywhere a character which is more of an enigma? Is there in all history a more thought-provoking irony than this, that the wisest of all men became the greatest of fools, that the man who had wealth and fame, and pleasure above all others, should write at the end, "Vanity of vanities!—all is vanity!"? Let us read, mark, learn, and inwardly digest!

ADDENDUM ON SOLOMON'S REIGN

We have said that Solomon's reign typifies the coming reign of Christ on earth. What then were the outstanding characteristics of Solomon's reign? First, throughout his reign there was *peace* and *rest.* Not one war or internal disturbance broke the serenity of that forty years. Second, there was surpassing *wisdom* and *knowledge*, as we see in 1 Kings iv. and x. Third, there was *wealth* and *glory*—such as excelled all that had gone before. Fourth, there was *fame* and *honour*, Solomon's name being the greatest in all the countries around Israel, and Israel being honoured by all peoples. Fifth, there was *joy* and *safety*. In 1 Kings iv. 25 we read: "Judah and Israel dwelt safely, every man under his vine and under his fig tree, from Dan even to Beersheba, all the days of Solomon." See also verse 20.

Now these are certainly the predicted marks of that kingdom which Christ will yet set up among the nations. There will be *peace* and *rest*: "Nation shall not lift up sword against nation, neither shall they learn war any more." "The wolf also shall dwell with the lamb, and the leopard shall lie down with the kid; and the calf and the young lion and the fatling together; and a little child shall lead them." There will also be unprecedented *wisdom* and *knowledge*; for "the earth shall be full of the knowledge of the Lord, as the waters cover the sea."

So, also, will there be *wealth* and *glory* such as have never been known before, for "the mountain (i.e. the kingdom) of the Lord's house shall be established in the tops of the mountains (i.e. kingdoms), and shall be exalted above the hills; and all nations shall flow unto it." And there will also be such *fame* and *honour*, and such empire, as no king has ever known before; for "He (Christ) shall have dominion, also, from sea to sea, and from the river unto the ends of the earth; yea, all kings shall fall down before Him; all nations shall serve Him." And there will also be *joy* and *safety* for all the privileged subjects in that eventual kingdom; for in Micah iv. 4 we read of it that "they shall sit every man under his vine and under his fig tree; and none shall make them afraid; for the mouth of the Lord of hosts hath spoken it." There is no more engrossing study in all the Scriptures than the study of those glowing passages in the prophets, which describe the glories of this Davidic and Solomonic kingdom of Christ which is yet to be on earth. Well may our daily prayer be, "Thy kingdom come!"

—*J. S. B.*

THE FIRST BOOK OF KINGS (3)

Lesson Number 34

NOTE.—For this concluding study in the First Book of Kings read again chapters xii. to xxii.

Solomon continued the policy and shared the blessing of his father. His dominions extended from the Mediterranean to the Euphrates. and from the Red Sea and Arabia to the utmost Lebanon (1 Kings iv, 21, etc.). The tributary states were held in complete subjection, and, as they were still governed by their own princes, Solomon was literally "king of kings." The Canaanites who remained in Palestine became peaceable subjects or useful servants. His treasures were immense, composed largely of the spoils won by his father from many nations, and treasured up by him for the purpose of building a temple to Jehovah. To these Solomon added the proceeds of oppressive taxation. The largeness of his harem transgressed the bounds of even Oriental licence, though possibly dictated by worldly policy.

The wisdom of Solomon is celebrated both in Scripture and in Eastern story. Three thousand proverbs gave proof of his virtues and sagacity. A thousand and five songs placed him among the first of Hebrew poets; while his knowledge of natural history was shown by writings which were long admired.

His very greatness betrayed him. His treasures, wives, and chariots were all contrary to the spirit and precepts of the Law (Deut. xvii. 16, 17). His exactions alienated the affections of his people; and, above all, he was led astray by his wives, and built temples to Chemosh, or Baal-Peor, the obscene idol of Moab; to Moloch, the god of Ammon; and to Ashtoreth, the goddess of the Sidonians. His later days, therefor, were disturbed by "adversaries," who stirred up revolt in the tributory states; the tribe of Ephraim became a centre of disaffection; Hadad did "mischief" in Edom; Damascus declared its independence under Rezon; and Ahijah was instructed to announce to Solomon himself that, as he had broken the covenant by which he held his crown, the kingdom should be rent from him and part of it given to his servant, 1 Kings xi. 31.

—*Angus, Bible Handbook.*

THE FIRST BOOK OF KINGS (3)

THE TWO KINGDOMS

WE COME now to the second half of the book. Immediately following Solomon's death the Disruption takes place; and from this point we follow the fortunes of the *two* kingdoms and the two lines of kings. To deal separately with each of these kings is not necessary to our present scheme of study: but let us try to pick out the ruling significances of the Disruption and the subsequent course of things.

The Disruption

Israel's Tragedy.

First, the Disruption was a *tragedy*. At the close of Solomon's reign Israel had become exalted to the highest dignity in its history. Worship, religion and public instruction had become, through the provision made by David and Solomon, such as had never been known before. As the late Principal Baylee says: "The theology of the Psalms, the practical wisdom of the Proverbs, the mystical suggestiveness of the Canticles, the patriarchal teachings of Job, the archæology of Genesis, the manifestation of God in history from Joshua to 2 Samuel, gave a fulness of instruction and guidance which was calculated to make Israel the centre of light and blessedness to the whole world." The high purposes of God through Israel were developing with increasing observableness; and we can only exclaim: "Alas, what might have been if the Disruption had not struck the nation with so deadly a wound!"

Solomon's guilt.

Second, it is well to grasp clearly that the Scriptures locate the *blame* for the Disruption with Solomon. As we saw in the book of the Judges, while God may confer many privileges, He never confers the privilege to *sin*—no, not even with such an elect personage as Solomon; and therefore, much as it must have grieved the God of the Davidic covenant, the Disruption was permitted. Solomon's guilt was great. It is an awful yet true indictment of him to say that "the whole after-history of the Disruption, the gradual decline of power and influence, the corruption of morals, and at times the almost total forgetfulness of God, were only the necessary developments of those pernicious principles and practices introduced by Solomon."

Rehoboam's folly.

Third, in chapter xii. the *actual occurrence* of the Disruption is explained. In the later years of Solomon's reign the extravagant expenses of the royal court had become such as to necessitate the levying of taxes which the people were ill able to yield. Therefore, on the death of Solomon and the accession of Rehoboam, the people, under Jeroboam's leadership, sought a redress of their grievance by a diminution of this burden. Their request seems to have been a reasonable one—"Thy father made our yoke grievous: now therefore make thou the grievous service of thy father, and his heavy yoke which he put upon us, lighter; and we will serve thee" (xii. 4). The stupid behaviour and fatuous reply of Rehoboam, however, reveal his utter inability to measure such a situation (xii. 5–15), and disclose a mental inferiority which stands in painful contrast with the mental superiority of his distinguished father. His senseless threat to outdo his father's severities towards his subjects was the last straw. The ten tribes renounced any further allegiance to the house of David; and Jeroboam became their king.

Jeroboam's innovations.

Fourth, the Disruption occasioned *grave innovations* in the ten-tribed kingdom. Jeroboam was as shrewd and unscrupulous as he was energetic and forceful. He quickly perceived that although he had fortified Shechem as his capital, Jerusalem would still be regarded as the uniting centre of all the tribes unless some drastic steps were taken to negative this. The temple and the ark of the covenant, and all those things which were emblematically sacred in Israel's religion, were in Jerusalem, as also was the principal seat of learning. If the people were to continue going up to the religious festivals there the result, sooner or later, would prove fatal to the throne of the ten-tribed kingdom.

Jeroboam therefore established two new centres of worship in the ten-tribed kingdom—the one at Dan in the north, and the other at Bethel in the south, professedly on the ground that it was "too much" for the people to keep going all the way to Jerusalem (xii. 28). In each of the two new centres he installed a golden calf, and proclaimed: "Behold thy gods, O Israel, which brought thee up out of the land of Egypt." Thus was Israel led into grave sin.

It is only fair to Jeroboam to allow that in setting up the golden calves he was not meaning to introduce the worship of gods other than Jehovah; for the calves were clearly understood by the people to be symbolical figures consecrated to Jehovah. Yet Jeroboam's guilt remains great, for he evidently had the episode of *Aaron's* golden calf in mind, seeing that he used the same words as Aaron himself had used—"These be thy gods, O Israel, which brought thee up out of the land of Egypt"; and Jeroboam knew well enough the anger of God and of Moses at that sin, besides knowing that all idol-representation of Israel's God was forbidden.

Jeroboam also built "high places" for the new worship, in-stituted sacrifices, and ordained a feast to correspond with the Feast of Tabernacles, though he put its observance one month later than that of the feast in Judæa. Moreover, he elected a new order of priests from the lowest of the people. This he did because the true priests and Levites, much to their credit, apparently preferred to lose their livings, and resort to Jerusalem, rather than be party to Jeroboam's illicit innovations (see 2 Chron. xi. 13). It would seem, also, that the evacuating priests and Levites were joined by other faithful souls in Israel (2 Chron. xi. 16); but the ten-tribed kingdom as a whole quickly fell in with the new arrangements (1 Kings xii. 30); and thus, besides the *political* disruption which had severed Israel and Judah from each other, there now came a *religious* cleavage.

Jeroboam was a shrewd and forceful man, as we have said; but he was entirely without the spiritual insight to see that since *God* had put him on the throne, God Himself would overrule those contingencies which seemed to threaten his throne. He went more and more deeply into sin, and dragged the people with him. His distinguishing epitaph is "Jeroboam, the son of Nebat, which made Israel to sin" (I Kings xxii. 52; 2 Kings iii. 3; x. 29, etc.). Thus, the ten-tribed kingdom had a sorry beginning; and it rapidly went from bad to worse.

The Two Lines of Kings

Compare now the two lines of kings, up to the point where this First Book of Kings ends. There is no need to go into a lot of details. The broad facts tell a clear story. As we have said, the second half of I Kings covers roughly the first *eighty* years of the two kingdoms, from the Disruption. During that period four kings reigned in Judah, and eight in Israel. Their names, along with the number of years they reigned, and the Scripture verdict on them, are as follows:

JUDAH Southern		ISRAEL Northern	
Rehoboam . . . evil	17 years	Jeroboam . . . evil	22 years
Abijam . . . evil	3	Nadab . . . evil	2
Asa . . . good	41	Baasha . . . evil	24
Jehoshaphat . . good	25	Elah . . . evil	2
Jehoram . . . (Although mentioned in chap. xxii. 50, Jehoram's reign did not begin until *after* Ahaziah's reign which is shown in the Israel column).	—	Zimri . . . evil	— (one week)
		Omri . . . evil	12
		Ahab . . . evil	22
		Ahaziah . . . evil	2
	about 86 years		about 86 years

From these figures it will be seen that, in the period covered, Israel had twice as many kings as Judah. Eight kings in about eighty years is not good for any nation. But what is far worse, of the eight kings who reigned over Israel, every one was *evil*— a tragic record. Of the four kings who reigned over Judah, the two who reigned the longest (covering sixty-six years out of eighty-six) were *good* kings.

The Prophet Elijah (xvii.-xxii.)

The last six chapters of 1 Kings are occupied with the ministry of the prophet Elijah in the *northern* kingdom, the kingdom of the ten tribes. This spectacular man of God rivets our attention to good purpose. He is one of the most remarkable figures in the whole story of Israel. His eminence is seen both in the religious reformation which he wrought, and in the fact that the New Testament speaks of him more often than of any other Old Testament prophet. [Moreover, it was he who was chosen to appear with Moses at our Lord's transfiguration.] And further, it is from this point that the ministry of the *prophets* in the two Hebrew kingdoms becomes more prominently emphasised. One of Israel's most startling and romantic characters, he suddenly appears on the scene as the crisis-prophet, with thunder on his brow and tempest in his voice. He disappears just as suddenly, swept skywards in a chariot of fire. Between his first appearing and his final disappearing lies a succession of amazing miracles. We here call attention to three things—his character, his ministry, his significance.

His Character.

The grandeur of Elijah's character is recognised by all. Even those critics who have disputed Elijah's miracles have allowed the greatness of his character. He seems to have been somewhat remarkable even *physically*. He was not a man of the city but of the open country. In fact he seems to have been a veritable bedouin, loving the haunts of the hills and the valleys, and roaming the broad, unsettled pasturages of Bashan. His rugged and austere appearance would be such as at once to attract the eye of the softer-clad townsman. When we read of Elijah's confronting Ahab, and announcing the coming drought, we must picture the shaggy-bearded, long-haired, weather-tanned sheik, or the gaunt, piercing-eyed dervish, clad with a rough sheepskin, striding into the king's presence, and lifting up a sinewy arm to heaven as he denounces the weak-willed king in tones sounding like awesome echoes from the mountains.

But Elijah is no less striking in his *moral* make-up. Three qualities are specially conspicuous—courage, faith, zeal. See his *courage*. Here is the Martin Luther of old-time Israel, who singlehanded challenged the whole priesthood of the state religion, and all the people of the realm, to the decisive test on Mount Carmel.

See also Elijah's *faith*. It was his faith which underlay his courage. What faith it required to go before Ahab and say, "There shall not be dew nor rain these years, but according to my word"! Dew and rain may be withheld through ordinary natural causes for days or even weeks or in very rare cases for some months; but for dew and rain to be suspended for years involved supernatural intervention.

Then see Elijah's *zeal*. Truly did he express his master passion when he said: "I have been very jealous for the Lord God of hosts." How much, this sun-bronzed, untutored child of the desert can teach us of jealousy for the Divine honour, of burning indignation at religious compromise, and of passionate loyalty to the word of God!

His Ministry.

Old Dr. Kitto remarks, "There were two sorts of prophets: prophets of deeds, and prophets of words. Of the latter the greatest is doubtless Isaiah. Of the former there has not been among men a greater than Elijah." This, then, is the first thing about Elijah's ministry: he was a prophet of *deeds*. So far as we know he wrote nothing; and this does not surprise us. Such devout impetuosity and tempestuousness as Elijah's seldom go with patient penmanship. Many of the most passionate and energetic reformers have been altogether ungifted as writers. They were men of action rather than diction. There is always need for such men.

But again, Elijah's ministry was one of *miracles*. At every turn miracles meet us. Because of this some recent "scholars" have summarily discarded this section of Scripture as largely mythical. Yet the narrative is so sober and circumstantial that had it not been for this miracle element in it the most destructive critic would never have questioned its veracity.

Again, Elijah's ministry was one of *reformation*. He did not originate anything. He was a protestant against the religious apostasy and resultant degradation of his nation; and he called

men back to the good old ways which Israel's covenant-keeping
God had marked out for them through Moses. There is need
today for such outright protestation.

His Significance.

First, Elijah demonstrates the truth that *God always has a
man to match the hour*. Things were dark enough when Ahab
began to reign, but he soon made them a hundred times worse.
It is written: "There was none like unto Ahab which did sell
himself to work wickedness in the sight of the Lord, whom
Jezebel his wife stirred up." Under the royal lead a grimly determined effort was made to stamp out the religion of Jehovah.
Of all hours in Israel's career this was the ugliest. Yet just at
zero hour God's champion arises. The same thing is seen again
and again in history. When the light of evangelical truth seems
on the point of being extinguished from Christendom, and
Popery smothers Europe's millions beneath its evil cloak, God
has his Martin Luthers and John Calvins to call back the con-
tinent to the faith once for all delivered to the saints. When
politics and religion and morals become so degraded in Britain
that the very vitals of the nation are jeopardised, God has His
John Wycliffes and William Tyndales and Whitefields and
Wesleys.

Another thing which Elijah illustrates is that *when wickedness
develops into extraordinary proportions God meets it with extraordinary measures*. The Phœnician gods which Jezebel and Ahab
had taught Israel to worship were largely emblems of the material
elements which produce dew and rain—Baal, Ashtoreth and
Ashere. Therefore the *true* God will show His superiority over all
the powers of nature by suspending rain and dew for three years
and six months! Over against the fake miracles of the false
religion Jehovah will now intervene with *real* miracles! This is
why the ministry of Elijah is one of miracles. God is meeting
an extraordinary situation by extraordinary measures. And I
believe that in the present days, when undoubtedly an extraordinary situation has begun to develop, we may expect God
again to meet the challenge by extraordinary measures.

There are other ways in which Elijah is significant for us today;
but we mention only one more. *Elijah is to come to this earth*

again! Strikingly enough we are told this in the very last words of the Old Testament (Mal. iv. 5–6). There are those who scorn such an idea just as they deny a visible return of the Lord Jesus. There are those who hold that the prophecies of Isaiah and Malachi concerning the coming of Elijah were fulfilled in John the Baptist, of whom our Lord said: "Elias is come already." But while John was an interim fulfilment, he was not Elijah personally; and our Lord said (after John's death) that the real Elijah was "still to come" (Matt. xvii. 11, literal translation). If we turn on to that strange eleventh chapter of Revelation we find that one of the two "witnessess" who are to come to earth just before the crash of the present world-system and the return of Christ is Elijah (as the delineation makes clear). Truly Elijah is a significant figure. When he came on the scene long ago things quickly moved; and when he reappears in the near future still bigger things will be on the move! The Lord's own return will be at hand!

THE SECOND BOOK OF KINGS (1)

Lesson Number 35

NOTE.—For this study read right through the Second Book of Kings once or twice.

The great empires of the East, Assyria, Babylon, and Persia, will now, almost exclusively, occupy our attention (i.e. onwards from this Second Book of Kings). They all alike exercised the greatest influence upon the destinies of ancient Israel; and it is among the most welcome surprises of recent times that this long period of Israel's history should now have found such a continuous and marvellous commentary in the recovered records of those great world-kingdoms. The confirmations are so numerous and so conclusive that the critics have had to confess that here at least the Bible must be recognised as history. This has been accompanied also with the overturn of some of their earlier and most confident conclusions. For, wherever the explorer and the discoverer bring back to us the past with which the Bible deals, the critic has to retire confounded and ashamed.

—*John Urquhart.*

THE SECOND BOOK OF KIN~

THIS Second Book of Kings, which opens with the translation of Elijah to heaven, and closes with the transportation of the captive Jews to Babylon, is more tragic than all which have preceded it. Nay, more than that, it is the most tragic national record ever written. The elect people, through whom the gracious purposes of God were to have been developed for the enlightenment and regeneration of the whole race, become more and more steeped in infidelity and moral degradation, until finally the measure of their wickedness is full, judgment falls, pitiless foes wreak vengeance on them, and drag them from their own land into humiliating captivity.

The Book of the Dispersion

In chapter xvii. we see the ten-tribed *northern* kingdom (Israel) going into the Assyrian captivity, from which they have never since returned; while in chapter xxv. we see Jerusalem sacked, the temple burnt, and the *southern* kingdom (Judah) going into the Babylonian captivity, from which only a remnant returned.

Although Judah did not go into captivity until over a century after the break-up of Israel, the two captivities are spoken of together as the *Dispersion*. We have seen how each of the historical books, so far, is distinguished by some controlling feature. It will repay us to fix these firmly in our memory.

1 Samuel is *the book of the Transition*—from theocracy to monarchy. 2 Samuel is *the book of David's reign*. 1 Kings is *the book of the Disruption*—of the one kingdom into two. And now, 2 Kings is always to be remembered as *the book of the Dispersion*.

We cannot read 2 Kings without thinking of Solomon's proverb —"The way of transgressors is hard." Paul's word—"The wages of sin is death," is here demonstrated on a national scale, and in clearly declared terms of poetic justice for all to see and heed. Sinning despite warning brings ruin without remedy. Inexcusable wrong brings inescapable wrath. Abused privilege incurs increased penalty. The deeper the guilt, the heavier the stroke. Correction may be resisted, but retribution cannot be evaded. "How shall we escape if we neglect . . ." God is not mocked: whatsoever a nation soweth, that shall it also reap. All these thoughts crowd in upon our minds when we read 2 Kings. As we see the battered, broken tribes of Israel dragged behind the chariots of their heathen conquerors, we surely cannot fail to see that the central message of this book is that *wilful sin brings a woeful end.*

Structure

Writers on these books of the Kings seem to find it very difficult to give a suitable analysis of their contents, because the two histories of Judah and Israel repeatedly overlap and interlock in the one narrative. But to ourselves the broad outlines are unmistakably clear. We have seen how in 1 Samuel the three parts clearly gather round Saul, Samuel, and David; and how, just as clearly, in 2 Samuel we first have David's triumphs and then David's troubles. We have seen, also, how 1 Kings is unmistakably divided into two main parts, the first part being wholly devoted to Solomon's forty years' reign, and the second part covering the first eighty years of the two kingdoms. And now we shall find that in this Second Book of Kings the main divisions are easily discoverable and just as easily rememberable.

It will be seen that the first ten chapters are practically wholly occupied with the *northern* kingdom, Israel (the only reference to Judah being purely incidental, to mention how two of Judah's kings joined Israel in two military actions, and because of connection by marriage with the house of Ahab). In these first ten chapters the ministry of Elisha to the northern kingdom is the predominant subject.

Then, in the next group of chapters, chapters xi. to xvii., we have alternating annals of *both* kingdoms, ending, in chapter xvii., with the passing of Israel into the *Assyrian* captivity.

Finally, in chapters xviii. to xxv., we have the history of *Judah only* (since the ten-tribed northern kingdom is now dispersed in captivity); and this third group of chapters ends with the passing of Judah into the *Babylonian* captivity. For the sake of making this clear both to the outward and the inward eye, we set it out as follows:

THE SECOND BOOK OF KINGS

The Book of the Dispersion

WILFUL SIN BRINGS A WOEFUL END

I. ANNALS OF ISRAEL, THE NORTHERN KINGDOM

(i.–x.).

THIS PART CONTAINS THE MINISTRY OF ELISHA, AND CONCLUDES WITH THE DEATH OF JEHU, ISRAEL'S TENTH KING.

II. ALTERNATING ANNALS OF BOTH KINGDOMS

(xi.–xvii.).

THIS PART RUNS UP TO THE ASSYRIAN CAPTIVITY OF ISRAEL. (JONAH, AMOS AND HOSEA PROPHESIED AT THIS TIME IN ISRAEL.)

III. ANNALS OF JUDAH, THE SOUTHERN KINGDOM

(xviii.–xxv.).

THIS PART ENDS WITH JUDAH'S BABYLONIAN CAPTIVITY BY WHICH TIME OBADIAH, JOEL, ISAIAH, MICAH, NAHUM, HABAKKUK, ZEPHANIAH, AND JEREMIAH HAD PROPHESIED IN JUDAH.

(For our present purpose there is no need for a more detailed analysis. It is the above three main movements which we ought to fix clearly in mind, to make the book as a whole more easily rememberable.)

Thus this second book of the Kings marks the end of both the Hebrew kingdoms, historically, though they still remain the subject of great prophecies which will be considered later on in our course of study. It is in the fulfilment of these prophecies that the final triumph of God in and through the Hebrew race will be achieved; but, viewed historically, the story of God's earthly people is one of heart-rending human failure and tragedy, as this second book of the Kings shows.

The Two Royal Lines in Completeness

Since this second book of the Kings records the dispersion and ruin of *both* the Hebrew kingdoms (the ten-tribed northern kingdom into the _Assyrian_ captivity, 721 B.C., and the southern kingdom, Judah, into the _Babylonian_ exile, 587 B.C.), it is well that we should scan the two lines of kings in their completeness, that is, at least, from the time when the ten tribes broke away at the "Disruption" to form their own kingdom, in 975 B.C.

It is noteworthy that nineteen kings, in all, reigned over the ten-tribed kingdom, and the kingdom lasted only some two hundred and fifty years; whereas Judah, which had twenty kings from the time of the Disruption, continued for some three hundred and ninety years from that point. Again, the nineteen kings of Israel came from no less than seven different dynasties, whereas all the twenty kings of Judah were of one and the same dynasty—the Davidic.

This leads us to make two observations.

First, although the successive kings are not dealt with in detail, but are viewed as kings rather than as men, it is noteworthy that in the case of Judah's kings *David is the standard according to which their character is estimated*. Again and again we have such words as "His heart was not perfect with the Lord his God as was the heart of David his father" (see 1 Kings xi. 4, 6, 33, 38); "Thou hast not been as My servant David" (xiv. 8); "His heart was not perfect with the Lord his God as the heart of David his father" (xv. 3); "Asa did that which was right in the eyes of the Lord, as did David his father" (xv. 11); and so on. This is a great tribute to David. Despite those personal sins which marred his life, his trust in God, his general integrity, his jealousy for the Divine honour, and his reverent recognition of responsibility as a theocratic king, were such as fully to justify his being called a man after God's own heart, and to make him a pattern to all his royal successors.

Second, it is clear that one of the ruling purposes of the Scripture history here is to show the faithfulness of God to the Davidic covenant (2 Sam. vii.), in *the preservation of the Davidic* line (see for instance 2 Kings viii. 19). Again and again the royal house of David seemed in peril of being cut off. It was threatened at the revolt of the ten tribes. Later, after the death of Ahaziah,

KINGS OF JUDAH AND ISRAEL

FROM THE DISRUPTION ONWARDS

Giving the number of years which each reigned, and showing roughly how the reigns in the two lines synchronised.

JUDAH	yrs	ISRAEL	yrs
Rehoboam . . .	17	Jeroboam . . .	22
Abijam . . .	3	Nadab . . .	2
Asa	41	Baasha . . .	24
		Elah . . .	2
		Zimri . .	1 week
		Omri . . .	12
Jehoshaphat . .	25	Ahab . . .	22
		Ahaziah . .	2
		Jehoram . .	12
Jehoram .	8	Jehu . . .	28
Ahaziah . . .	1		
Athaliah . .	6		
Joash . . .	40	Jehoahaz . . .	17
Amaziah . . .	29	Jehoash . . .	16
Azariah (Uzziah) .	52	Jeroboam II . .	41
		Interregnum . .	12
		Zechariah . .	½
		Shallum . .	1 month
		Menahem . . .	10
		Pekahiah . . .	2
Jotham . . .	16	Pekah . . .	20
Ahaz . . .	16	Hoshea . . .	9
Hezekiah . . .	29		
Manasseh . . .	55		
Amon . . .	2		
Josiah . . .	31		
Jehoahaz . .	3 months		
Jehoiakim . . .	11		
Jehoiakin . .	3 months		
Zedekiah . . .	11		

when the royal city was held by a usurper, and the survival of
the Davidic line through Solomon hung on the preserving of the
child Joash from the usurper's sword, the woman Jehosheba
saved the child and the line continued. Still later, when the as
yet childless king Hezekiah was sick and apparently dying, and
Jerusalem was besieged by the Assyrians, and it seemed as though
the Davidic line was imperilled both by sword and sickness, God
intervened, and the line continued. Still later, when the kingdom
of Judah fell, on account of its sinning, the faithfulness of God
continued and the line was preserved; for although God had
to say of the wicked king Jeconiah, "Write this man childless,"
and the line of David through Solomon failed, a subsidiary line
had been preserved from David through Nathan, into which
line the succession now ran. And even after the Captivity in
Babylon the line continues in Zerubbabel, under whose leadership the temple was rebuilt; and from him the genealogical record
is preserved right down to the birth of the Lord Jesus Christ,
David's Son and Lord, in whom the Davidic line is perpetuated
for evermore, and by whom, at His second advent, the throne
of David shall be set up on earth again in the city of Jerusalem,
in fulfilment of that covenant made with David long ago.

We hear that since Israel recently became constituted and
acknowledged as an independent State again in Palestine, en-
quiries have been set going, and certain pretensions made, with
the idea of establishing a present day lineal link with the Davidic
throne. Whether there be truth in this we do not know for certain;
but one thing which *is* certain is that Israel will never be an
independent *kingdom* again until the King himself returns, even
our Lord Jesus Christ. He, and He alone, will re-establish the
Davidic throne, for since His birth at Bethelehem He alone is
the true Heir, according to the Scriptures of both Old and New
Testaments.

> Jesus is king! Jesus is king!
> True king of Israel; David's great Son;
> Hope of the fathers; Heir to the throne;
> Lion of Judah; Lamb that was slain;
> True king of Israel, yet shall He reign.
> Jesus is king! Jesus is king!

THE SECOND BOOK OF KINGS (2)

Lesson Number 36

NOTE.—For this further study in 2 Kings, read again the first ten chapters and chapter xiii.

The newest knowledge cannot be said to be drawing us away from the Bible; on the contrary it is bringing us back to it. Our foremost scientists are feeling and finding their way through a vast undergrowth of materialistic facts towards a world horizon much more in harmony with Holy Scripture. And it has further become clear that the leaders of Science a generation ago both overestimated and overemphasized the limited knowledge of their time, and neglected to look beyond it. Because education reflects the beliefs of leading minds of the previous generation, and not those of the present, so today we are suffering from those miscalculations. But in the light of facts not then observed, or whose significance had been overlooked, scientists of the present have ceased to overestimate human knowledge; on the contrary they are emphasizing human ignorance. So-called Miracles are no longer being laughed at, they are being recognised.

—*Sir Charles Marston.*

THE SECOND BOOK OF KINGS (2)

THE PROPHET ELISHA (i.–x.)

THE PREDOMINANT subject in the first ten chapters of 2 Kings is the ministry of the prophet Elisha; and we would here call careful attention to it. The ministry of Elisha is equally remarkable as that of Elijah, and, in certain typical ways, is even more so. In our last study but one we spoke about Elijah in a threefold way—his character, his ministry, his significance. Perhaps we cannot do better than employ these three headings in connection with Elisha, laying the emphasis on the last of the three, namely, his peculiar and far-reaching significance.

His personal character.

It is always good to consider the personal character of God's outstanding servants, for by so doing we come to see the kind of persons whom God chooses and uses in signal ways. We pick out the following traits in Elisha's moral make-up as being at once noticeable.

We mark first a *spirituality of desire.* When Elijah says: "Ask what I shall do for thee," Elisha's request is, "Let a double portion of thy spirit be upon me" (ii. 9). There is no grasping after earthly advantages, though such might certainly have been chosen.

We note also *filial affection.* "Let me, I pray thee, kiss my father and mother, and then I will follow thee" (1 Kings xix. 20). There is no parallel here with the would-be disciple of Luke ix. who offered before he was called, and whom our Lord knew to be superficial. Elisha at once made a clean break from home ties; but the way he did it evinces family affection. Those who combine true family affection with their supreme love for Christ are those who usually make the sincerest and fittest servants of the Lord.

We observe further Elisha's *humility.* It would seem as though for some time his services were of a very humble sort. He is

spoken of as "the son of Shaphat, which poured water on the
hands of Elijah" (2 Kings iii. 11)—an allusion to the old-time
Oriental custom of the servant pouring water from a ewer over
his master's hands to wash them.

And again we are impressed with Elisha's _courage._ See, for
instance, his first meeting with king Jehoram (iii. 13, 14). Very
unlike the empty compliments of the quack diviners who fawned
around Jehoram were Elisha's stinging words of denunciation.
Only a brave and honest messenger of God could have spoken
them.

Nor can we travel through these ten chapters with Elisha
without seeing again and again his strong _faith._ Right from that
first moment when he struck Jordan's waters with Elijah's
mantle, believing that they would obey him as they had obeyed
Elijah, we see his faith riding on from exploit to exploit. It was
this faith which gave fuel to the fire of his courage. Real faith in
God always makes a man fearless.

And, once more, we mark Elisha's _disinterestedness._ How
rich he might have made himself by such gifts as that which was
suggested by Naaman the Syrian (v. 5, etc.) and that which was
sent by royal Ben-hadad (viii. 9)! But this prophet's eye is on
no such rewards. He lives for one thing only—the will and the
honour of Jehovah. May the Spirit of God reproduce these
qualities in our own hearts and lives!

His prophetic ministry.

Elisha's ministry is an extraordinary one. Again and again the
supernatural flames out through it in the most arresting ways.
It is even more interspersed with miracles than was the fiery
ministry of Elijah. It has been truly observed that there are no
miracles in the Old Testament, except those of Moses, which can
be compared in number or variety with the wonders that Elisha
did. In these first ten chapters of 2 Kings there are no less than
seventeen such phenomena on record. The full list, including the
strange miracle at Elisha's grave, totals twenty.

How many other miracles were wrought through Elisha,
without being recorded, we do not know. There may have been
many. The principle of purposive selection and exclusion which

is consistently observed by the Spirit-guided writers of the Scriptures, and on which we have commented in an earlier study, implies that those miracles of Elisha which have been recorded are specially noteworthy, either because of their importance at the time or because of their latent spiritual significances.

So far as we know, Elisha, like Elijah, wrote nothing; but his miracles must have created no little stir. Kings and leaders, both inside and outside Israel, were obliged to take note of him. For instance, in 2 Kings viii. 4, we read: "And the king talked with Gehazi, the servant of the man of God, saying: Tell me, I pray thee, all the great things that Elisha hath done." And all Elisha's mighty acts, let it be remembered, were unmistakable and unanswerable evidences of the reality and sovereign power of Jehovah, Israel's true God, from whom the nation had now outrageously apostatised. Elisha's ministry fell in a period which bears ominous parallels with today. The very fact that the ministries of Elijah and Elisha were so full of supernatural wonders is itself intense with meaning. God is meeting a critical situation by supernormal measures. Apostate and degenerate as the nation has become, a final bid shall be made, by special messengers and startling miraculous signs, to recall the sinning people to Jehovah and to the true faith of Israel. Even to the last, God will seek to turn His idolatry-infatuated people from their corruptions, and thus avert the culminating catastrophe of the Dispersion which must otherwise overtake them.

Alas, the louder the warning and the clearer the sign, the deafer and blinder do the unwilling people become! "The heart of this people is waxed gross." Not even the ministries of prophets like Elijah and Elisha and Jonah could turn the nation from its deadly downgrade. Doubtless there was an overridden godly remnant; but the bulk of leaders and people were wedded to their idolatries and immoral ways, and were brazen both to the appeals and the alarms of Jehovah's prophets.

Pretty much the same state of things can be seen even now developing as the present age plunges on to Armageddon. Great signs and judgments are in the earth today. All who have eyes to see *can* see if they *will*. Yet the greater are God's signs, the bolder are man's sins. The heavier the judgments, the more blindly stubborn do the nations officially become against our God and His Christ. The malady has now got beyond any gentle remedy. Accentuated apostasy and anti-Godism, going with ever-more-dangerous scientific knowledge, call for decisive Divine intervention. Judgment and destruction are again necessary; and they are even now speeding upon this present world-system. Meanwhile, however, God is gathering out His "little flock" to whom it is His "good pleasure" to "give the kingdom."

His peculiar significance.

We cannot thoughtfully linger over Elisha's ministry and miracles without sensing that there is somehow a latent typical and mystical significance clinging about him and his actions. Again and again we seem to detect that the Holy Spirit has invested him with subtle anticipations of our Lord's own ministry.

We get a hint of this in *the contrast between Elijah and Elisha*. We find the same kind of dissimilarity between Elijah and Elisha as that which is seen between John the Baptist and our Lord Jesus. This is too pronounced not to be noticed; and there is more in it than might appear at first. We know that the correspondence between Elijah and John the Baptist is more than coincidental. There is a specifically stated typological link between the two. It was announced by the angel Gabriel that John, as the Lord's forerunner, should "go before Him *in the spirit and power of Elias*" (Luke i. 17); and our Lord Himself later said of him: "*This is Elias which was for to come*" (Matt. xi 14; see also xvii. 10–12). It is not unnatural, therefore, that the question should suggest itself as to whether there may be a similar type-connection between Elisha and our Lord Jesus. And what do we find? Well, there is no actual statement anywhere to that effect, but the adumbrations are too definite to be accidental. Elijah, like John the Baptist, came "neither eating nor drinking," and was in the deserts, solitary and apart from men. Elisha, on the other hand, like our Lord Jesus, "came eating and drinking" and mingling freely among the people. There were no shaggy locks and sheepskin mantle, and there was no being fed by ravens in the lonely grot of Cherith, but a man normally shorn and clad, having a gentle and sociable presence, and a house of his own in Samaria. Instead of the fire, the storm, the sternness and judgment, there are healing acts and gentler words.

Then again, there are special features in Elisha's ministry which give it a resemblance to that of our Lord. In Elisha's recurring ministries beyond the bounds of Israel we seem to see a suggestion of Him who, besides being "the glory of His people, Israel," was to be "*a light to lighten the Gentiles.*" While again, Elisha's miracle with the twenty barley loaves, and his multiplying the widow's pot of oil, easily remind us of Him who took the five barley loaves to feed the hungry multitude in New Testament times. And yet again, the miracle of Naaman's cleansing from leprosy, at the word of Elisha, is one of the greatest Old Testament illustrations of the Gospel way of salvation. Nor can we fail to add that Elisha's weeping over the evils which he saw coming upon his nation, but which he was unable to avert (viii. 11, 12), is almost the only scene in the Old Testament which affords a parallel to our Lord's weeping over Jerusalem, as related by Luke.

We find the same parallel suggested by *the main emphasis* in Elisha's ministry. The distinctive insistence in *Elijah's* ministry, of course, like that in the preaching of John the Baptist, is the stern call to repentance, accompanied by the warning of impending judgment; but the main emphasis all through *Elisha's* ministry is that of resurrection and hope of new life, if only the people will respond. The nation has now sunk into such a state that it can scarcely be recovered except by something equal to resurrection. Therefore, through the ministry of Elisha, the people are given to see, in a succession of symbolic miracles, the power of resurrection at work, and the hope of new life which is theirs in Jehovah, if they but return to him.

Just let the mind run through some of Elisha's miracles. See how characteristic is this suggestion of life out of death. His very first miracle is the healing of the death-giving waters of Jericho, so that what had given death now gave life (ii.). Then comes the saving of the armies from death by miraculous water-supply (iii.). And in the next chapter we find the raising of the Shunamite woman's son from death to new life (iv.). This is followed by the healing of the poisoned pottage: "Death in the pot" is changed to life and wholesomeness (iv.). And in the same chapter we have the miraculous multiplication of the barley loaves. Then comes the healing of Naaman, by that symbolic baptism in Jordan, with its washing away of death, and the coming up in new life (v.). The miracle of the recovered axe-head, which next follows, speaks of the same thing in a different way. "The iron did swim"—a new life-power overcoming the downward pull of death. Finally, not to mention the intervening miracles, we have the strange miracle in which the man is brought to life at Elisha's grave, by accidental contact with the deceased prophet's bones! The emphasis on resurrection and new hope running through these miracles is surely clear to see.

But this latent typical significance which clings to Elisha reaches its most striking expression when we take Elijah and Elisha and Jonah together. These three prophets came in quick succession during the last period before the dispersion of the northern kingdom—Jonah probably lived well into the reign of Jeroboam II, after whose reign the ten-tribed kingdom only survived about another sixty years. Such "signs" were given through these three prophets as had never been given before, with the purpose of arresting the nation. Alas, the nation did not respond; but the "signs" remain, and they make these three prophets together a kind of type-trio.

It will be noticed that the idea of *resurrection* is expressed and illustrated with peculiar force through the ministry of these three. In the case of Elijah there is the raising up of the Zarephath widow's son from death to new life. Such a miracle had never been known in Israel before. Miracles had happened again and again since the days of Moses; but never had a dead person been brought back to life. The unheard-of had happened. No wonder that this man who could raise the dead could call his countrymen to Carmel! Yet that crowning miracle was repeated in the ministry of Elisha, in the raising of the Shunamite's son. Indeed it was more than repeated. An even stranger thing happened: a dead man was suddenly quickened into life again through contact with Elisha's own corpse! But, most amazing of all, there next comes *Jonah's* experience of something stranger even than death, and stranger even than being brought back to life— a resurrection not merely from bodily death, but from "the belly of Sheol"!

Now take these three prophets together. *Elisha* died and was buried—as Christ died and was buried. *Jonah*, in miraculous symbol, did more than die and become buried; he went down into Hades itself, as Christ also went into Hades. *Elijah* triumphantly smote assunder the waters of Jordan (here a type of death), passed through them, and then ascended to heaven—as Christ also overcame death, and then ascended to heaven.

But look at these three men again. *Elisha* dies and is buried, yet in his death gives life to another—as Christ, through his death, gives life to those who come into union with Him. *Jonah* goes down into "hell" itself, yet is brought up that he should not see corruption—as Christ himself was not left in Hades nor suffered to see corruption (Acts ii. 27). *Elijah,* in ascending, cast down his mantle and a "double portion of his spirit" so that his follower on earth might do "greater works" than he himself had done— as Christ also, when He ascended up on high, poured forth the Spirit so that His followers might do the "greater works" of which He had spoken.

Are all these correspondences quite fortuitous? Or were they not rather designed—strangely clear yet strangely subtle—so that godly souls, willing to be taught by God's Spirit, might be enabled to perceive Divine truths which could never be sought out by the wise and prudent of this world?

We shall speak more fully about the unique type-teachings concealed and yet so conspicuous in the story of Jonah when we come to study the little book which bears that prophet's name. Meanwhile, let us duly appreciate the significance of Elijah and Elisha and Jonah as a trio. How wonderfully, through the supernatural works and experiences of these three prophets, God prepared the minds of His earthly people for that super-miracle which was yet to be, namely, the resurrection of the Lord Jesus, Israel's Christ and the world's Saviour!

In 1 Corinthians xv. 4, Paul says that Christ "rose again the third day *according to the Scriptures.*" But to what Scriptures of the Old Testament was he referring? Perhaps he had in mind Psalm ii. 7 (which he also quoted in the same connection at Antioch in Pisidia: see Acts xiii. 33); or perhaps he was thinking of Psalm xvi. 10, 11 (which verses Peter cited as resurrection prophecies on the day of Pentecost: see Acts ii. 25–36); but we feel pretty certain that he also had in mind these three men, Elijah and Elisha and Jonah; for during those "silent" three years which Paul spent in Arabia (Gal. i. 17, 18), when the Spirit taught him "in all the Scriptures" the things concerning Christ,

Paul must have come to see in these three prophets wonderful gleamings which he had never even guessed at before! All of the more prominent features in our Lord's resurrection are fore-enacted by these three prophets, even to the three days and nights in Hades and the coming forth again on the third day: so that Paul could even say that our Lord's rising again *the third day* was truly "ACCORDING TO THE SCRIPTURES"!

THE SECOND BOOK OF KINGS (3)

Lesson Number 37

NOTE.—For this third study in 2 Kings read again chapters ix. to xvii. twice.

The Second Book of Kings has been much more extensively confirmed and illustrated through recent research than any other book of the Old Testament. This is due to the fact that the annals of Assyria and of Babylon, covering the same period as 2 Kings, have been so largely recovered. Light has poured in from the monuments of those two great empires, and in that light we note, with grateful astonishment, how one unexpected confirmation after another shows us the absolute fidelity and the minute accuracy of the sacred history. The lesson taught by this ought to be heeded and remembered. We have less confirmation of other parts of the Old Testament history, because we have less information regarding the countries and the times with which the Scripture narrative deals. But wherever the curtain *is lifted* we see the very things chronicled in the Bible. Could there be any fuller proof of its reliability?

—John Urquhart.

THE SECOND BOOK OF KINGS (3)

Evil Kings of the Northern Kingdom

As ALREADY noted (see lesson 34), up to the point at which the *First* Book of Kings closes, all the eight kings who had reigned over the northern kingdom were *"evil"* kings. What, now, of the further *eleven* who figure in this *Second* Book of Kings? The answer is as revealing as it is deplorable. It is chronicled of every one of them that "he did evil"—(with the exception of Shallum) and *he* reigned only one month! Here are the references: iii. 2, 3; x. 31, 32; xiii. 2, 3, 11; xiv. 24; xv. 9, 18, 24, 28; xvii. 2. What a record! And what ruin the result!

Think of this wretched line of kings in parallel with the Davidic line of kings who reigned over Judah. We have already observed that in the annals of the kings of *Judah* the standard according to which each king is estimated is the example of *David*. It is interesting to trace this out. We see it in the case of Solomon (1 Kings xi. 6), Abijam (xv. 3), Jehoshaphat (2 Chron. xvii. 3), Amaziah (2 Kings xiv. 3), Ahaz (xvi. 2), Hezekiah (xviii. 3), Josiah (xxii. 2). Thus did David "cast his shadow" for good, even three hundred and seventy years onward, over his royal successors.

But now, returning to this unrelieved succession of "evil" men who reigned over the *ten-tribed northern kingdom*, we find an even more emphatic standard of comparison. Alas, it is no noble standard such as that which was set by David: it is the very reverse. There is no David in *this* line, to strike a norm of true godliness, or to cast any lingering lustre over the throne. The standard according to which these *Israel* kings are judged is the shameful reign of *Jeroboam*, the first king who occupied the throne of the northern kingdom after the split of the ten tribes from Judah; and the distinguishing epitaph of this brazen offender, Jeroboam, is: "*JEROBOAM, THE SON OF NEBAT, WHO MADE ISRAEL TO SIN.*" Again and again, in these records of the kings, Jeroboam is referred to by this horrible distinguishment, until the words become almost a refrain. And here is a fact as striking as it is tragic: it is written of no less than fifteen out of the eighteen kings who followed Jeroboam on the throne of the ten-tribed kingdom that "he did evil" after the example of this "Jeroboam, the son of Nebat, who made Israel to sin." Here are the references: Nadab (1 Kings xv. 26), Baasha (xv. 34), Zimri (xvi. 19), Omri (xvi. 25, 26), Ahab (xvi. 31), Ahaziah (xxii. 52), Jehoram (2 Kings iii. 2, 3), Jehu (x. 31), Jehoahaz (xiii. 2), Jehoash (xiii. 11), Jeroboam II (xiv. 24), Zechariah (xv. 9), Menahem (xv. 18), Pekahiah (xv. 24), Pekah (xv. 28).

Thus did the wicked Jeroboam project *his* deadly shadow over the throne and the throes of the ten-tribed kingdom for two hundred and fifty years ahead, until at last, degraded and denuded and deported, it was torn to pieces by the Assyrian dragon.

We do well to reflect, in passing, on the shadows cast by these two men, David and Jeroboam. All of us are casting shadows as we go through this present life. Just as our bodies cast their shadows quite involuntarily, so are we continually and quite involuntarily casting the shadow of our moral and spiritual influence upon other lives. We can no more detach ourselves from this involuntary and often unconscious influence upon others than our bodies can rid themselves of their own shadows. What we *can* determine is the *kind* of shadow which we cast. Our influence, quite apart from any speech of the lips, may contribute either to the eternal salvation or the eternal damnation of other souls. God save us from casting a shadow like that of Jeroboam! Amid both the younger and the older everywhere around us there are always those who, from one cause or another, are in that sensitive poise of mind which makes them susceptible to the shadow of some influence falling upon them from another personality.

It is a solemn reflection that the shadow of our silent influence may have results reaching on even into eternity. It is well to remember, too, that our shadow often lingers here when we ourselves have passed beyond, as was the case with David and Jeroboam. Are Voltaire and Paine and Ingersol and Huxley dead, and other infidels who kept step to their music? Do not their shadows still stalk the earth, gibbering their old blasphemies in new phraseology within the walls of our schools and colleges? And, on the other hand, are Luther and Calvin, and Wesley and

Whitefield and Moody and Spurgeon dead? Do not the Christ-filled shadows of these seraphic evangelists still fall with enduring benediction upon our national life?

Is it objected that these whom we have picked on are all outstanding men, and that the same does not apply to the inconspicuous? Well, if we are thinking *that*, we are wrong. Adolph Hitler's vile shadow, remember, includes in itself the shadows of all those other men whose names will never be published but who influenced Hitler in his earlier years, and made him what he afterwards became. We speak of Wesley and Whitefield, and the other sanctified geniuses of the Methodist revival; but remember that the heavenly shadow of that glorious epoch is really the composite influence of those thousands of obscure but consecrated men and women who are simply an anonymous multitude to the historian.

Perhaps some who read these lines are even now thanking God for the still lingering shadow of a departed saintly father or mother, or of some other departed Christian loved-one. Or perhaps some who now read these lines suffer and weep because of a darksome shadow cast over their lives by departed predecessors of a different sort. What kind of shadows are *we* going to cast today and leave tomorrow? Our lingering influence will certainly out-stay us. God keep us near to Christ! God help us to cast the shadow of a sanctified influence which will linger on to heal and bless, as Peter's shadow, long ago in Jerusalem, healed the sick ones on whom it fell!

The Dispersion of the Northern Kingdom

chp 17

2 Kings xvii. records one of the most tragic anticlimaxes of history. With what prospect of high destiny had the Hebrew tribes entered Canaan under Joshua! With what wretchedness are the tribes of the northern kingdom now dragged away and dispersed! Here, in this seventeenth chapter, is the final indictment of the ten-tribed kingdom, and the deportation of its thrashed and battered people into a captivity which for ever ended their existence as a separate kingdom.

The sins for which this monster calamity was allowed to crush them are here written indelibly, as with a "pen of iron" or the "point of a diamond," so that all who come after may know the real cause of what happened, and justify the ways of God with men. Read verses 7 to 23 again. What a catalogue of outrages against Israel's covenant God! What insatiate idolatry! What stiff-necked implacability! What depth of degradation! Note specially verses 20–3. Here, right at the end of the Divine indictment, and in that last, awful, zero hour of ruin, there falls again the ugly shadow of that wicked man, the first king who sat on the throne of the ten-tribed kingdom—"Jeroboam, the son of Nebat, who made Israel to sin."

"The Lord rejected all the seed of Israel, and afflicted them, and delivered them into the hand of spoilers, until He had cast them out of His sight . . . For the children of Israel walked in all the sins of Jeroboam which he did: they departed not from them until the Lord removed Israel out of His sight."

There are certain facts of outstanding importance which we ought now to note in connection with this obliteration of the ten-tribed kingdom.

First, we see here, written in bold and terrible lines, *the operation of "poetic justice."* That is, we see Divine judgment falling upon a nation in direct correspondence to its sin, just as one line of poetry answers to another. Unfalteringly, this chapter attributes the Dispersion to the avenging hand of God Himself. If, then, this chapter is an *inspired* explanation, no philosophy of history is true which does not recognise the sovereign hand of God controlling all events and developments. There are those today who affect to scorn the idea that God thus directly visits the sins of nations back upon themselves. Well, if the Bible is the word of God, they are wrong. The God who laid this Israel kingdom low by the penal stroke of the Dispersion is still the God who rules and arbitrates above the nations. There is but the one true God. He has not abdicated. His power has not declined; and His nature is still the same. He is the Jehovah who says, "I change not." Those of us who believe and know the Bible to be the word of God have been able to grasp at least something of the meaning behind what has happened to the nations of Europe in the last few years of war and upheaval. To us, indeed, those people who say they cannot see any evidence of supernatural control in the strange anomalies of the past war and its aftermath are afflicted with a strange blindness. As truly as God overruled the revolutions of history in the days of Egypt and Assyria and Babylon and Israel, so does He now, in the history of modern Russia and Germany and America and Britain ; and as certainly as God visited the sins of nations with judgment *then*, so does He *now*.

Second, we ought to note that *the dispersion of the ten tribes occurred in two stages*. Some years before the final break-up of the kingdom, two and a half of the tribes had already been carried away captive. These were Reuben and Gad and half the tribe of Manasseh, which occupied territory on the *eastern* side of Jordan, and which therefore first fell prey to the Assyrians. Their deportation is thus narrated in 1 Chronicles v. 25, 26: "And they transgressed against the God of their fathers, and went a whoring after the gods of the people of the land, whom God destroyed before them. And the God of Israel stirred up the spirit of Pul, king of Assyria, and the spirit of Tilgath-pilneser, king of Assyria, and he carried them away, even the Reubenites and the Gadites and the half tribe of Manasseh, and brought them unto Halah and Habor and Hara and to the river of Gozan, unto this day." We learn from 2 Kings xv. 29 that the tribe of Naphtali, to the north-east, also suffered with them.

Away back in our studies in the Book of Numbers we noted that these tribes, Reuben and Gad and half the tribe of Manasseh, instead of crossing Jordan as God had directed, pleaded permission to occupy the Gilead area *east* of Jordan. The request sounded reasonable, as do most arguments which excuse compromise, but it *was* compromise none the less. Their true place was with the other tribes across the Jordan, in the covenanted place of blessing. But they chose by the sight of their eyes (Num. xxxii. 33), instead of by faith and according to the will of God, and were content with a portion just outside the place of promised blessing. They are types of so-called "worldly" Christians today. We see the after-effects of their choice. They quickly bowed to the gods of the nearby peoples ; and now *they are the first to go into captivity*. Compromise always seems an easy way out of difficulty, but it is always costly afterwards, and only too often proves fatal.

The Assyrian king who carried away these tribes is called *Tiglath-pileser* in 2 Kings xv. 29, and also *Pul*, in 1 Chronicles

v. 26. Controversy has raged around these two names. It was
thought that they referred to two different persons, though the
Bible seemed to use them both of one. But an ancient "Babylonian Chronicle" discovered by the late Dr. Pinches, among
tablets in the British Museum, some years ago, ended the uncertainty; for it refers to Tiglath-pileser by this other name of Pull
or Pulu. So the Bible is again confirmed, in yet another historical
detail.

The deportation of the *other* tribes of the northern kingdom
took place about thirteen years after that of the two and a half
tribes, that is, *about* 721 B.C. By that time Tiglath-pileser had
passed away and had been succeeded by Shalmaneser IV. See
again chapter xvii. 3–6. That Samaria should withstand the
practised and daring soldiery of Assyria for three years (verse 5)
is remarkable. Provisions and munitions must have been accumulated in anticipation. Help, also, was daily expected from Egypt
(verse 4), which, however, never came. At last the city fell.
We can imagine the state of its inhabitants, and the treatment
they would receive from the notoriously cruel Assyrians, who
seem to have been of all oppressors the most inventive of torture-
cruelties. The whole population was carried off, never to see
Samaria again.

Third, this dispersal of the ten tribes *fully accords with what
we know of Assyrian practice at that time.* The late Mr. John
Urquhart, in his *New Biblical Guide,* says: "A marked feature of
the campaigns of Tiglath-pileser III is this very carrying away
captive to Assyria of the original populations of a conquered
country, the planting in their stead populations which were
likewise carried from a far distance, placing Assyrian officials
over them, and annexing the lands in this way to Assyria. From
broken men, with no common ties and with no fatherland to
defend, no resistance was to be feared. The policy put an end
effectually to the plottings and the alliances which had formerly
sprung up in the conquered districts as soon as the Assyrian
armies had withdrawn. And this policy may be said to have been
Tiglath-pileser's own invention." The long-buried Assyrian
inscriptions which have now been disinterred and interpreted by
archaeologists show us that this policy was ruthlessly carried out.
Again and again there are references to it. We have not space to
quote here, except just one as an example: "I took 155,000

people and children from them. Their horses and cattle without number I carried off. Those countries to the boundaries of Assyria I added . . . like clay I trampled and the assembly of their people to Assyria I sent." Tiglath-pileser's policy was followed by those who succeeded him. It solved the problem which had hitherto baffled every conquering power, namely, how to preserve lands in cultivation by peoples who should enrich the empire without having either the spirit or the means to revolt. It would seem that Shalmaneser who besieged Samaria died the year that the city fell, and that the conquest was claimed by Sargon, his successor. Inscriptions made by Sargon have been found which actually tell of his deportation of the Israelites from Samaria (27,290 is the figure he gives), and his settling of foreigners in the land.

Fourth, *from this dispersion there has been no return*. Descendants of these exiles may have found their way back to Judaea two hundred years later, at the time when the Jewish "remnant" returned under Ezra and Nehemiah; but apart from that there has been no return, and the ten-tribed kingdom has remained non-existent. Attempts to identify these Israel tribes have been made in more recent times. The American Indians, the Armenians, and others have been suggested. The "British Israel" theory, which identifies them with the British and American peoples throughout the world, is attractive, but the more carefully we have gone into that theory, the more difficult have we found it to accept. That, however, we cannot discuss here. We confine ourselves to the historic *fact* of the dispersion of these tribes. *That* was real enough, and was a heart-rending tragedy at which one could weep even today. Among the many Assyrian writings now recovered is a deed of sale (made about fourteen years after the Israel dispersion) in which two Israelite men and one woman are sold by a Phœnician to an Egyptian for three minas of silver (about £27). This condition of perpetual slavery must have been the lot of thousands. Truly, "the way of transgressors is hard" (Prov. xiii. 15). Israel had refused to accept the ennobling service of God. She must now suffer and weep in degrading servitude to men. Oh, those words of Jesus, as He wept over Jerusalem centuries later, have a long and wide application—" I *would* " —" Ye would *not* "—" Ye *shall* not "!

THE SECOND BOOK OF KINGS (4)

Lesson Number 38

NOTE.—For this further study in 2 Kings read again from chapter xviii. to the end of the book. All these eight chapters are of great importance, leading up as they do to the culminating Divine judgment which fell on Judah by way of the Babylonian exile. They should be well read and pondered.

Those who are acquainted with critical commentaries on the Old Testament will appreciate the extent to which their contents are contradicted by this fresh evidence (i.e. of archaeology)—such, for example, as the fact that Monotheism was the original religion, and Polytheism a by-product from it. Or that the Habiru were, after all, the Hebrews and the Israelites under Joshua. Indeed, if at the present time some cynic, or candid friend, sought to make the punishment fit the crime, and proceeded to compile an Encyclopaedia of the mistakes that had been made by critics and commentators on the Old Testament, and placed beside each the real facts that have recently come to light, it would surely run into volumes.

—Sir Charles Marston.

THE SECOND BOOK OF KINGS (4)

Later Course and Downfall of Judah

THE TEN-TRIBED kingdom is no more. Its cities have been plundered, its capital laid low, its royal house swept away, its pleasant land literally scraped of Israelite inhabitants and repeopled by a mongrel mixture imported from afar by the Assyrian overlord. And now, with the history of the ten-tribed kingdom forever closed, the last stretch of chapters in this Second Book of Kings (xviii.–xxv.) is occupied solely with the later course and downfall of *Judah*. These last eight chapters of the book, therefore, run from the fall of Samaria (721. B.C.) to the sack of Jerusalem (587. B.C.), a period of about one hundred and thirty years.

Could anything have given the sister kingdom graver cause for penitent reflection and amendment than what had now happened to the ten tribes? The long-threatened but mercifully postponed judgment had at length fallen. The warnings uttered by Jehovah's faithful prophets had materialised with tragic exactness. Israel had over-presumed upon her covenant relationship with Jehovah, and He had now utterly cast her off. The news of what had happened must have stabbed many a heart and conscience in Jerusalem with strange apprehensiveness. Yet the fact is that this terrible object-lesson in Divine vengeance had little deep or lasting effect upon Judah. Except for the reign of Hezekiah, and in a lesser way of Josiah, it is the same story of apostasy and downgrade until Jerusalem pays the agonising penalty bemoaned by Jeremiah in his "Lamentations."

So, then, we now look through these remaining eight chapters of 2 Kings. From the time of the Disruption of the ten tribes from Judah (1 Kings xii.) up to the point at which this eighteenth chapter of 2 Kings commences, twelve successors of David have occupied the throne of Judah. Eight are still to come before Jerusalem falls. These are, Hezekiah, Manasseh, Amon, Josiah, Jehoahaz, Jehoiakim, Jehoiachin, Zedekiah. Of these there are three which call for special comment. First, and by far the most commanding, is king Hezekiah.

Hezekiah

Good king Hezekiah was a really remarkable man. Soldier, statesman, architect, poet, saint—he was all these. His reign was the greatest since the days of David and Solomon. While pondering the three chapters which here tell of him (xviii.–xx) we certainly ought to read the parallel account in 2 Chronicles xxix.–xxxii. It is a noble record. Immediately upon his accession he reopened and repaired the Lord's House, he re-organised the priesthood and the Levitical services. He recalled his subjects to the worship of the true God, and led the way by his own illustrious example. Throughout the land he destroyed idols and groves and false altars. He gathered his people to a great national observance of the Passover, of which it is written, "Since the days of Solomon, the son of David, king of Israel, there was not the like in Jerusalem." He also smote Israel's enemies and extended his borders, and became "magnified in the sight of all nations" (2 Chron. xxxii. 23). Indeed, it is said of him, "He trusted in the Lord God of Israel so that after him was none like him among all the kings of Judah, nor any that were before him." Oh, what solid benefactions always result when men and kings and nations walk in the ways of the true God! Those golden hopes begin to materialise which politics, economics, legislation and education by themselves can never bring to fulfilment.

Hezekiah and the Scriptures

But Hezekiah's importance is not limited to his own reign and time. Although few may realise it, his impact is still felt in our modern world. He is really one of the *very* important men of history, and the repercussions from his labours will last to the end of the age.

It seems clear that in good degree we owe to Hezekiah *the arrangement and transmission of the Old Testament Scriptures.* Think what that has meant to the nations and to history. Note some of the evidences of Hezekiah's activities in connection with the Scriptures. We mark his zeal for the *house* of Jehovah (2 Chron. xxix. 3–19), and for the *worship* of Jehovah (verses 20–36), and his strict adherence to the Davidic pattern (verses 25, 27, 30).

Clearly, his delight was in the *word* of Jehovah. And, further, 2 Chronicles xxxi. 21 speaks of the *"work"* which he commenced *"in the Law and in the Commandments."* Nor is this all; he formed a *guild* of men for this devout literary work. A reference to Proverbs xxv. 1 will show that these "men of Hezekiah" had a good hand in shaping the Book of Proverbs into its present form. Their work would scarcely begin and end with that one book! It has been well said that in Hezekiah's age "Israel reached its golden literary prime" with Hezekiah himself as the royal patron of piety and letters. Isaiah and Shebna and Joah were leaders among these "men of Hezekiah" (2 Kings xviii. 18, xix. 2).

There seems to be a curious confirmation of Hezekiah's work on the Scriptures in the form of a certain peculiarity which perhaps few people may know about. At the end of many books in the Old Testament, in the Hebrew originals, three capital letters occur which no transcriber has dared to omit, even though their meaning was lost. They are the three Hebrew letters corresponding to H, Z, K, the first three in the Hebrew name, Hezekiah. Nothing is more likely, says the late J. W. Thirtle, than that when "the men of Hezekiah" had completed their work of transcribing the different books, Hezekiah should have thus affixed his own sign-manual in royal confirmation. When we come to study the Book of Psalms we shall find not only that Hezekiah had much to do with the shaping of that collection, but that he himself was a composer of psalms and songs.

Now Hezekiah's reign is made unique by the fact that an extra fifteen years were added to his life (2 Kings xx.; Isa. xxxviii.). It was in those extra years that Hezekiah's literary activities reached their high point. There is more in this than at first meets the eye. Judah's days were numbered. Only five more kings were to reign before the deportations to Babylon began, and four out of the five were to prove ungodly failures. The moment had certainly come for the bringing together and editing of the inspired Scriptures, with a view to their preservation and transmission; and who should be God's man for this purpose? Who was more suitable and willing than Hezekiah? We have good cause to thank God for Hezekiah, and for those added fifteen years, and for his labours in the Scriptures which were to mean so much to posterity. Yes, Hezekiah is a great figure.

Manasseh

Talk about "studies in contrasts"! Was there ever an extremer
contrast between father and son than that between Hezekiah
and Manasseh? How is it that sometimes the best of fathers have
the worst of sons, and the worst of fathers the best of sons? That
is a nice study for the psychologists! We ourselves will not try
to solve the problem, but we will try to caution ourselves by it.
If men like Samuel and Hezekiah could have sons like Joel and
Abiah and Manasseh, we will be careful before we allow our lips
to scourge godly parents of today who have worldly-minded sons
and daughters.

A short time ago we heard two Christian women harshly
criticising a saintly, elderly Christian man who was known for
his keenness in winning souls to the Saviour. "He would do far
better to begin at home with his own unconverted son and
worldly daughter," said one to the other. "His children's behaviour doesn't say much for his Christianity in the home." We
were much pained by our overhearing of those caustic words,
for we knew how that dear man had prayed for his children,
how consistently he had lived before them, how he had pleaded
with them, and how he had wept about them in our own presence
only a few days earlier. Oh, what sharp-edged swords the tongues
of some Christians are! How they wound the heart of Jesus every
time they cut into the good name of some other Christian! We
do well, changing the metaphor, to beseech the Holy Spirit to
"set a watch" at the "door of our lips"! It is so easy to add cruel
pangs to godly hearts which are already torn with grief over
wayward sons and daughters.

And now, about this Manasseh: what a character he is! And
what a grim enigma that the wickedest of all Judah's kings
should be the longest-reigning one! Fifty-five years is a long
stretch. In that more-than-half-a-century Manasseh wrought
such things as almost defy the pen. We need not here dilate on
his extremes of idolatry and spiritism, his offering of human
sacrifices, his making the very streets of Jerusalem run with
innocent blood (including that of the martyred prophet Isaiah),
and so on. It is even said that he did wickedly "above all that
the Amorites did" whom God cast out before the chosen people.

What the effect of all this would be on the nation requires little imagination to appreciate.

But there are three remarkable features which are peculiar to Manasseh, which we ought particularly to note. For these we need to turn to the parallel account in 2 Chronicles xxxiii.

First, we are told that *Manasseh was carried captive to Babylon*. Verse 11 reads: "Wherefore the Lord brought upon them the captains of the host of the king of Assyria, which took Manasseh among the thorns, and bound him with fetters, and carried him to Babylon." This verse has been a "bone of contention" to Bible critics. Had it been a Babylonian king who took Manasseh captive to Babylon all would have been normal; but that a king of *Assyria*, whose capital city was *Nineveh* away on the Tigris, should carry Manasseh captive to *Babylon*, which was three hundred miles south on the Euphrates—well, that is most decidedly a blunder! But once again the Bible proves right, and the critics themselves the blunderers. We know that the Assyrian king who reigned contemporaneously with Manasseh's father, Hezekiah, was Sennacherib, and that Sennacherib's son, who reigned during part of Manasseh's reign, was Esarhaddon (2 Kings xviii, xix; 2 Chron. xxxii.). Well, recent findings by Assyriologists have shown that of all the Assyrian kings *this Esarhaddon alone built a palace at Babylon, and lived there*!

Second, in captivity *Manasseh repented and was forgiven of God*. He thus becomes one of the most amazing instances of the pardoning love of God to extreme sinners. See verses 12 and 13. Manasseh was truly converted.

Third, *Manasseh was restored to Jerusalem*, and made amends, as far as possible, for all the evil he had done. See verses 14 to 20. Manasseh is one of the gravest warnings to all wicked-doers, for just as judgment fell on him as a direct retribution for his evil, so will it be with all others like him: yet Manasseh is also one of the most wonderful encouragements to all who are really penitent, for he shows us that, however we may have outraged God, such is the love of God that He delights in mercy to the worst.

Josiah

We skip the evil reign of Manasseh's son, Amon. After two years he was murdered by his own servants (2 Kings xxi. 19–26).

We come to the noble reign of *Josiah*. This was the one bright interval during the last hundred years of the Judah kingdom, that is, between the death of king Hezekiah in 698 B.C. and the sack of Jerusalem by the Babylonians in 587 B.C., at which time the bulk of Judah's people were carried into exile. Alas, the brightness of Josiah's reign is that of sunset. It is the final flash of a departing glory, just before the throne of David is trodden in the dust.

Josiah came to the throne about 641 B.C., when he was but eight years old. In the early years of his reign, therefore, the queen-mother, with the help of trusted advisers, would largely direct the course of government. At the age of sixteen, "while he was yet young, he began to seek after the God of David his father" (2 Chron. xxxiv. 3); and the promise of those early years was splendidly fulfilled. We shall not linger here over the noble progress of his reign. His repairing of the temple, the strange discovery of the strangely lost Pentateuch, his reading of the Law to the gathered people of his realm, his renewal of the covenant with Jehovah on behalf of the nation, his firm measures against moral evils, and his organising such a national observance of the Passover as had not been held "from the days of the Judges"—all these things are there in the record, and speak for themselves. But there are two important facts which we would pick out for special comment, as follows.

First, *Josiah's lead to his people did not really check the national downgrade.* The apparent "revival" consisted rather in outward measures taken by the king himself than in a hearty desire on the part of the people in general. There was much outward reform but no real inward return. The king's lead was deferentially respected, but there was no real heart-penitence toward the God who had been so brazenly wronged. Judah had gone too far. The moral sense of the people had now become so blurred that the popular power to respond genuinely to the king's lead was gone. Through prophet after prophet and providence after providence God had pleaded with His people, but they had repeatedly shown that they "*would* not," until now, by that deadly process which ever operates in human nature, they had reached the point where they *could* not. Apostasy and idolatry had now become ingrained in the national character. The people had lost the sense of Jehovah. The meaning of the earthly throne

in Judah had been lost because they had lost the vision of the
throne in the heavens. The ever-persistent stupidity of idolatry
which more and more depraved the nation was the muddle-
brained effort to fill the vacuum created by the lost sense of
Jehovah. The moral sensitiveness of the people had now degen-
erated into a gross callousness. As things grew worse, great
prophets were raised up; yet the mightiest and tenderest of these
were left saying, "Who hath believed our report?" It is quite
clear that the changes under Josiah were superficial, for the people
were quite ready to sink back into idolatry and infidelity again
immediately afterward. People who could imperviously spurn
such messages as those of Isaiah and Jeremiah were ripe for
judgment; and judgment was even now at the door. All this is
only too sadly corroborated in the prophecies of Jeremiah.
That great-hearted prophet commenced his ministry in the
thirteenth year of Josiah, and continued until after the fall
of Jerusalem (Jer. i. 1–3). The earlier chapters of Jeremiah
refer to Josiah's reign. See chapter iii. 10, for the superficiality
of the "revival" under Josiah. Yet it is good to detect the
noble influence of Jeremiah upon the king himself, all through
his reign. Perhaps Josiah would not have been what he was
but for Jeremiah.

Second, *Josiah's reign occurred at one of the most fateful turning
points in history.* Events of the greatest magnitude were in progress. These were—(1) The fall of the Assyrian empire after an
existence of hundreds of years and after maintaining complete
mastery over the other nations for about two hundred years;
(2) the rise of the new Babylonian empire under Nabopolassar
and his son Nebuchadnezzar, by which the most ancient mistress
of the nations laid her hand once more upon the sceptre of the
kingdoms; (3) the formation of the Median empire, which, a
little later, as the Media-Persian empire, was to overthrow
Babylon, and, through the famous "decree of Cyrus," was to
bring about the rebuilding of Jerusalem and the restoration of
the Jewish "Remnant," as told in the Book of Ezra; (4) the
dissolution of the kingdom of Judah as an independent kingdom
(the destruction of Jerusalem and the final deportation of the
Jews to Babylon took place in 587 B.C., only twenty years after
Josiah's death, since which time Judah has never again existed
as an independent kingdom).

When later, in 536 B.C., the Babylonian empire was over-thrown by Cyrus, and the Persian empire took its place, the various regions over which Babylon had held sway thereby passed under the Persian rule; and the hundreds of thousands of scattered Jews—both those of the ten-tribed kingdom (Israel) which had been swept off by Assyria in 721 B.C. and those of the southern kingdom (Judah) who had been carried off more recently by Babylon—thereby similarly passed under the Persian rule. The same kind of transition took place when the Persian empire gave place to the Alexandrian and then lesser empires and then the Roman empire.

Only about 50,000 of them returned to Judaea when, in 536 B.C., Cyrus gave them liberty to return. Scattered through the nations the Jews nevertheless remained a distinct people, were preserved through successive epochs of trouble, and largely increased in numbers. We find them in their millions scattered throughout the Roman world in the days of our Lord and the Apostles. James addressed his epistle to "the twelve tribes which are scattered abroad"; and Peter similarly commences his writing, "Peter. . . . to the strangers scattered throughout Pontus, Galatia, Cappadocia, Asia and Bithynia". As remarked above, however, from the time of the Babylonian Exile until our own day, Judah has never again existed as an independent kingdom. In May, 1947 Israel once again became constituted (and later acknowledged) as an independent state; but as we observed in a former study, Israel will never become an independent *kingdom* again until the King Himself returns, even our Lord Jesus Christ. He alone is the true Heir according to the Scriptures of both Old and New Testaments.

THE SECOND BOOK OF KINGS (5)
Lesson Number 39

NOTE.—For this final study in 2 Kings read carefully again chapters xviii. to the end of the book, with concentration on the last part, that is, chapters xxiii. 31 to xxv. 30.

The reformations were superficial. Immediately Hezekiah had passed away, the people returned to their old way of evil. When Hezekiah began his reformation he commenced with the temple, and before anything else could be done it took the whole company of priests and Levites sixteen days to carry rubbish therefrom, which simply means that the temple had become a lumber store. In the days when Josiah carried out his reformation, the book of the Law was found. Mark the significance of this fact that it had to be found! Moreover, its teaching so astonished Josiah that he halted in the middle of his work to enquire from the prophetess Huldah. The people had so forgotten the law of their God that, when it was found, they were absolutely unfamiliar with it.

—*G. Campbell Morgan.*

THE SECOND BOOK OF KINGS (5)

THE FALL OF JERUSALEM AND JUDAH

THE YEAR that king Josiah died, the Assyrian empire died also (608 B.C.), and with the downfall of that empire there died Judah's one earthly hope of protection against Egypt on the one hand and Babylon on the other. The Babylonian, Jehovah's avenger whose advent had been fore-announced through Isaiah over a hundred years earlier, had now appeared. The fatal stroke was to fall at last on Judah. The Babylonian exile was at hand. In the Scripture account of how this fearful retribution fell upon Jerusalem and Judah there are many incidental matters which attract our eye; but we adhere to our present purpose, and simply pick out certain facts which are of key significance.

First, we call attention to the fact that *the destruction of Jerusalem and the captivity of Judah are most emphatically ascribed to the sovereign hand of Jehovah.* Not to appreciate this is to miss nine tenths of the meaning. "Surely at the commandment of Jehovah came this upon Judah . . ." (2 Kings xxiv. 3. See also 2 Chron. xxxvi. 16, 17, 21). Because of their unique relationship with God, because they were a people chosen to embody a special revelation of God to the nations, and because God's dealings with them are permanently transmitted to the nations through the inspired Scriptures, the judgments which felled them become history's supreme object-lesson in the ways of God's government among the nations. Our statesmen of today could do nothing more profitable than to study the principles of God's disposings among the earth's peoples as revealed in the Scriptures, and as exemplified in the nation Israel. What suffering might thus be averted! But our modern statesmen are too wise to become *really* wise.

As with the judgment which fell on the ten-tribed kingdom, so with that which now falls on Judah—we see in it the operation of "poetic justice." Let those smile who will. They are welcome to their educated nonsense which would make history all a matter of blind chance. We ourselves stand with the Scripture. We

believe that God orders things in history according to the behaviour of nations. He allows free rein to the human will within
wide limits, so that men and nations are always fully responsible
for their course; but He super-controls all other controlling powers,
and works His sovereign will among earth's peoples, both to
reward the good and to requite the evil. This is as true today as it
was when Jerusalem fell beneath the blows of Nebuchadnezzar.

Second, it is well to note that *the deportation of Judah's people
was in three stages.* The first of these fell in the third year of king
Jehoiakim; and among the captives then taken from Jerusalem
to Babylon was the then youthful Daniel (Dan. i. 1–4 with 2
Kings xxiv. 1, 2; and 2 Chron. xxxvi. 5–7). The second deportation occurred some eight years later, just after the death of
Jehoiakim and the accession of Jehoiachin, when Nebuchadnezzar deposed Jehoiachin after a short reign of only three
months, and put Zedekiah on the throne instead. Since this
coincided with the beginning of Zedekiah's reign it must have been
eleven years before the destruction of Jerusalem. At this second
deportation Nebuchadnezzar carried off ten thousand captives
comprising all the most useful and better-class Jerusalemites
(2 Kings xxiv. 8–16); and among these was the priest (and later
the prophet) Ezekiel—for Ezekiel himself tells us that at the
destruction of Jerusalem he had already been in Babylonia for
eleven years (Ezek. xl. 1).

The final deportation took place in 587 B.C. It was precipitated
by a futile rebellion on the part of Zedekiah. Nebuchadnezzar
now decided to break up this troublesome Jewish city and
kingdom once for all. After a siege of eighteen months "a breach
was made" in the city wall (2 Kings xxv. 4 R.V.). King Zedekiah
and his men of war fled by night, but were overtaken. The sons
of Zedekiah were slain before his eyes; then Zedekiah himself
was blinded, put into brass fetters, and carried to Babylon (all
of which procedure finds its parallels in the annals of eastern
conquerors of that period). Jerusalem was utterly stripped of all
its treasures and valuables; the temple was thoroughly dis-
mantled and all its vessels carried away; the city walls were
broken down; and then the whole city, with its desecrated
temple, its desolated palaces, and its now deserted dwellings,
was set on fire. All this is recorded in 2 Kings xxv. and 2 Chronicles xxxvi.

What the people suffered during and after the siege who can describe? Something of what was endured may be gathered from Lamentations and Ezekiel and Josephus. The complexions of the men grew black with famine, their skin having become shrunk. and parched; the noble women searched dunghills for scraps of offal; the children died or were eaten by their parents (Lam. ii. 20; iv. 3–10); a third of the inhabitants died of this famine, and of the plague which grew out of it (Ezek. v. 12). Nearly all the remaining population were then carried off into exile, only the poorest of the land being left, to be vinedressers and husbandmen (2 Kings xxv. 11, 12).

Third, *after the Babylonians had withdrawn from Jerusalem there was a conspiracy among the Jews left in the land, which resulted in a further flight of Jews from Judæa into Egypt.* This is recorded in 2 Kings xxv. 22–6; but to understand these verses thoroughly we need to read Jeremiah xl.–xliii. (Jeremiah by his own choice stayed on with those who were left in the land). The following quotation gives the gist of what transpired.

"Nebuchadnezzar, when he carried off Zedekiah to Babylon, appointed, as governor of Judæa, a certain Gedaliah, a Jew of good position, but not of the royal family. Gedaliah made Mizpah, near Jerusalem, his residence; and here he was shortly joined by a number of Jews of importance, who had escaped from Jerusalem and hidden themselves until the Babylonians were gone. Of these the most eminent were Johanan the son of Kareah, and Ishmael, a member of the royal house of David. Gedaliah urged the refugees to be good subjects of the king of Babylon, and to settle themselves to agricultural pursuits. His advice was accepted and at first followed; but presently a warning was given to Gedaliah by Johanan that Ishmael designed his destruction; and soon afterwards, as Gedaliah took no precautions, the murder was actually carried out. Other atrocities followed; but after a time Johanan and the other leading refugees took up arms, forced Ishmael to fly to the Ammonites, and then, fearing that Nebuchadnezzar would hold them responsible for Ishmael's act, fled (against Jeremiah's remonstrances) with the great mass of the Jews that had been left in the land, from Judæa into Egypt. Here our writer leaves them (verse 26), without touching on the calamities which befell them there according to the prophetic announcements of Jeremiah (see Jeremiah xliv. 2–28)."

Thus, even those Jews whom Nebuchadnezzar left were dispersed from Judæa, and the land became utterly desolate.

Fourth, *the date on which the siege of Jerusalem began is one of utmost significance, and should be very carefully observed.* 2 Kings xxv. 1 gives the date with a noticeable preciseness: "And it came to pass in the ninth year of his (Zedekiah's) reign, in the tenth month, in the tenth day of the month, that Nebuchadnezzar, king of Babylon, came, he and all his host, against Jerusalem, and pitched against it, and they built forts against it round about." This is the first time in these historical books that an event is thus dated to the very day. Apart from anything else, therefore, the carefully-given date would catch our eye; but the fact is that this same event is referred to with a similarly impressive exactness in other parts of Scripture. At the time when Nebuchadnezzar came and invested Jerusalem, the prophet Ezekiel was far away in Babylonia where he had then been an exile for over nine years. On the day that the siege of Jerusalem began, a special message was delivered about it from God to Ezekiel. In Ezekiel xxiv. 1, 2, we read—

"IN THE NINTH YEAR, IN THE TENTH MONTH, IN THE TENTH DAY OF THE MONTH, THE WORD OF THE LORD CAME UNTO ME, SAYING: SON OF MAN, WRITE THE NAME OF THE DAY, EVEN OF THIS SELFSAME DAY. THE KING OF BABYLON HATH SET HIMSELF AGAINST (i.e. HATH BESIEGED) JERUSALEM THIS SELFSAME DAY" (see R.V.).

Is not that striking? At the very hour when the Babylonian troops were arriving to encircle the Jewish capital, the fact was revealed of God to Ezekiel those hundreds of miles away. And Ezekial was commanded to write down that date emphatically, for observation and preservation—the tenth day of the month Tebeth, 589 B.C. The day has been observed by the Jews as an annual fast ever since.

But besides this, the prophet Jeremiah marks the date with the same kind of particularity. See Jeremiah lii. 4. And *why* is such attention fixed on this day? The answer to that question is also found in Jeremiah, or, rather, is found in a comparison of Jeremiah with Haggai and Daniel. The twenty-fifth chapter of Jeremiah predicts a seventy years' period of "desolations" on

Jerusalem. We find this, later, exercising the mind of Daniel (Dan. ix. 1, 2), and mentioned again by Zechariah (Zech. i. 12). Now that seventy years' period begins from that carefully emphasised day when the Babylonian army beset Jerusalem—and this fact will help to interpret much to us a little later on in our studies.

There can be no doubt that the prophetic year in Scripture is one of 360 days (see our article on Daniel's prophecy of the "seventy weeks"). If, then, we reckon seventy years of 360 days each, from the tenth day of the month Tebeth, 589 B.C., when the siege of Jerusalem began, we come down to the twenty-fourth day of the month Chisleu, 520 B.C. Does anything special happen on that latter date? Well, turn to the little book of the prophet Haggai, chapter ii. 15–19, and see what he says to the returned exiles after their Babylonian captivity. Note the prophet's deliberate stress on the words, besides our own emphasis by the use of capitals—

"CONSIDER, *FROM THIS DAY* AND UPWARD, FROM BEFORE A STONE WAS LAID UPON A STONE IN THE TEMPLE OF THE LORD . . . CONSIDER NOW *FROM THIS DAY* AND UPWARD, FROM *THE FOUR AND TWENTIETH DAY OF THE NINTH MONTH*, EVEN FROM THE DAY THAT THE FOUNDATION OF THE LORD'S TEMPLE WAS LAID, CONSIDER IT . . . *FROM THIS DAY WILL I BLESS YOU.*"

Haggai's pronouncement marked the end of that seventy years' period. We shall refer more fully to this later. Meanwhile, let us mark well that significant emphasis on the year and month and day when Jerusalem was invested.

Fifth, let us also be clear about this, that *judgment did not fall upon the chosen people only because they had committed evils as other peoples had, but signally because they had fouled a sacred covenant.* Note a few major instances of this. (1) Israel was to keep a Sabbatic year every seventh year, and the Jubilee Sabbatic year every fiftieth, when all slaves were to be freed and all debts cancelled. See Leviticus xxv. Where is there any record of Israel's keeping these Sabbaths? See Jeremiah xxxiv. 8–22. It was because of unfaithfulness here that the seventy years of "desolations" came as a long Sabbath of judgment. See the

remarkable connection between Jeremiah xxv. 11 and 2 Chronicles xxxvi. 21; and then read Leviticus xxvi. 32–5 as explaining
both. (2) Israel was not to make any covenant with the surrounding nations, but to be separate (Exod. xxxiv. 12–17, etc.).
Yet from the first Israel defaulted (Joshua ix. 14–16; Judges
ii. 2; and many other references). And (3) Israel was to shun
idolatry and the use of religious images. There is scarcely need
to give references. The record is shameful. But see 2 Kings
xvii. 17–23. Other examples might be given, as for instance
failure in tithing, Passover observance, and so on. It was in these
ways that Israel fouled the Covenant, and, in a peculiar way,
merited judgment. It should be clearly grasped that all the
judgments which came upon the chosen people were strictly
in accord with what was threatened, under such circumstances
of default, when the Covenant was first enunciated (see Lev.
xxvi. 14–39).

Final Impressions

"Conquered, captive, castaway"—thus, as one has put it,
ends the story of Judah as an independent kingdom. Let us now
glance back over 2 Kings, and gather up our main impressions.
There is always the double aspect to be kept in view—the human
and the Divine. In the foreground, and in the immediate sense,
is the human failure, as seen in the kings and the multitude; but
in the background, and in the ultimate sense, is the Divine triumph
as seen in the prophets and their messages—for let it be remembered that all the great prophets whose writings have come down
to us prophesied in the period covered by 2 Kings, and it is the
writings of these prophets which finally interpret to us both the
present and the future tense of the Israel story.

On the human side we see, above all else, that "where there is
no vision, the people perish." With departure from a simple,
sincere worship of Jehovah comes a lost sense of His presence,
accompanied increasingly by idolatry, ruinous alliances, inability
to discern the hand of God even when it chastises, a losing of the
true ideal of national life, so that moral values are belittled, and
a conscience eventually so desensitised that even such messages
as the inspired prophets delivered failed to arouse response.
Yes, this is the message on the human side. Where the vision of
God is lost there inevitably ensue, as Dr. Campbell Morgan puts

it, "degraded ideals, deadened consciences, defeated purposes." That lesson is as true for Britain and America today as it was for Judah and Israel long ago.

But on the Divine side there is the picture of ultimate triumph. The greatest prophet of the era writes of Jehovah, "*HE* shall not fail, nor be discouraged" (Isa. xlii. 4). When the throne on earth falls to pieces the throne in the heavens rides the storm. The chosen people may fail on earth, but the chosen purpose spans the centuries, and the predetermined consummation is beholden through prophets' eyes. The Babylonian exile which came as a judgment on the Jews cured them for ever of their idolatries, and strangely recovered to them their lost sense of Jehovah. The Law of Jehovah became exceedingly precious to them, and the true ideal of their nationhood began to be discerned again. That ideal is preserved to this day. They are still the chosen people. What a study they are! Scattered over the face of the earth, yet strangely one; ever persecuted, yet ever preserved; mixed in with all races, yet the most distinct people in the world; their history is a mystery apart from the explanation given in Scripture. Other peoples of far greater national dimensions than they have passed away and become extinct (as, for instance, the Assyrians and the Babylonians), yet they, the children of Abraham, are still preserved, according to covenant-promise, and *will be* preserved until all human failure is completely eclipsed in the Divine triumph when David's greater Son, even the Lord Jesus, sits on the throne in Jerusalem, and reigns in world-wide empire.

THE BOOKS OF THE CHRONICLES (1)
Lesson Number 40

NOTE.—For this study read the First Book of the Chronicles through twice.

ABOUT THOSE GENEALOGIES!

Nine chapters of genealogical tables! What waste of space! Nay, rather, what blindness to think so! No part of the Chronicles is more important. Such lines of descent were of sacred importance to all godly Jews, and rightly so, for they knew that their nation, besides being the repository of a special Divine revelation, was the possessor of wonderful Divine promises reaching on to unborn generations. The chronicler himself knew well enough that these genealogies reveal the selective process of Divine election right from Adam downwards, and that the covenant line of redemptive purpose was to culminate in the Messiah. Especially did the preservation of the trunk and main branches of Israel's family tree become vital after the Babylonian exile (when the Chronicles were written). Families had been uprooted by the thousand. Connections had been broken. Many records had been lost (see for instance Ezra ii. 59), and Judah's archives must have become largely disintegrated even where not actually destroyed. Our chronicler's lists link the *pre*-Exile with the *post*-Exile period; for (as should be clearly grasped) chapter ix. 2–34 concerns the resettlement in Judæa *after* the Exile. The break is marked by the first verse of that chapter, which should really be the last verse of the preceding chapter. The Angus *Bible Handbook* remarks: "These tables give the sacred line through which the promise was transmitted for nearly 3,500 years, a fact unexampled in the history of the human race."

—*J. S. B.*

THE BOOKS OF THE CHRONICLES (1)

THE SECOND Book of Kings has left us with a strange and gloomy sadness oppressing our minds. We feel like sitting down with Jeremiah, in sackcloth and ashes, and lamenting amid the ruins, "How doth the city sit solitary! How is she become a widow! How is the gold become dim! How are the precious sons of Zion esteemed as earthen pitchers!" The city is sacked. The temple is burnt. The country is laid bare. The nation is deported.

And yet we would not linger here. We would follow the thousands of Judah into the land of their exile, would sit and weep with them by the banks of the Chebar as Ezekiel did, or mingle with their captive princes in the Babylonian capital as Daniel did; and then, leaping the decades, we would return to Jerusalem and Judæa with the "Remnant," under the leadership of Ezra and Zerubbabel.

However, before we can do this, the two books of the "Chronicles" lie before us; and we may well be grateful that they do. Our Bible would certainly be the poorer without them. In one quick span, from Adam to Nehemiah, they give us the main genealogies of the Israelite nation, and the main events of the Davidic kingdom down to the time of the Babylonian exile.

Having gone carefully through the books of Samuel and the Kings we shall not need here to give more than a brief survey of 1 and 2 Chronicles. But the shortness of our treatment must not be misinterpreted as suggesting unimportance. On the contrary, not only are these "chronicles" alive on every page with sheer interest—yes, even those opening lists of genealogies!—they are of high importance to a right grasp of the Divine significance running through the story of the Israel nation. The one simple reason why we treat 1 and 2 Chronicles thus briefly is that they cover practically the same ground as 2 Samuel and the two books of the Kings.

This may sound as though they consist of repetition. So they do; but it is no "vain" repetition. It is a re-outlining of the story already told in the books of Samuel and the Kings, but from a

different standpoint, with new emphases and new aspects, with
significant additions and omissions, and supplying completive
interpretations. In fact, it is in this repetition, with its characteristic additions and omissions, that the peculiar *viewpoint
and significance* of the Chronicles are perceived; for if we read these
"chronicles" side by side with the earlier accounts in Samuel and
the Kings, we soon begin to notice that the additions and omissions all seem of the same sort, that is, they all seem to conform
to one focal purpose. What, then, is the unifying idea running
through these additions and omissions? And what is the central
purpose of the Chronicles?

The Unifying Idea

First, as to *the unifying idea or emphasis,* all who have studied
and written on these two books of the Chronicles are unanimous
in observing the prominence given to the *temple* and matters
connected with it. As representative of many others, take the
following quotation from the late Dr. A. T. Pierson: "While
much contained in the Books of Kings is repeated or restated
in the Chronicles, much is omitted because foreign to the author's
purpose. But whatever bears on the *temple*, its preservation and
restoration, the purity of its worship, the regularity and order-
liness of its services; whatever makes idolatrous rites or relics
hateful, or lifts God to His true throne in the hearts of the people,
is here emphasised."

If we have carefully read the *first* of these two books of the
Chronicles, as directed at the beginning of this present study,
examples of this emphasis on the temple and associated topics
will quickly come to mind. For instance, beginning with chapter
xi., the whole of the remaining nineteen chapters of 1 Chronicles
are occupied with the reign of David. In these chapters there
is no repeating the familiar tale of David's romantic adventures,
or of his reign at Hebron, or of his grief over Saul and Jonathan,
or of his sin against Bathsheba and Uriah, or of the revolt of
Absalom (these, not to mention others, are some of the significant
major *omissions*); but, on the other hand, we are given with great
fulness the following matters which are *not* mentioned in Samuel
and Kings—David's abundant preparation of material in advance
for the temple (xxii.), his preparatory numbering and distributing
of the Levites and the priests (xxiii.–xxiv.), his appointment

and arrangement of singers and players and porters (xxv.-xxvi.)
—all in anticipation of the *temple* (these, not to mention others,
are some of the significant major *additions*).

This feature persists right through the *Second* Book of the
Chronicles. The account of Solomon's reign is much shorter
here than in 1 Kings, yet no less than six out of the nine chapters
given to it in 2 Chronicles refer to the *temple*. The same significance attaches to the fact that onwards from chapter x., which
marks the disruption of the nation into the two kingdoms, the
northern ten-tribed kingdom is throughout ignored, as being
founded upon apostasy from the nation's true worship as well as
from the house of David. It is solely with Judah and Jerusalem
that the Chronicles are concerned, because it is that kingdom and
that city which hold the *temple*. And not only do all these remaining chapters (x.-xxxvi.) confine themselves to Judah, they
still further confine themselves to that viewpoint which subordin-
ates all political and military and personal facts to the interests
of that holy religion of which the temple was the great symbol.
Thus, for instance, the reigns of Asa, Jehoshaphat, Joash, Hezekiah, and Josiah are given prominence because of the religious
reforms and temple restorations associated with them. In Kings
only *three verses* are given to Hezekiah's reforms, as against *three
chapters* in the Chronicles.

Everywhere in the Chronicles the *temple* is emphasised as the
vital centre of the nation's true life; and even where the temple
itself is not mentioned, it is obvious that the emphasis is always
upon that *religion* which the temple represented. We pick out
just one instance of this. Dr. J. H. Moulton says: "No single
incident brings out the contrast of the two versions better than
the reign of Abijah (called in the Kings Abijam). The prophetic
account (i.e. that in the Kings) of the reign is a brief notice
of the wickedness of the king, so great that only for David's
sake was the succession continued in the family. Also mention
is made of wars between Israel and Judah. The *Chronicler* relates
these wars at length, and in particular gives a fine address of
Abijah to the enemy, in which the whole spirit of the Chronicles
is concentrated "—

*"Ought ye not to know that the Lord, the God of Israel, gave the
kingdom over Israel to David for ever, even to him and to his sons*

*by a covenant of salt? Yet Jeroboam the son of Nebat, the servant
of Solomon the son of David, rose up, and rebelled against his
lord. And there were gathered unto him vain men, sons of Belial,
which strengthened themselves against Rehoboam the son of
Solomon, when Rehoboam was young and tender-hearted, and
could not withstand them. And now ye think to withstand the
kingdom of the Lord in the hand of the sons of David; and ye be
a great multitude, and there are with you the golden calves which
Jeroboam made you for gods. Have ye not driven out the priests
of the Lord, the sons of Aaron, and the Levites, and have made
you priests after the manner of the peoples of other lands? so
that whosoever cometh to consecrate himself with a young bullock
and seven rams the same may be a priest of them that are no gods.
But as for us, the Lord is our God, and we have not forsaken
him; and we have priests ministering unto the Lord, the sons of
Aaron, and the Levites in their work; and they burn unto the
Lord every morning and every evening burnt offerings and sweet
incense: the shewbread also set they in order upon the pure table;
and the candlestick of gold with the lamps thereof to burn every
evening: for we keep the charge of the Lord our God; but ye have
forsaken him. And behold, God is with us at our head, and his
priests with the trumpets of alarm to sound an alarm against
you. O Children of Israel, fight ye not against the Lord, the
God of your fathers; for ye shall not prosper"* (2 Chron. xiii
5–12, R.V.).

Even the genealogies in the first nine chapters lead up to the
allocation of the returned "Remnant" in Jerusalem and Judæa
(after the Exile) necessary as a basis for the *temple* service, and
the dues by which that service was to be supported (for it should
be clearly grasped that chapter ix. 2–34 refers to the *post*-Exile
resettlement. Verse 1 marks the break).

So then, without need for more illustrations, we see the unifying
emphasis which runs through the Chronicles. They are not merely
repetition. Nor are they merely supplemental, supplying numerous
items omitted from Samuel and Kings. They relate the history
of the elect people in a new way, and from a new standpoint.

The Central Purpose

But we are still left asking: "*Why* this unifying new emphasis? What is the *purpose* behind it? Here, to some degree, we must part company with the commentators. The usual reason given for the peculiar religious emphasis in the Chronicles is that the writer, or rather the compiler, was a *priest*, a priest with a very ecclesiastical outlook, to whom, quite understandably, all matters relating to organised worship and especially to the temple were of unequalled importance. For instance, Angus's *Bible Handbook* says: "It must be remembered all through that the Books of Chronicles are essentially *Levitical*. To all, therefore, that concerns the house and service of Jehovah especial prominence is given." And Moulton's *Modern Reader's Bible* says: "The whole succession of Chronicles is animated by the conscious *ecclesiastical* spirit." And Ellicott's *Commentary* says: "From the entire tone and spirit of the work it is reasonably inferred by most critics that it was the production of a Levite attached to the temple." Most others seem to take the same view.

Now the Chronicles may or may not have been compiled by a priest or Levite; but to say, as do the many, that the peculiar emphasis in the Chronicles is simply *because* the compiler was a priest or Levite, anxious to magnify his own line of things, is to miss the overruling *Divine* design in this part of Scripture, and to reduce the significance of the Chronicles to the limited outlook of an ecclesiastic who was no bigger than the office he held. If we would really appreciate the central purpose of the Chronicles, we must bear thoughtfully in mind the time and circumstances in which they were issued.

The Chronicles were compiled *after the Babylonian exile*, when the "Remnant" had returned from Babylonia to Judæa, under Ezra and Zerubbabel. This is made absolutely certain by statements and references in the Chronicles themselves, as we shall show in our next study. The Chronicles were specially written for these repatriated Jews and their descendants who were to reconstitute the Jewish national life in the homeland; and it was because of certain new circumstances which now confronted the Jewish people that the Chronicles were compiled with the unifying emphasis running through them which we have already noted, and for a special purpose which we now mention.

If we imagine ourselves back in Judæa with that "Remnant," we soon realise that there is one very great lack which forces itself upon the mind, namely, *there is no king*. That is the crucial fact to grasp, and the first key to the purpose of the Chronicles—

THE DAVIDIC THRONE IS GONE!

What that meant to all thoughtful Jews does not require much imagination to appreciate. The throne of David was unique in the earth. It was a throne founded in a Divine covenant. We have dwelt on that in a former study, and need not linger over it again here. It must have been a sore problem to thoughtful Jews, that the throne of David was no more. What we stress here, however, is that the people were returning, not to rebuild a throne, but a *temple*. Indeed, the rebuilding of the temple was the thing for which pre-eminently the Persian emperor, Cyrus, had issued the edict precipitating the return of the Jewish "Remnant" to Jerusalem and Judæa (Ezra i. 1–4). Perhaps there is here a lesson as timely as it is vital for our own days. Note it well—even before Nehemiah is sent to rebuild the *city*, Ezra and Zerubbabel are sent with the "Remnant" to rebuild the *TEMPLE*. In any national reconstruction we must begin *there*—with the temple, that is, with *GOD*! Our politicians and reconstructors of the present post-war period will not learn. They persist in the worldly-wise idea that the *city* must be built before the temple. Well, *they are wrong*.

But now, realising vividly that the throne is gone, let us see what remains. There were three things remained which meant more than all others—

1. First, there was *the teaching of the past*, a past such as no other people had ever had, with a significance attaching to it such as did not attach to the history of any other nation. The teaching of that past had reached a point of completeness in the Exile from which the "Remnant" were now just returned; that is, certain processes in the nation's past had worked themselves out completely, to their ultimate issue, and to their bitter end. In retrospect, the covenant people could now see, in grimly complete lines, just where those processes of apostasy had brought them, and it was

vital that they should now learn unforgettingly the teaching of their nation's past.

2. Second, there was *the prophetic promise for the future.* Although the Davidic 'throne was no more among them, the Davidic *line* was; and of this line the Messiah was to come, according to Divine promise and covenant, who should lift the Davidic throne to unprecedented splendour, and consummate Jehovah's purpose in and through Israel, by bringing in a wonderful world-rule, with its centre at Jerusalem. It was vital that they should keep this great hope ever before their eyes as they now resettled in Jerusalem and the covenant land.

3. Third, there was *the presence of Jehovah with them in the present.* That presence had been strikingly guaranteed to them in the edict of Cyrus, the Persian emperor, calling on the Jews to return to their native land and to rebuild the temple of Jehovah in Jerusalem (Ezra i. 1-4). What must have been the feelings of the Jews during the last years of their exile in Babylonia, when the fame of Cyrus the Persian began to spread?—when Babylon fell?—and when the new emperor, Cyrus, who had been actually forenamed by Isaiah two hundred years earlier, gave his edict for the rebuilding of the Temple at Jerusalem, exactly as Isaiah had foretold? (see Isa. xlv., also our article on the date of Isaiah). This, in addition to Nebuchadnezzar's proclamation of his conversion to Jehovah (Dan. iv. 1-3, 34-7), and Jeremiah's prophecies as to the exact duration of the servitude to Babylon (see Jer. xxix. 10, and the comment on it in our study of Haggai), must have shown the Jews beyond all doubt that Jehovah was with them in their return to Judæa.

These, then, were the three transcendent factors which remained—the teaching of their national past, the prophetic promise for the future, the presence of Jehovah in the present. What was now necessary? It was above all things needful that the nation should read its past and its present and its future in the true way, that is, from the Divine standpoint; *and it was with this very thing in mind—to meet this need and attain this end —that the "Chronicles" were compiled.*

Three things were naturally very important in this connection

—(1) In view of the nation's unique calling and the Davidic covenant, it was most important to retain unimpaired the nation's principal genealogies; and these are therefore carefully presented in the first nine chapters. (2) In view of the catastrophes which had occurred, it was important to recast the nation's history exclusively from a religious standpoint, at least from the beginning of the Davidic kingdom; and this we find from the tenth chapter of 1 Chronicles onwards. (3) In view of the fact that the temple represented the holy religion which had come to Israel by special Divine revelation, and the disregard of which had brought such evils on the nation, and in view of the fact that the temple was the supreme surviving link between the nation's great past and its still greater prophesied future, it was greatly important to emphasise the temple and its observances in the regard of the people; and this emphasising of the temple we find all through the Chronicles, as already noted.

The temple was now, above all things, (a) the symbol of the unity of the nation, the more so now that the earthly throne had disappeared; (b) the reminder of the nation's high calling and function; (c) the sign that Jehovah was still with His chosen people; (d) the focus of the true emphasis in the national life. It was in the light of that temple that all the past was to be read, and the present reconstructed, and the future anticipated. Hence the compiling of the Chronicles, with their sustained emphasis on the temple and the religious aspects of things. And hence the central *purpose* of the Chronicles, namely, to bring home afresh to the covenant people *where the true emphasis in Israel's national life lay*, to convince them as to *where their first duty and their only true safety lay, and thereby to challenge the elect race to a renewed consecration* as the Divinely-appointed Priest of the nations.

Perhaps we cannot do better than conclude this present study by quoting some very telling words from the pen of the late John Urquhart. "These Books of the Chronicles . . . are not mere repetitions of information supplied by pre-existing Books; nor are they made up of odds and ends left by former writers. Israel's story is told afresh with clear, distinct intention. That intention is as evident in the silence of the Books as in their speech. The story of the ten tribes is left out, and Judah alone is dealt with. In the light of the evident purpose of *Chronicles,* the reason is plain. Judah alone preserved the Divine ordinances. And for the returned Israelites was not this—name it 'ecclesiastical tone,' or whatever one may choose to call it—the one thing that the replanted people had to keep constantly before them? *Israel, unlike the other nations, has no destiny apart from God's service.* This has been proved by these more than eighteen centuries of what may be named national existence, but cannot be called national life. It will be more gloriously shown in the coming day of Israel's renewed consecration. But there is enough even now to teach the higher criticism, and also a modified rationalism, that *Chronicles* saw clearly, what is now becoming apparent as a historical phenomenon, that Israel has not existed, and cannot exist, for itself. It is the Divinely-appointed Priest of the nations. When it recognised its mission, it impressed and led the nations. When it neglected it, it sank into insignificance. When it renounced it, Israel was bereft of fatherland and of spiritual perception and power. It wanders among the nations today in its blindness, disinherited, disrobed, and yet with ineffaceable marks of its priestly destiny. The Book which proclaimed that destiny to restored Israel four-and-twenty centuries ago, not only read to them the one lesson of their past; it also read to the Israelites the story of their future. This one fact is quite enough to show the Book to be prophetic: it stamps it as Divine."

THE BOOKS OF THE CHRONICLES (2)

Lesson Number 41

NOTE.—For this further study in the Chronicles read 2 Chronicles right through twice.

As with 1 and 2 Samuel and 1 and 2 Kings, these two books of the Chronicles formed one continuous work in the Hebrew original, with the title, *Dibrê Hayyâmîm*, "Events of the Days." The division into two parts dates back to the Septuagint Version (third century B.C.), which named the two parts the first and second books of "Things Omitted." The division certainly occurs at the most suitable point, but the title, "Things Omitted," is very inadequate: it makes the Chronicles merely supplemental, and quite misses their special intent. Our own title, "The Chronicles," dates from the time of Jerome, who translated the Hebrew Scriptures into the Latin about A.D. 385–405. This famous translation is known as the "Latin Vulgate" because, from the time of Gregory I (A.D. 540–604), and with the confirmation of the Council of Trent (A.D. 1562), it was accepted as the generally authentic and current text (*vulgatis* = general, common). In some of the editions of the Latin Vulgate we find the title, *Chronicorum Liber*, that is, "Book of Chronicles," as now in our English version. Even this title is not over-commendable, for the Chronicles are really more in the nature of a retrospective and interpretative epitome than merely annals.

—*J. S. B.*

THE BOOKS OF THE CHRONICLES (2)

THUS FAR our survey of the Chronicles has been concerned with their unifying emphasis and purpose. We wish now to glance over their contents, but first there are several preliminary matters which attract attention.

Originals of Compilation

Plainly the Chronicles are a compilation from earlier documents, some of which seem to be quoted literally (see "unto this day" in 2 Chron. v. 9; viii. 8). About fourteen of these are named—

1. Book of the Kings of Israel and Judah (2 Chron. xxvii. 7).
2. A Midrash (commentary) on the above (2 Chron. xxiv. 27).
3. Words, or History, of Samuel the Seer (1 Chron. xxix. 29).
4. Words, or History, of Gad the Seer (1 Chron. xxix. 29).
5. Words, or History, of Nathan the Prophet (2 Chron. ix. 29).
6. The Prophecy of Ahijah the Shilonite (2 Chron. ix. 29).
7. The Visions of Iddo the Seer (2 Chron. ix. 29).
8. Words, or History, of Shemaiah the Prophet (2 Chron. xii. 15).
9. Work of Iddo the Prophet on genealogies (2 Chron. xii. 15).
10. A Midrash (commentary) of Iddo the Prophet (2 Chron. xiii. 22).
11. Words, or History, of Jehu, son of Hanani (2 Chron. xx. 34).
12. Acts of Uzziah, by Isaiah the Prophet (2 Chron. xxvi. 22).
13. The Vision of Isaiah the Prophet (2 Chron. xxxii. 32).
14. Words, or History, of Hozai (or the Seers) (2 Chron. xxxiii. 19).

These sources of compilation are more revealing than might seem in passing. They indicate (*a*) that the author was well-informed for his task; (*b*) that he was using well-known documents which proved the *bona-fide* nature of his work; (*c*) that many consultable writings by competent scholars had accumulated during the nation's history, which fact the more confirms to ourselves the reliability of the records that have now come down to us in our Bible; (*d*) that Israel's archives were by no means the spurious, spasmodic, almost fungus growth which some of our recent "scholars" have supposed, but a body of literature carefully composed, collected, compared, and compiled.

Note that first book in our list—"The Book of the Kings of Israel and Judah." Three times we find this title (2 Chron. xxvii. 7; xxxv. 27; xxxvi. 8). Four times we find the title partly reversed to "The Book of the Kings of Judah and Israel" (2 Chron. xvi. 11; xxv. 26; xxviii. 26; xxxii. 32). The two titles refer to the same work. This is clear, for whichever way the title occurs, the reference is to a king of *Judah*. It seems to have been a remarkable repertory of historical and biographical data (2 Chron. xxvii. 7). It is well to realise that when the chronicler refers to this "Book of the Kings" he is not meaning the earlier book in our Bible which *we* now call by that name. On the contrary, there is reason to think that both Kings and Chronicles in our Bible quote this same work. This is indicated in the fact that the books which *we* now call the Books of the Kings do not contain those matters to which the chronicler calls attention in the book which *he* knew as the Book of the Kings.

Date and Authorship

Unless we are to swallow the assumption of certain moderns, that the Chronicles are blotched all over by interpolations, we shall not be long in finding verses which settle the approximate date of their compilation. Chapters vi. 15 and ix. 1 make clear that they were put together after the carrying away to Babylon. The genealogy in iii. 16–24 shows the same. The very last words of 2 Chronicles make even the edict of Cyrus, which officially ended the Exile, a thing of the past. Most conclusive of all, unless we gratuitously label the whole of 1 Chronicles ix. a later addition, the work is brought right down to the period after the return of the "Remnant" and their partial resettlement "in the cities" and "in Jerusalem" (as is made plain by comparing this chapter with Nehemiah xi. 3–32; vii. 45; xii. 25, 26; Ezra ii. 42). And, just once again, the genealogy of Zerubbabel, in chapter iii. 17–24, brings us at least to a point very late in the life of Ezra or Nehemiah. Hebrew scholars, we may add, are agreed that the language and orthography of the Chronicles also fits this post-Exilic period. Aramaisms mark the corruption of the pure Hebrew by the Chaldean language learned by the captive Jews in Babylon.

Who the compiler was is an unsettled question. The Talmud says Ezra. We cannot here go into the discussion which clings round the matter; but we mention three points which impress us in favour of the Ezra tradition. (1) We have not yet met any weighty reason *against* it. (2) Scholars seem unanimous in tracing a single hand through the three books now called Chronicles, Ezra, and Nehemiah; and all agree it is Ezra's in at least much of the book which bears his own name. (3) No one was more fitted than Ezra; nor does our claiming him as compiler of the bulk of the work exclude completive additions by some subsequent editor.

Relation to Preceding Books

As already noted, although the Chronicles cover much the same ground as the books of Samuel and the Kings, they were written at a later date, from a different standpoint, giving a special emphasis, and having a purpose peculiar to themselves. We may now crystallise the contrastive aspects between the Chronicles and the preceding historical books, as follows. Samuel and Kings are more *biographical*; the Chronicles are more *statistical*. The former are more *personal*; the latter are more *official*. The former are more from the standpoint of the *prophet*; the latter are more from the standpoint of the *priest*. The former give the history of both the northern kingdom (Israel) and the southern kingdom (Judah) after the Disruption of the nation into the two kingdoms; whereas from the Disruption onwards the Chronicles give only the history of *Judah*. In the books of Samuel and the Kings the emphasis is upon the *throne*. In the books of the Chronicles the emphasis is upon the *temple*. In their total effect the books of Samuel and the Kings are an *indictment* of the nation, exposing its guilt; whereas the Chronicles are meant to be an *incitement* to the nation, encouraging new loyalty. The books of Samuel and the Kings are simple, faithful records of things that happened; whereas the Chronicles are a purposively selective succession of extracts all chosen to press home one focal idea. All the books of our Bible thus far, from Genesis to 2 Kings, have pursued a chronological succession of events, right from Adam's creation to Judah's captivity; but now, with the Chronicles, we come to a writing which does not carry us further forward (except in odd touches here and there which reveal its post-exilic compilation), but goes back and *reviews* the whole story in order to derive and apply a vital lesson, namely, that *the nation's response to God is the decisive factor in its history and destiny*. And this lesson, we may add, is just as true of modern Britain and America as it was of old-time Israel and Judah.

Relation to Ensuing Books

Ellicott says: "Examination of the Hebrew text of Chronicles, Ezra, and Nehemiah soon reveals that the three resemble each other very closely, not only in style and language, which is that of the latest age of Hebrew writing, but also in the general point of view, in the manner in which the original authorities are handled and the sacred Law expressly cited, and above all in the marked preference for certain topics, such as genealogical and statistical registers, descriptions of religious rites and festivals, detailed accounts of the sacerdotal classes and their various functions, notices of the music of the temple, and similar matters connected with the organisation of public worship. . . . There are other facts which combine with the above to prove that Chronicles, Ezra, and Nehemiah originally constituted a single great history." Perhaps this is confirmed by the strange termination of the Chronicles in an unfinished sentence, which the opening verses of Ezra complete; and there is actually extant part of a Greek version of these three books which shows no division between them.

Now this close affinity between Chronicles, Ezra, and Nehemiah has certain values for us. Long ago, when the Jews formed their canon of sacred writings, they put the Chronicles right at the end; and we find certain Bible teachers today who would have us think that the Chronicles ought still to come right at the end of our Old Testament, so as to show more easily the connection of their genealogies with those given by Matthew. But no, the Chronicles *must not be separated from Ezra and Nehemiah*. The right place for them is just where they come in our Bible. Surely this is *obviously* so. They belong to the *historical* books; and they are *the true link* between the pre-Exile and post-Exile periods. They look back summarisingly over the throne period, and relate it to the throneless new period. We certainly must not separate the four post-exilic books—Chronicles, Ezra, Nehemiah, and Esther; nor must we miss seeing how their distinctive subjects go together to form one progressive group, thus—

Chronicles—Retrospection.
Ezra   —Restoration.
Nehemiah—Reconstruction.
Esther   —Preservation.

Contents and Structure

And now, most interesting of all, let us try to get a quick, "all in" view of the contents of the Chronicles. Perhaps "interesting" is scarcely the best word. These Chronicles are *fascinating*, if with a little imagination we catch our author-compiler's idea, and see the purpose behind his pen taking carefully chosen form through each successive section.

Take the first section of 1 Chronicles (i.–ix.). To say that these chapters are genealogies is correct, but it is putting it in a very colourless way. They are part of our chronicler's scheme as a whole, and when seen as such they assume new meaning. What we are mainly meant to see is the family tree of a certain *people*—the people of Jehovah. The stock of Adam shoots out three great branches: the sons of Japheth, Ham, and Shem. In the electing purpose of God, the eldest is passed by, and Shem, the youngest, is chosen. So is Abram, the youngest son of Terah, selected; so is Isaac, in preference to Ishmael; and so is Jacob, in preference to Esau. All this is in chapter i. Next, in chapter ii., the redemptive line and selective progress descends through Jacob to Judah, then away down to Jesse, and thus to David. The chronicler here interrupts himself to preserve the genealogy of Caleb, that hero of faith who was also of Judah (ii. 18–25); but with chapter iii. he resumes the Davidic line—right down to the last of Judah's kings, Zedekiah. Finally, having shown the selective process from Adam down to Abraham, Isaac, Jacob, Judah, David, he reviews the genealogies of the Israel tribes in general, and their allotments in Canaan (iv.–viii.), for all share in the covenant promises. So, in these first chapters, we have, distinctively, the *PEOPLE* of Jehovah.

Now take chapters x. to xii. Here begins the reign of David, the *anointed* of Jehovah. Chapter x. (which obviously is simply transitory) tells of Saul's death (all else about him is designedly excluded), and how thereupon God "turned the kingdom unto David." Chapters xi. and xii. tell *how* David became king, how he made Jerusalem the capital, who were his mighty men, and how all the tribes were "of one heart" to make him king. Saul had been king rather by *human* choice. David was king by *Divine* choice. Saul had possessed high *natural* qualities, yet was without true faith, and could not please God (x. 13); so his house was set aside, and the throne given to the man of *God's own choice* (x. 14). Here, then, we have the *ANOINTED* of Jehovah.

Now take chapters xiii.–xvi. Here is the first-recorded outstanding public act of king David—the bringing of the *ark* of Jehovah to Jerusalem. David sensed keenly that the secret of the nation's blessing was Jehovah's presence in the midst. Saul had never grasped this in the same way. He had let the ark of Jehovah, symbol of Immanuel ("God with us"), remain neglected (xiii. 3), which in essence was a despising of Israel's birthright, and proved Saul unworthy of the kingship. Very different is it with David, the man of faith. He plans at once to put the ark of Jehovah at the centre of His people's life. After a setback (xiii. 9–13) the ark is at length brought with due reverence to Jerusalem; and although Saul's daughter might see no glory in this act of faith, and might despise the man of God (xv. 29), God blesses this man on every side (xiv.), and David, in an inspired psalm (xvi. 7–36), can teach the people to see covenant mercy in this sacred symbol of promise. In this third section, then, see the *ARK* of Jehovah.

And next, in chapters xvii.–xxi., see the *covenant* of Jehovah. It pleased God to choose out of the race one nation—Israel, then out of that nation one tribe—Judah, then out of that tribe one family—the house of David, and to make with that house a wonderful covenant. See chapter xvii. for this covenant. Then see chapters xviii.–xx. for the immediate Divine implementing of that covenant in David's full establishment and high-point of prosperity. And although David later fell prey to a stratagem of Satan (xxi.), even this lapse was overruled to further God's plan, for it led to the fixing of the spot where the future temple was to stand (xxi. 28 with 2 Chron. iii. 1). Thus, in these chapters we have the *COVENANT* of Jehovah.

This brings us to the last group of chapters (xxii.–xxix.), which are occupied with the *temple* of Jehovah. David was not allowed to build it, but he amply prepared for it—materials (xxii.), Levites (xxiii.), priests (xxiv.), singers, porters, and other officers (xxv.–xxvii.), and a final charge in anticipation of it to Solomon and the nation (xxviii.–xxix.). Plainly, the subject here is the *TEMPLE* of Jehovah. And thus, in this first book of the Chronicles we have—

> The *PEOPLE* of the Lord (i.–ix.).
> The *ANOINTED* of the Lord (x.–xii.).
> The *ARK* of the Lord (xiii.–xvi.).
> The *COVENANT* of the Lord (xvii.–xxi.).
> The *TEMPLE* of the Lord (xxii.–xxix.).

The *subject* of these Chronicles is *the house of Jehovah*. In the larger sense that house is the whole nation Israel; in a more centralised sense it is the house of David; in the centre-most sense it is the temple. The central lesson may be expressed in the words of 1 Samuel ii. 30: "Them that honour Me, I will honour." To the man who would build God a house God says: "The *LORD* will build *thee* an house" (xvii. 10). There is no need for a minute analysis. The following will fix the framework for us.

THE FIRST BOOK OF CHRONICLES
THE HOUSE OF JEHOVAH

RESPONSE TO GOD THE DETERMINING FACTOR

---

1. ISRAEL'S MAIN GENEALOGIES (i.–ix.)

ADAM TO JACOB (ALSO ESAU'S LINE) (i.).
JACOB TO DAVID (ALSO CALEB LINE) (ii.).
DAVID TO ZEDEKIAH (AND POST-EXILE) (iii.).
TRIBE GENEALOGIES AND ALLOTMENTS (iv.–viii.).
Post-Exile resettlement (ix.).

2. DAVID'S REIGN AT JERUSALEM (x.–xxix.).

THE ANOINTED OF THE LORD (x.–xii.).
THE ARK OF THE LORD (xiii.–xvi.).
THE COVENANT OF THE LORD (xvii.–xxi.)
THE TEMPLE OF THE LORD (xxii.–xxix.).
Death of king David (xxix. 26–30).

And now we come to the *Second* Book of the Chronicles. For our present purpose it may be summed up very briefly. It is a tragic book, with a glorious opening and a terrible ending. The first nine chapters give us the forty years' reign of Solomon. The remaining chapters (x.–xxxvi.) give us Judah's history down to the Exile.

As for Solomon's reign, the larger part of the account is taken up with the *temple*. We need not speak here about the temple as a building: we have already done so in our study of 1 Kings. Nor need we speak again about Solomon personally, nor of the type aspects of his reign. Let us try to catch the *national* and *moral* significances of the chronicler's outline.

The Davidic covenant had provided that the seed of David should (1) inherit a firm kingdom; (2) build the temple; (3) be subject to discipline. All these three provisions begin to have fulfilment in Solomon's reign. The kingdom reaches unprecedented splendour; the glorious temple is built; and, alas, discipline has to be exercised. The promises of God concerning *ultimate* issues never have an "if" in them, because they find their final goal in *Christ* (see our note on 2 Sam. vii.); but promises concerning the intermediate processes toward those ultimate issues often *do* have an "if" in them. Thus, as someone has aptly observed, "Solomon was promised wisdom, wealth, and power, and he received them. He was promised 'length of days' *if* he persevered in his walk with God (1 Kings iii. 14). This latter gift he forfeited, and died at fifty-nine."

And what a story *after* Solomon's death—from Rehoboam and the "Disruption" to Zedekiah and the "Dispersion"! There is no need here to give each of the twenty kings separate mention. We have read the chronicler's account. We know the story. But again let us grasp the centre-point of significance. In the preceding chronicles there have risen up before us a *THRONE* founded in a Divine covenant, and a *TEMPLE* made glorious by a Divine descent into it. The throne and the temple are meant to uphold and glorify each other; but a condition of apostasy develops, and goes from bad to worse despite occasional checks, in which the throne becomes the worst *enemy* of the temple, until a point is reached where one of the two must go, and as it cannot be the temple it must be the throne. Hence the Exile and the suspension of the Davidic throne. The temple too is allowed to be burnt, for it had already been profaned far more by Jewish sinning than it now could be by Babylonish burning: and a new temple must be built in the throneless new period after the Exile.

Such is the centre-point of national significance; but let us catch the *moral and spiritual* truth of the book. Running right through the story of these kings, with its occasional reforms and ever-worsening relapses, is the solemn, vital, urgent truth that *a nation's response to God is the really determining factor in its history and destiny.* This was specially true of Israel, but it is universally true of the earth's people today. "As long as Uzziah sought the Lord, God made him to prosper" (xxvi. 5); "Jotham became mighty because he prepared his ways before the Lord his God" (xxvii. 6)—this is the stress all through 2 Chronicles. In the two books of the Chronicles taken together, we have the full historical view of the Davidic monarchy; and in it we see high calling, great blessing, ill doing, bad ending. We are meant to see, through the alternating ups and downs of the nations' history, that when king and people honoured God there was prosperity, whereas whenever they behaved unfaithfully to Him there came adversity. On page after page this truth is driven home that the nation's response to God is the really decisive factor in its history and destiny.

This truth may not seem so immediately perceptible in our modern world with its international complicatedness; but when we look at processes over a period we find it still in operation. Moral principles and spiritual convictions are the *first*-important things as regards national progress or decline, not politics and economics—as seems to be the fashionable thought in Government today. The place we give to *GOD* is that which determines our prosperity or adversity, our history and our destiny. Israel of old—kings, leaders, people—deceived themselves into thinking that they could sin with impunity, imagining that because Jehovah could not be seen He could not see: but they did not deceive God; nor can we. "God is not mocked." He rules, He chooses, He forbears; but He will not spare the persistent exploiting of privilege. The abuse of high calling by low living always brings ruinous ending. Oh, that nations, leaders, peoples, might realise that today!

The following outline will help to fix the main points in mind.

THE SECOND BOOK OF CHRONICLES
The Temple versus the Throne

RESPONSE TO GOD THE DETERMINING FACTOR

1. SOLOMON'S FORTY YEARS' REIGN (i.–ix.).

   Solomon's early establishment (i.).
   Solomon rears the Temple (ii.–vii.).
   Solomon in all his glory (viii.–ix.).
   Death of Solomon (ix. 29–31).

2. JUDAH'S HISTORY TO THE EXILE (x.–xxxvi.).

   The "Disruption" of the kingdom (x.).
   The twenty kings of Judah (xi.–xxxvi.).
   Deportation to Babylon (xxxvi. 15–21).
   Edict of Cyrus (xxxvi. 22, 23).

Concluding Reflections

In our brief survey of the Chronicles we have had to leave many interesting points untouched. Perhaps a few hints or suggestions may be acceptable as we close.

These Chronicles are an endless mine for preachers. Every part is full of spiritual suggestion. As just one instance, in 2 Chronicles, take the four deliverances wrought for Judah— (1) under Abijah against Jeroboam; (2) under Asa against the Ethiopians; (3) under Jehoshaphat against the Moabites; (4) under Hezekiah against the Assyrians; and note how in every case the victory is attributed to God's fighting for Judah (see xiii., xiv., xx., xxxii.). Or go through the chapters noting the two persistent perils to the temple and the true worship—(1) neglected, or (2) corrupted. Or again, the reforms under Hezekiah are a grand study, showing the first steps to be taken, both negatively and positively, in *any* national reconstruction.

Again, as Dr. J. H. Moulton says, "There can be few better exercises in the study of historic literature than to compare these two divisions of Bible history (Chronicles *versus* Samuel and Kings), in their treatment of the same incident." We give overleaf a list of the parallel passages.

PARALLEL PASSAGES

A comparison with the books of Samuel, Kings and certain chapters in Isaiah is necessary in the study of Chronicles. To assist in this, we give a complete list of the parallel passages with which Chronicles should be studied.

1 Sam. xxvii. .	.	1 Chron. xii. 1–7
xxix. 1–3	.	xii. 19–22
xxxi,	.	x.
2 Sam. v. 1–5 .	.	xi. 1–3
v. 6–10 .	.	xi. 4–9
v. 11–16 .	.	xiv. 1–7
v. 17–25 .	.	xiv. 8–17
vi. 1–11 .	.	xiii.
vi. 12–23 .	.	xv. and xvi.
vii.	.	xvii.
viii.	.	xviii.
x. .	.	xix.
xi. 1–27 .	.	xx. 1
xii. 29–31 .	.	xx. 1–3
xxiii. 8–39 .	.	xi. 10–47
xxiv. 1–9 .	.	xxi. 1–6
xxiv. 1–9 .	.	xxvii. 23, 24
xxiv. 10–17 .	.	xxi. 7–17
xxiv. 18–24 .	.	xxi. 18–xxii. 1
1 Kings ii. 1 .	.	xxiii. 1
ii. 1–4 .	.	xxviii. 20, 21
ii. 10–12 .	.	xxix. 23–30
ii. 46 .	.	2 Chron. i. 1
iii. 4–15 .	.	i. 2–13
v. .	.	ii.
vi. .	.	iii. 1–14 ; iv. 9
vii. 15–21 .	.	iii. 15–17
vii. 23–6 .	.	iv. 2–5
vii. 38–46 .	.	iv. 6, 10, 17
vii. 47–50 .	.	iv. 18–22
vii. 51 .	.	v. 1
viii.	.	v. 2 ; vii. 10
ix. 1–9 .	.	vii. 11–22
ix. 10–28 .	.	viii.
x. 1–13 .	.	ix. 1–12
x. 14–25 .	.	ix. 13–24
x. 26–9 .	.	ix. 25–8 ; i. 14–17
ix. 41–3 .	.	ix. 29–31
xii. 1–19 .	.	x.
xii. 21–4 .	.	xi. 1–4
xii. 25 .	.	xi. 5–12
xii. 26–31 .	.	xi. 13–17
xiv. 22–4 .	.	xii. 1
xiv. 25–8 .	.	xii. 2–12
xiv. 21, 29–31 .	.	xii. 13–16
xv. 1 .	.	xiii. 1, 2
xv. 6 .	.	xiii. 2–31
xv. 7, 8 .	.	xiii. 22 ; xiv. 1
xv. 11, 12 .	.	xiv. 1–5
xv. 13–15 .	.	xv. 16–18
xv. 16–22 .	.	xvi. 1–6
xv. 23, 24 .	.	xvi. 11–14
xxii. 1–40, 44 .	.	xviii.
xxii. 41–3 .	.	xvii. 1 ; xx. 31–3
xxii. 45 .	.	xx. 34
xxii. 47–9 .	.	xx. 35–7
xxii. 50 .	.	xxi. 1

PARALLEL .PASSAGES (*continued*)

2 Kings i. 1 ; iii. 4, 5	.	.	2 Chron. xx. 1–3
viii. 16–19	.	.	xxi. 2–7
viii. 20–2	.	.	xxi. 8–15
viii. 23, 24	.	.	xxi. 18–20
viii. 25–7 .	.	.	xxii. 1–4
viii. 28, 29 ; ix. 1–28.	.	.	xxii. 5–7, 9
x. 11–14 .	.	.	xxii. 8
xi. 1–3 .	.	.	xxii. 10–12
xi. 4–20 .	.	.	xxiii.
xi. 21 ; xii. 1–3	.	.	xxiv. 1–3
xii. 6–16 .	.	.	xxiv. 4–14
xii. 17, 18	.	.	xxiv. 23, 24
xii. 19–21.	.	.	xxiv. 25–7
xiv. 1–6 .	.	.	xxv. 1–4
xiv. 7 .	.	.	xxv. 11–16
xiv. 8–14	.	.	xxv. 17–24
xiv. 17–20	.	.	xxv. 25–8
xiv. 21, 22 ; xv. 1–4 .	.	.	xxvi. 1–15
xv. 6, 7, 27, 28	.	.	xxvi. 22, 23
xv. 32–5 .	.	.	xxvii. 1–8
xv. 38 .	.	.	xxvii. 9
xxvi. 1, 2.	.	.	xxviii. 1, 2
xvi. 3, 4, 6	.	.	xxviii. 3–8
xvi. 7 .	.	.	xxviii. 16–19
xv. 29 .	.	.	xxviii. 20
xvi. 8–18 .	.	.	xxviii. 21–5
xvi. 19, 20	.	.	xxviii. 26, 27
xviii. 1–3	.	.	xxix. 1, 2
xviii. 13 .	.	.	Isa. xxxvi. 1
xviii. 14–16	.	.	2 Chron. xxxii. 2–8
xx. 1–11 .	.	.	{ 2 Chron. xxxii. 24 ; { Isa. xxxviii.
xx. 12–19.	.	.	Isa. xxxix. 1–8
xviii. 17–37	.	.	{ 2 Chron. xxxii. 9–19 { Isa. xxxvi. 2–22
xix. 1–5 .	.	.	{ 2 Chron. xxxii. 20 { Isa. xxxvii. 1–4
xix. 6, 7 .	.	.	Isa. xxxvii. 6, 7
xix. 8–19 .	.	.	{ 2 Chron. xxxii. 17 { Isa. xxxvii. 8–20
xix. 20–37	.	.	{ 2 Chron. xxxii. 21 { Isa. xxxvii. 21–38
xx. 20, 21	.	.	2 Chron. xxxii. 32, 33
xxi. 1–16	.	.	xxxi. 1–9
xxi. 17, 18	.	.	xxxiii. 18–20
xxi. 19–26	.	.	xxxiii. 21–5
xxii. 1, 2 .	.	.	xxxiv. 1–7
xxii. 3–20	.	.	xxxiv. 8–28
xxiii. 1–3	.	.	xxxiv. 29–32
xxiii. 21–3	.	.	xxxv. 1–19
xxxiii. 24–6	.	.	xxxiv. 33
xxiii. 28–30	.	.	xxxv. 20–7
xxiii. 30–3	.	.	xxxvi. 1–3
xxiii. 34–7	.	.	xxxvi. 4, 5
xxiv. 8, 9	.	.	xxxvi. 9
xxiv. 15–17	.	.	xxxvi. 10
xxiv. 18, 19	.	.	xxxvi. 11, 12
xxiv. 20 .	.	.	xxxvi. 13–16
xxv. 8–21	.	.	xxxvi. 18–21

The above list of parallel passages we have taken the liberty of reproducing from the *Annotated Bible*, by the late A. C. Gaebelein, which work we are happy to recommend.

Gloria Johnson
Stevens
Row York
tomorrow at 9 oclock

It is good to know that recent archaeological discovery has wonderfully confirmed the Chronicles. See the late John Urquhart's *New Biblical Guide*, volumes 6 and 8, and other books on Bible archaeology.

Most of all, may that central message of the Chronicles grip our minds, namely, *that response to God is the really decisive factor*. It is true both nationally and individually. It was true of old: it is true today. The first *duty* and the only true *safety* of the *throne* lies in its relation toward the *temple*. Our national leaders of today might well ponder that fact. When God is honoured, government is good and the nation prospers. But when God is *dis*honoured, the cleverest statesmanship cannot avert eventual disaster. The call to our nation today, as clearly as in the Edict of Cyrus quoted at the end of 2 Chronicles, is to "*go up*" and *REBUILD THE TEMPLE.*

THE BOOK OF EZRA (1)

Lesson Number 42

NOTE.—For this study read through the Book of Ezra twice. Make a note of problematical points or references. Some of these, at least, will be found dealt with in the two ensuing studies. For a note on the Jewish "months" see appendix to our next study in Ezra.

It is maintained by many that the Book of Ezra is the work of several different hands, and that such unity as it possesses has been given to it by a compiler. The compiler is by some believed to have been Ezra, by others an unknown Jew contemporary with him. This latter theory rests upon the fact of the curious transitions from the third to the first person, and back, which occur in the later chapters (vii. 28; x. 1). . . . In the earlier portion of the Book it is supposed that different styles may be traced. . . . The simple view that Ezra, who is admitted to have written at least one section, really composed the whole, using for the most part his own words, but in places inserting documents, is to the full as tenable as any other hypothesis. The general harmony of the whole Book, and the *real* uniformity of its style, are in favour of this view. The objection from the changes of person is of no great importance, changes of this kind often occurring in works admitted to be the production of a single writer, as in Thucydides and in Daniel. Moreover, tradition ascribes the whole Book to Ezra; and if Ezra wrote Chronicles, which is the view of many critics, then the connection of the Book with Chronicles will be an additional argument in favour of Ezra's authorship.

—Rev. George Rawlinson, M.A., in " Pulpit Commentary."

Note: The above quotation refers to " curious transitions " (plural) from third to first person and back, as though they occurred several times. The actual fact is that there is one complete section in which the change to first person is sustained throughout, without alternation (vii. 27—ix. 15). We mention this because it seems yet further to strengthen the likelihood that Ezra was the author-compiler, rather than that " unknown few contemporary with him."

—J.S.B.

THE BOOK OF EZRA (1)

THE THREE little books which now lie before us—Ezra, Nehemiah,
Esther—complete the seventeen historical books which form the
earlier part of the Old Testament. These three belong together
as the three books which record God's dealings with the Jews
after their going into captivity. Ezra and Nehemiah deal with
the "Remnant" which returned to Jerusalem and Judæa, while
the book of Esther has to do with those who stayed on in the
land of their captivity. While we are reading these three sketches
at the end of the seventeen *historical* books, we ought to read
the three prophets at the end of the seventeen *prophetical* books,
namely, Haggai, Zechariah and Malachi, for these were the three
prophets whom God raised up among His people in the post-
Exile period.

The Return of the Remnant

The subject with which this Book of Ezra deals is one of the
most important in Jewish history, namely, *the return of the
Remnant.* This event took place about the year 536 B.C., that
is, at the end of the seventy years' servitude to Babylon. Both
the Exile and the return were predicted before ever the Exile
began (see Jer. xxv. 11-12, and xxix. 10, 11); and the Book of
Ezra recognises this in its opening words—"Now in the first year
of Cyrus, King of Persia, *that the word of the Lord by the mouth
of Jeremiah might be fulfilled*, the Lord stirred up the spirit of
Cyrus, King of Persia, that he made a proclamation throughout
all his kingdom, and put it also in writing, saying:

"JEHOVAH, GOD OF HEAVEN, HATH GIVEN ME ALL THE KING-
DOMS OF THE EARTH; AND HE HATH CHARGED ME TO BUILD
HIM AN HOUSE AT JERUSALEM WHICH IS IN JUDAH. WHO IS
THERE AMONG YOU OF ALL HIS PEOPLE?—HIS GOD BE WITH
HIM, AND LET HIM GO UP TO JERUSALEM WHICH IS IN JUDAH,
AND BUILD THE HOUSE OF JEHOVAH, GOD OF ISRAEL (HE IS
THE GOD) WHICH IS IN JERUSALEM."

At the outset, then, let us clearly note these two facts—first, that the return was foretold in prophecy; and second, that it was actually set on foot by the decree of Cyrus.

The Size of the Remnant

As to the *size* of the returning Remnant, in the second chapter of Ezra thirty-three family groups are enumerated, making a total of 24,144. Then follow four groups of priests totalling 4,289. Then come groups of Levites and others to the number of 1,385. These three totals added together give the combined total of 29,818. This total, however, seems to be the aggregate of the *males only*; for in verses 64–5 we read: "The whole congregation together was forty and two thousand, three hundred and three score; beside their servants and their maids, of whom there were seven thousand, three hundred, thirty and seven." Thus, the final total of males, females, and servants is 49,697; and we may therefore put the size of the Remnant at the round figure of 50,000.

Such a number, out of the national total, was very small. It was, indeed, merely a "*remnant.*" During the years of captivity in Babylonia many of the older generation had died off, and the new generation of Jews who had grown up amid their foreign environment would not feel just that smarting sense of strangeness, humiliation, and resentment which their parents had felt. Understandably, therefore, though not excusably, the pull of their fatherland was not so strong upon these latter as it had been upon their exiled parents. Historic changes, also, had taken place during those years of Jewish exile. The power of Babylon had crumpled and perished before the resistless spread of the Persian empire (which accounts for the fact that it was a Persian king, Cyrus the Great, who issued the edict which precipitated the return of the Jewish remnant to Jerusalem); and the Jews seem to have fared none too badly under the Persian rule. Thus when the providential opportunity came for repatriation, the bulk of the nation, to their shame, preferred their tolerable and perhaps even lucrative life under Persian rule, to which they had now become quite accommodated.

A Further Return

So, then, there was this return of fifty thousand, in response to the decree of Cyrus, in 536 B.C.—which return was under the leadership of Zerubbabel (see ii. 2), who was a lineal descendant of the kings of Judah. But about *eighty years later*, in the year 456 B.C., there was a further return, though of a very much smaller number, under the leadership of Ezra, the priest and scribe. It was occasioned by a decree of Artaxerxes, the then reigning Persian king; and the twelve groups of those who comprised the expedition along with the Nethinims (viii. 20) totalled about 2,000, though this is said to be the number of males only (viii. 3., etc.). With this further expedition under Ezra in mind, we may say that the repatriating of the Remnant was in two stages. It was *commenced* under Zerubbabel, in the first year of Cyrus (536 B.C.), and was *completed* eighty years later, under Ezra, in the seventh year of Artaxerxes (456 B.C.).

The further return under Ezra is described in chapters vii. and viii., and marks off this book of Ezra into its two main parts: Part I—The Return under Zerubbabel (i.–vi.); Part II—The Return under Ezra (vii.–x.).

The " Book " of Ezra

As we pointed out in our study of the Chronicles, there is reason to believe that 1 and 2 Chronicles, Ezra, and Nehemiah were originally one undivided work. The Jewish and early Christian view is that Ezra was the author-compiler of that original. Perhaps we may profitably mention here again three points in favour of the Ezra tradition: (1) we have not yet encountered any weighty reason *against* it; (2) scholars agree that a single hand may be traced through Chronicles, Ezra, and Nehemiah, and that it is certainly Ezra's in part of the book which bears his own name; (3) it is difficult to find an alternative. Who was more fitted or more likely? And as for that over-refined critical expertness which professes to discern *several* different "styles" in the original, it is surely answer enough that Ezra's being the author-compiler of the work in bulk does not rigidly exclude God-guided completive touches here and there by some competent hand a little later, nor does it exclude that the autobiographical parts in the Book of Nehemiah were written by Nehemiah himself.

As to the *date* of the book, obviously, it must have been written after the latest event which it records, and that is the reformation under Ezra, the year after his arrival at Jerusalem, 456 B.C. Probably it was written a few years after that event.

Perhaps the central *spiritual* significance of the book may be best expressed in the words of Lamentations iii. 32—"*Though He cause grief, yet will He have compassion.*" God had certainly brought grief upon His elect people, for judgment had become necessary, and the grief was richly deserved: but now the span of exile was over; God had not forgotten to be gracious, and there was a compassionate restoration made possible. Oh, that most wonderful truth—that the God of Israel, and of the universe, is a *compassionate* God! Let us never forget it, especially in times when men's sins bring vast calamities upon the world.

The *structure* of the book is simple and interesting. As already mentioned, it is in two clearly divided parts. In chapters i. to vi. we have the return under Zerubbabel, and what ensued; then in chapters vii. to x. we have the further return under Ezra, and what ensued. It should be most definitely understood that between these two parts (i.e. between the end of chapter vi. and the beginning of chapter vii.) there intervenes *a gap of sixty years*. The return under Zerubbabel was in the first year of Cyrus (i. 1) which was 536 B.C. The return under Ezra was in the seventh year of Artaxerxes (vii. 1, 8) which was in 456 B.C., that is, *eighty* years later. The first six chapters of the book cover the first *twenty* years (approximately) after the return under Zerubbabel, which leaves about *sixty* years between the end of chapter vi. and the opening of chapter vii. During the earlier part of this sixty years' gap the critical events narrated in the Book of *Esther* took place.

There is a noticeable parallelism between the two main parts of this Book of Ezra. In preference to an ordinary paragraph-by-paragraph analysis, we ought to get into our minds a picture of the book in this parallel form. Part 1 begins with the decree of Cyrus; part 2 begins with the decree of Artaxerxes. In part 1 the central figure is Zerubbabel; in part 2 the central figure is Ezra. In both parts we are given a careful list of the persons who returned, and of the sacred vessels. In part 1 there is the ministry of the prophets, Haggai and Zechariah; in part 2 there is the ministry of the priest-scribe, Ezra. At the end of part 1 the main outcome is the temple rebuilt; at the end of part 2 the main outcome is the people re-separated.

THE BOOK OF EZRA
THE BOOK OF RESTORATION

"Though He cause grief, yet will He have compassion."

THE RETURN UNDER ZERUBBABEL (i.–vi.)	THE RETURN UNDER EZRA (vii.–x.)
The decree of Cyrus (i. 1–4)	The decree of Artaxerxes (vii. 1, 11–26)
The leader, Zerubbabel (i. 8; ii. 2)	The leader, Ezra the scribe (vii. 1–10)
Names and number of Remnant (ii. 3–65)	Names and number of company (viii. 1–20)
Sacred vessels and gifts (i. 6–11; ii. 68–70)	Sacred vessels and gifts (vii. 15–22; viii. 24–35)
The coming to Jerusalem (iii. 1)	The coming to Jerusalem (viii. 32)
Prophet ministry: Haggai, Zechariah (v. 1–vi. 14)	Intercessory ministry of Ezra (ix. 1–15)
Main outcome — Temple rebuilt (vi. 15–22)	Main outcome — People re-separated (x. 1–44)

The Two Leaders

If this book of Scripture were named according to its subject
rather than after its author, it would be called "The Book of
the Remnant," or "The Book of the Restoration," or "The Book
of the Repatriation," rather than "Ezra." Or, if it were named
after its leading parts or personalities, it would be "The Book
of Zerubbabel and Ezra," rather than of Ezra alone. This is
worth mentioning, lest from repeated reference to the book as
"The Book of Ezra" we fall into thinking of Ezra himself as
the principal actor in the story. Ezra certainly is the leader of
the expedition and re-separation in chapters vii. to x., but the
real leader of the Remnant, eighty years before Ezra's expedition,
and the chief administrator of affairs among the Remnant after
the resettlement in Judæa, was Zerubbabel. The contemporary
prophet, Haggai, uniformly addresses him as "Zerubbabel,

governor of Judah." Since he must have been well into adult
years when he led the Remnant back to Judæa, we presume that
he must have been dead a considerable time when Ezra came
to Jerusalem, eighty years after the Remnant. The last historical
reference to Zerubbabel is in chapter v. 2. Both these leaders
are very important figures in the story of Israel.

Zerubbabel.

In this Book of Ezra, Zerubbabel is also called by two other
names—"Sheshbazzar" (i. 8, 11; v. 14–16), and "The Tirshatha"
(ii. 63). The former is his Babylonian or Chaldee name; the
latter is a Persian title meaning governor. His personal name,
"Zerubbabel," means *descended of Babylon,"* which indicates
that he was actually a child of the Exile, born in Babylonia, or
probably in the city of Babylon itself. This also suggests that
in the case of Zerubbabel personally, the coming to Jerusalem
with the 50,000 Remnant was not a "return" but *his first coming*.
There is nothing to suggest that he had ever seen Jerusalem or
Judæa before.

He is called, "Zerubbabel, the *son of Shealtiel"* (elsewhere
called Salathiel). His full lineage is given in 1 Chronicles iii.
That he was indeed one of the generation born in captivity is
definitely shown in 1 Chronicles iii. 17–19 (see R.V. for verse 17).
His lineage makes his leadership of the Remnant the more noteworthy. He was directly in the royal line of David, being the
great-grandson of king Jeconiah (who began to reign at the age
of eighteen but was carried captive to Babylon three months
later: see 2 Kings xxiv. 8–16). So important does the chronicler
deem Zerubbabel's lineage that, after connecting it right back
with David, he carries it down several generations *after* Zerubbabel—in fact to the latest point of time anywhere in Chronicles,
Ezra or Nehemiah. When we turn on to the New Testament
we at once find Matthew completing the links, until, of David
and Zerubbabel's line, according to the flesh, *CHRIST* is born.

Of Zerubbabel's personal character we know nothing except
by inference from scantiest data. His religious zeal is implied,
of course, in his very leadership of the Remnant. We note his
care to conform the restored worship to the word of God (Ezra
iii. 2–5, 11), and his response to the two prophets (v. 1, 2; Hag.

i. 12). But the threefold glory which immortalises him is that he (1) captained the Remnant back to Judæa, (2) laid the foundation of the new temple, (3) completed the erection of the new temple (compare iii. 8 and vi. 15 with Zech. iv. 9).

Ezra.

Jewish tradition, via the Talmud, has made Ezra one of the most celebrated personages in all the history of his people. Five great works are attributed to him: (1) The founding of the so-called "Great Synagogue," or synod of learned Jewish scholars —concerning which see the note sub-joined to our next study; (2) the settlement of the sacred "canon," or recognised list of authoritative Hebrew Scriptures, and its threefold arrangement into the Law, the Prophets, and the Writings; (3) the change-over from the writing of the Hebrew Scriptures in the old Hebrew script to the new, with its square Assyrian characters; (4) the compilation of the Chronicles, along with the book which now bears his own name, and the Book of Nehemiah; (5) the institution of local synagogues.

If these five big accomplishments provenly and directly originated with Ezra, then he certainly is of a stature to be eyed with some wonder; but *did* they all originate with him? Scholarly investigators into these Jewish traditions have pronounced them largely legendary. This much, however, is quite factual, that these far-reaching developments took shape in or near the period of Ezra's moral and literary leadership, and that he had no small part in them. Thus, it is not without reason that he should be regarded as something of an epochal figure.

But let us glance at Ezra *personally*. He was one of the captives in Babylonia, where, also, almost certainly, he was born. He was a lineal descendant of Israel's first high priest, Aaron; and all the links in the chain of descent are given in chapter vii. 1–5. So he was a *priest*. Also, he was a *"scribe"*—a "ready scribe in the Law of Moses" (vii. 6), which really means that he was an *expert instructor* in the Scriptures. Apart from this, Ezra would never have become the leader that he was. He shows us how God can use a man who studies to a proficient grasp on the written word of God. He shows us what a noble and vital qualification for highest leadership it is to have a full and careful knowledge of the Scriptures. In his personal *character*, also, Ezra is a fine example. See his *godly purpose* (vii. 10) ; his *godly thankfulness* for success (verses 27, 28) ; his prayerful *dependence on God* (viii. 21–3) ; his acute *grief* at the sin of the people (ix. 3, 4) ; his *deep humility* before God (verses 5–15) ; his prompt, brave *action against that which was wrong* (x.). These aspects of Ezra's character richly repay reflection, and may well send us to our knees with the prayer that the same qualities may be reproduced in ourselves, through the sanctifying ministry of the Holy Spirit.

THE BOOK OF EZRA (2)

Lesson Number 43

NOTE.—For this further study read the Book of Ezra through again, at one sitting.

One of the most brilliant French scientists of our time—Dr. Alexis Carrel, of the Rockefeller Institute of New York—has lately . . . affirmed that the negative attitude towards miracles *can no longer be sustained* in the face of the facts observed by Science during the last fifty years. And this authority in medical research goes on to accept miracles of healing through prayer, including even organic diseases, such as cancer. The evidences for unusual happenings in human life have always existed, but they are only now at last being recognised, recorded, and vouched for by Science. Since this is being done, it follows that the well informed and unprejudiced cannot henceforth reject the Bible narrative because it records the occurrence of unusual happenings some thousands of years ago. A section of our clergy who call themselves Modernists might make themselves familiar with this advance in knowledge if they desire to retain their title; otherwise they have clearly become " Ancient Modernists ".

—*Sir Charles Marston.*

THE BOOK OF EZRA (2)

THIS BOOK of Ezra contains remarkable spiritual lessons, some of which we wish to mention; but before we come to these, we ought perhaps to touch on several points in the narrative which may not be quite clear to the minds of some readers. The story of the book becomes all the more interesting when these obscure bits here and there are cleared up, and when certain sidelights are brought to bear upon it.

Explanatory Notes and Sidelights

Duration of the Exile.

The Jewish exile in Babylonia is often spoken of as the *seventy years'* exile, on the basis of Jeremiah xxix. 10 and 2 Chronicles xxxvi. 21. But it will occur to any thoughtful reader that if the Exile lasted seventy years, practically none of those who went into it as adults could have been alive, let alone physically able, to join the returning "Remnant" at the end of it. Yet chapter iii. 12 says: "But many of the priests and Levites and chief of the fathers, who were ancient men, that had seen the first house (Solomon's Temple), when the foundation of this (the new) house was laid before their eyes, wept with a loud voice." Are we then to think that these "many" were all men of ninety and over? No, for the Exile lasted fifty-one years only, not seventy. It began in 587 B.C., and ended with the decree of Cyrus, 536 B.C. In Jeremiah xxix. 10, the words "at Babylon" should be "*for* Babylon" (as in R.V.). God did not say His people would be *at* Babylon seventy years, but that there would be a seventy years' rule *for* Babylon (which came true exactly: see our note re this in the study on Haggai). These older men who came back to Jerusalem with the "Remnant" need not have been more than the three-score-years-and-ten. Even so, they were brave and zealous to caravan those seven hundred miles from Babylon to Jerusalem, a journey which meant five months of daily travel.

Assyria, Babylon, Media-Persia.

That part of Israel's history which is recorded in the latter part of the Kings and the Chronicles, and in Ezra, Nehemiah, and Esther, has for its successive background three world-empires—Assyria, Babylon, and Media-Persia. With the Book of Ezra before us we have reached a point in our Bible study where we ought to have at least a skeleton sketch of this background in our minds. This is the more so because in this little book of Ezra no less than seven different kings are mentioned, representing all three world-empires, and the story means so much more when these references are intelligently distinguished. For instance, we must not think that the emperor Darius here is the king Darius of the book of Daniel; nor must we think that the Artaxerxes of chapter iv. is the Artaxerxes of chapter vii. So, then, a few words about Assyria, Babylon, and Media-Persia will be useful.

First comes the *ASSYRIAN EMPIRE*. The story of the kingdom of Assyria begins a long, long way back, and runs in three periods, the first being from about 1430 to 1000 B.C., and the second from about 880 to 745 B.C., in both of which there was a period of rise to power followed by long decline. It is the *third* period which has so much to do with *Israel*, in which Assyria became world-mistress. This period began in 745 B.C., with the able and cruel usurper-general, Pul, who took the reigning name of Tiglath-Pileser III, and it continued till Nineveh was finally destroyed, about 612–608 B.C., when Babylon took the lead. Here are the Assyrian emperors and their connections with Scripture history:

Tiglath-Pileser III (745–27). 2 Kings xv. 19, 29; xvi. 7, 10; 2 Chron. v. 26.

Shalmaneser IV (727–22). 2 Kings xvii. 3; xviii. 9.

Sargon (722–05). 2 Kings xviii. 11; Isa. xx; x. 12, 28–34 (R.V.).

Sennacherib (705–681). 2 Kings xviii.–xix.; 2 Chron. xxxii.; Isa. xxxvi.–xxxvii.

Esar-haddon (681–68). 2 Kings xix. 37; 2 Chron. xxxiii. 11; Ezra iv. 2.

Assur-bani-pal (668–26). Ezra iv. 10 ("Asnapper")?

With the death of Assur-bani-pal this greatest period of

Assyria fell into decline. In 625 B.C. Babylon regained independence under Nabopolassar (Nebuchadnezzar's father) who reigned at Babylon till 606 B.C. Also the kingdom of the Medes regained independence. Later the Medes and Babylonians made alliance and overthrew Nineveh about 608 B.C., which ended the Assyrian empire for ever (see further on this in our study of Nahum).

Now comes the *BABYLONIAN EMPIRE*. On the fall of Nineveh, the even more ancient city of Babylon laid her hands once more to the sceptre of the nations. Her new lead began in 606 B.C. with the young and brilliant Nebuchadnezzar; yet it only lasted until 536 B.C., thus exactly fulfilling Jeremiah xxix. 10. During the latter fifty years of this time the Jews were captives in Babylonia. Had the undermentioned kings who followed Nebuchadnezzar been as imposing as their names, perhaps the empire might have had better fortunes!

Nebuchadnezzar (606–562).

Evil-Merodach, or Amil-Marduk (562–559). 2 Kings xxv. 27.

Nergal-sharezer, or Neriglissar (559–55). Jer. xxxix. 3. 13.

Labashi-Marduk, or Laborisoarchod (555, 9 months)

Nabonidus, or Nabunahid (*whose viceroy was the "Belshazzar" of Daniel v.*) (553–36).

And now the *MEDIA-PERSIAN EMPIRE* succeeds Babylon. We have already mentioned how the kingdom of the Medes regained independence and made alliance with Babylon to overthrow Assyria. That alliance ended with the end of Nebuchadnezzar's reign. Two or three years later the Medes and the Persians became one empire, under Cyrus the Persian. The Medes and the Persians were akin to each other, and followed the same customs and religion. An insurrection dethroned the last *Median* king, in 559 B.C., and the taking of the throne thereupon by Cyrus transferred the supremacy to the Persians. Cyrus had a wonderful career of conquest. To quote the words of another—"In but twelve years, with his handful of Persians, he destroyed for ever three great empires—Media, Lydia, and Babylonia, conquered all Asia, and secured to his race for two centuries the dominion of the world." This is the Cyrus with whose edict for the restoration of the Jews to Judæa the Book of Ezra opens.

After conquering Babylon, Cyrus made a certain Gobryas viceroy there. This Gobryas is seemingly the "Darius" of the

Book of Daniel. Also, Cyrus reversed the policy of transportation which the Assyrians and Babylonians had practised since the time of Tiglath-Pileser, and permitted subject peoples to return to their own countries, and to restore their own religions and institutions. His idea was to attach them to his government by gratitude instead of fear. It was in keeping with this that the Jewish state was resuscitated in Judæa, though, of course, it still remained vassal to Persia.

The Persian empire lasted from 536 B.C. (first year of Cyrus) until 330 B.C., when it was overthrown by Alexander the Great, and gave place to the *Greek* empire. Here follow its kings, except for two or three minor usurpers in its later years. The names in brackets are the *personal* names or stigmas of these kings, as apart from their *throne* titles.

Cyrus the Great (536–29). Ezra i., etc.; Isa. xlv.
Cambyses (529–21). Ahasuerus of Ezra iv. 6.
Gaumata (pseudo-Smerdis) (7 mths). Artaxerxes of Ezra iv. 7.
Darius I (Hystaspis) (521–486). Re-allowed Temple: Ezra v., vi.
Xerxes I (485–64). Ahasuerus of Esther.
Artaxerxes I (Longimanus) (465–24). Ezra vii. 1; Neh. ii. 1; v. 14.
Xerxes II (424–24).
Darius II (Nothus) (424–04). Neh. xii. 22?
Artaxerxes II (Mnemon) (404–359).
Artaxerxes III (Ochus) (359–38).
Darius III (Codomanus) (336–30). Neh. xii. 22?

The Decree of Cyrus.

One cannot read such books as Ezra, Nehemiah, Esther, without being struck by the wonderful way in which God over-rules during times of trouble and crisis. Let us not miss the point that in Ezra i. 1 the "proclamation" of Cyrus which occasioned the return of the Remnant is directly attributed to Divine constraint—"The LORD stirred up the spirit of Cyrus, king of Persia, that he made a proclamation. . . ." Men and nations are free agents, and God permits them, within wide limits, to work out their own history, yet never so as to elude His own super-control. There are Divine intervenings, sometimes visible but more often invisible, which, without violating the free-will of man, ensure the fulfilment of the ultimate Divine purposes. In these later days of this present age it is well to keep this truth firmly in mind, that human freedom does not rule out Divine control. It has a steadying effect when evil and exciting developments seem to run on unchecked. High above God's *permissive* will is His *directive* will which can never know defeat.

The *wording* of Cyrus's proclamation is certainly remarkable: "Jehovah, the God of heaven, hath given me all the kingdoms of the earth; and He hath charged me to build Him an house at Jerusalem which is in Judah." How came this Persian emperor to have such knowledge of, and reverence for, and guidance from the God of Israel? Note particularly his later words in the proclamation: "Jehovah, God of Israel, He is *the* God." Modernist critics have felt that their only escape from the problem of the surprising wording here is to depreciate it as "a Judaizing paraphrase of the original." Once again they would insinuate that the Bible writers resort to distortions and misrepresentations. But the problem of these critics then becomes: If this edict of Cyrus was *not* as it is worded in the Scripture transcription of it, then *why* did Cyrus issue this proclamation of his favour to the Jews at all? There certainly was no *political* reason for it, for the Jews, unlike the Babylonians and certain other peoples conquered by Cyrus, were quite powerless either to help or to harm the new dominion.

The fact is that in some way or other *Cyrus had come under the influence of Jewish religious teaching*. The Jewish historian, Josephus, tells us how. He tells us that after Cyrus's conquest of Babylon, the new emperor was shown the remarkable prophecy of Isaiah xliv. 24—xlv. 6, written two hundred years earlier, in which Cyrus is actually named in advance as the destined restorer of the Jews and rebuilder of the temple. Josephus tells us that Cyrus, having seen the Isaiah prediction, was at once seized with "an earnest desire and ambition to fulfil what was so written." And there is much more which Josephus tells us about Cyrus and his edict, not all of which, perhaps, we need accept. But there can be absolutely no doubt about the *fact* of the edict or that the Bible transcription of it is literally *exact*; and this implies, of course, that Cyrus (as Josephus actually states) had come to recognise Jehovah as the supreme God. To say the least, it is understandable that the Isaiah prophecy would stir up a keen appetite in the mind of Cyrus to know more of Israel's inspired Scriptures.

How wonderful then, indeed, is the Divine overruling! Even
that black calamity, the Babylonian exile of the Jews, is overruled to the conversion of Nebuchadnezzar, the Babylonian
emperor, and of Cyrus, the Persian emperor; moreover it cured
the covenant people of their idolatry once for all, and, by spreading
the knowledge of the one true God throughout the nations of the
ancient world, prepared for the coming of the Gospel of our Lord
and Saviour, Jesus Christ.

What about those "ten tribes"?

If we read this Book of Ezra carefully we find ourselves again
running counter to that fanciful theory according to which the
so-called "lost ten tribes" are Britain and America. This is not
a place where we can discuss the British Israel case separately;
but there are certain features in the Book of Ezra which directly
bear upon it, and which ought to be noted. The British Israel
position is that the Jews are one tribe only (Judah), and that the
other tribes are the British and American peoples. It is claimed
that only the tribe of Judah returned to Palestine under the
decree of Cyrus, and that the other tribes (ten apart from the
Levite tribe) became "lost." The whole theory bristles with
difficulties, but just to take one aspect alone, let us see what the
Book of Ezra says about the composition of the Remnant.

First, in chapter i. 3, the edict of Cyrus is to *all* Israel. Let
it be remembered that Assyria (which took the ten-tribe kingdom
into captivity) had later become absorbed in the Babylonian
empire, which in turn had now become part of Cyrus's dominion:
so *all* the tribes were now in his domain. Understandably, the
chiefs of Judah and Benjamin responded, seeing that it was to
Jerusalem and Judah that the Remnant was to return; but
with these were "*all* whose spirit God had stirred" (verse 5, R.V.).

Now see chapter ii. 2. In this verse we are given the leaders of
the Remnant. Compare it with Nehemiah vii. 7. There were
twelve leaders. Is anything more reasonable than to understand that
these twelve were heads of the twelve tribes? If not, why twelve?

Next go to chapter ii. 70. Not only was Jerusalem reoccupied,
but so were the other Judæan cities (see ii. 1); and so we now read
that "*all* Israel" dwelt "in their cities." Can this mean less than
that the return was participated in by all the tribes?

Pass on to chapter vi. 17. Is it without significance that at the dedication of the new temple the number of the he-goats offered for a sin-offering was twelve, and was for "all Israel"? And is it without significance that again in viii. 35 there are twelve bullocks and twelve he-goats offered for "all Israel"?

And in chapter viii. 29, what can be meant by "the princes of the fathers' houses of Israel" if the whole of the tribes were not represented? Nothing can be clearer than that the Return was participated in by all the tribes, even though, understandably, Judah and Benjamin took the lead. It was not, as the British Israel advocates say, simply a return of Judah-ites.

Moreover, these indications that the Remnant was composed from all the twelve tribes are strengthened by two important facts outside the Book of Ezra. The first of these is that before ever the ten tribes were carried away there had been large infiltrations from them into Judah (2 Chron. xi. 13–17; xv. 9; xxxiv. 6–9). The second is the fact that the names "Jew" and "Israelite" became synonymous during the Exile. Who can doubt this when the Book of Esther speaks of the "Jews" as scattered right through the one hundred and twenty-seven Persian provinces from India to Ethiopia (Esther i. 1; iii. 8, 12, 14)? The Book of Esther makes no distinguishment between Jew and Israelite; nor does our Lord Jesus, nor do the writers of the New Testament. Remember, it was only a small part, even in the case of the Judah tribe, who returned to Judæa. We have practically as much reason, therefore, to speak of the major part of Judah as "lost" as we have of the other tribes. When the apostle James, five and a half centuries later, writes to "the twelve tribes which are scattered abroad" (Jas. i. 1), he writes to a scattered people who were *all* known as "Jews"; and, similarly, those people who are known to us *today* as the Jews are the posterity of *all* the Israel tribes, not just of Judah.

Chapter iv. 4–24.

This passage presents a problem which it is well just to note. Through artful misrepresentation, adversaries cause a suspension in the rebuilding of the Temple. Verse 5 says they "hired counsellors" against the Jews, "to frustrate their purpose all the days of Cyrus, *even unto the reign of Darius*." This Darius came next-but-two after Cyrus. Glance back at our list of Persian kings. The frustration lasted from the second year of Cyrus (iii. 8) to the second year of Darius (iv. 24), about fourteen years.

The problem begins at verse 6: "And in the reign of *Ahasuerus*, in the beginning of his reign, wrote they unto him an accusation against the inhabitants of Judah and Jerusalem." Then verse 7 says: "And in the days of *Artaxerxes* wrote Bishlam," etc. It is these two names, Ahasuerus and Artaxerxes which make the problem. See our list of Persian kings again. The two thus named did not reign until *after* Darius in whose second year the rebuilding suspension was ended; and, therefore, if these are the two who are really meant in Ezra iv. 6, 7, then verses 6 to 23 are a long *parenthesis* telling of what happened thirty years later, and then again what happened another twenty years or more after that.

Not a few have adopted this parenthesis idea; but in our own view it is wrong and needless. It has really nothing in its favour but the sequence of the royal names, which in this case is of very doubtful weight, for Persian kings often had more than one name. Moreover, such a parenthesis here seems a quite foreign and pointless interruption. But what is clearly fatal to the idea is the nexus of verses 23 and 24. That last verse of the chapter says: "*Then* ceased the work of the house of God which is at Jerusalem. So it ceased unto the second year of the reign of Darius king of Persia." That "*then*" surely connects with what immediately precedes. We need have no headache, therefore, about the poser of those two royal names in verses 6 and 7. They are the Cambyses and Gautama who reigned between Cyrus and Darius, or else *both* names refer to Cambyses alone.

Who were the "Nethinims"?

Seventeen times in Ezra and Nehemiah we read of the *Nethinims*. They are mentioned only once elsewhere (1 Chron. ix. 2, which also refers to the post-Exile resettlement). Strictly, the "s" is not needed at the end of the word, for the ending "im" is itself the Hebrew plural. Who, then, were these Nethinim? The Hebrew word means "the given ones." Ezra viii. 20 calls them "the Nethinim whom David appointed for the service of the Levites." That seems a sufficient clue. In both Ezra and Nehemiah they are closely connected with another order—"the servants of Solomon," who seem to have been descendants of the Canaanites Solomon used in building his Temple (2 Chron. ii. 17), and whose duties were possibly even humbler than those of the Nethinim. Maybe the Nethinim were originally captive foreigners who had been given from time to time by the kings for the more menial work of the temple. Certainly, the personal names of some of them seem to indicate a non-Israelite diversity of origin. Only about the time of the Return does the name "Nethinim" seem to have definitely crystallised upon this class of helpers—presumably because their services then became so much the more needed. Nehemiah xi. 21 points to their having been organised into a sort of guild under their own leader. They are not mentioned in Scripture again. Probably, with other groups, they became gradually incorporated into the general body of Levites.

ADDENDA

THE "GREAT SYNAGOGUE"

According to Rabbinic tradition, a great council was convened some time after the return of the Jewish Remnant from Babylon, to reorganise the religious life of the people. Smith's smaller *Bible Dictionary* gives the following summary. "It consisted of 120 members, and these were known as the men of the Great Synagogue, the successors of the prophets, themselves, in their turn, succeeded by scribes prominent, individually, as teachers. Ezra was recognised as president. Their aim was to restore again the *crown*, or *glory* of Israel. To this end they collected all the sacred writings of former ages and their own, and so completed the canon of the O.T. They instituted the feast of Purim. They organised the ritual of the synagogue, and gave their sanction to the *Shemôneh Esrêh*, the eighteen solemn benedictions in it. Much of this is evidently uncertain. The absence of any historical mention of such a body, not only in the O.T. and the Apocrypha, but in Josephus, Philo, and the *Seder Olam*, so that the earliest record of it is found in the *Pirke Aboth*, circ. the second century after Christ, has led some critics to reject the whole statement as a Rabbinic invention."

It is true that many recent scholars have rejected this tradition; yet, as the late Dr. James Orr says, "It is difficult to believe that declarations so circumstantial and definite have no foundation at all in actual history." The excessive scepticism of certain modern schools in such matters is an intellectual *fashion*, rather than a product of scholarly cautiousness.

JEWISH MONTHS IN EZRA, NEHEMIAH AND ESTHER

In Ezra, Nehemiah, Esther, Jewish "months" are referred to thirty-five times. We ought to familiarise ourselves with the Jewish calendar. There were really *two* Jewish "years"—sacred and civil. Originally the new year began in the autumn (Exod. xxiii. 16), but from the Exodus the seventh month (Nisan) was made the first month (Exod. xii. 2). Josephus says: "Moses appointed that Nisan should be the first month of their festivals because he brought them out of Egypt in that month; so that this month began the year as to all solemnities they observed to the honour of God; although he preserved the original order of the months as to selling and buying and other ordinary affairs." Mostly in Scripture the months are those of the sacred year. The pre-exilic names of most of them have not come down to us; but they seem to have been based on the seasons, *Abib* meaning grain in the ear, and *Ziv* the beauty of spring flowers. The twelve months were lunar; and therefore every three years or so a thirteenth, inter-calary month was added to readjust the year with the sun.

Month	Sacred	Civil	English
Abib or Nisan	1st.	7th.	Mar.–Apr.
Ziv or Ivar	2nd.	8th.	Apr.–May
Sivan	3rd.	9th.	May–June
Tammuz	4th.	10th.	June–July
Ab	5th.	11th.	July–Aug.
Elul	6th.	12th.	Aug.–Sept.
Ethanim or Tisri	7th.	1st.	Sept.–Oct.
Bul or Marchesvan	8th.	2nd.	Oct.–Nov.
Chisleu	9th.	3rd.	Nov.–Dec.
Tebeth	10th.	4th.	Dec.–Jan.
Shebat	11th.	5th.	Jan.–Feb.
Adar	12th.	6th.	Feb.–Mar.

THE BOOK OF EZRA (3)
Lesson Number 44

NOTE.—For this study read the book again, noting the course things took in chapters ii.–vi.

When people say that the doctrine of plenary or full inspiration of the Bible fails to do justice to the individuality of the Biblical writers. they simply show that they do not know what they are talking about, Yes, what a wonderful variety there is in the Bible. There is the rough simplicity of Mark, the unconscious yet splendid eloquence of Paul, the conscious literary art of the author of the Epistle to the Hebrews, the matchless beauty of the Old Testament narratives, the high poetry of the Prophets and the Psalms. How much we should lose, to be sure, if the Bible were written all in one style! We believers in the full inspiration of the Bible do not merely admit that. We *insist* upon it. The doctrine of plenary inspiration does not hold that all parts of the Bible are alike; it does not hold that they are all equally beautiful or even equally valuable; but it only holds that all parts of the Bible are equally true, and that each part has its place.

—*J. Gresham Machen.*

THE BOOK OF EZRA (3)

WE DID not intend our Ezra studies to run into a third instalment. It is an important tract of Scripture, however, marking a major turning-point, and well merits this further consideration. In this final study we review it exclusively from a spiritual point of view. It is replete with spiritual lessons of ever-fresh relevance; but we here limit ourselves to that *main* spiritual lesson which develops as the story of the book itself develops.

MAIN SPIRITUAL APPLICATIONS

The subject of the book, as we have seen, is the repatriation of the Jews, under the edict of Cyrus. It is the book of the *Restoration*. What we ought not to miss is that this historical restoration of the Jews strikingly exemplifies the laws and factors which operate in all true *spiritual* restoration.

First of all, the very *fact* of the Jewish restoration is spiritually eloquent. It speaks deep comfort concerning the restoration of Christian believers who become "bewitched" by this "present evil world," or ensnared by Satan's "devices," and fall into "backsliding." God had permitted great grief to engulf the covenant people, even to the extreme expedient of disintegrating the twelve tribes in the lands of heathen captors. Their being the covenant people did not immunise them from the penalty of sinning. Nay, their privilege increased their responsibility. Their apostasy and presumption were answered by unsparing chastisement. Yet even under the lash they were still Jehovah's people. The covenant still stood, and God did not go back on it. He had cast them out, but He did not cast them off; and He now made a way of return and restoration for all who would avail themselves of it.

And as this was true of Israel nationally, so it is true of God's people in Christ individually. We may wander from the place of blessing. We may lose our first love and grow spiritually cold. We may backslide into worldliness and become lured away by its deceptive glamour. God may allow heavy chastisement to reduce us to sore straits. He may allow evil powers to lead us captive in some degree. The grieved Spirit of God may withdraw all consciousness of His presence from us. Yet if we are truly the Lord's by a genuine conversion, if we are truly born of the Spirit and sprinkled with the covenant blood of Calvary, then God will never utterly cast us off or allow us finally to "fall from grace." However sadly we may have backslidden there is a way of return and restoration. God has made that truth plain in His Word; and the restoration of the Jews illustrates it. Indeed, in the case of the Jews, God not only opened up the way of return, but it was He who also "stirred" the hearts of those among His people who responded (i. 5). And even so does the Holy Spirit still minister in the hearts and consciences of backslidden believers. The very desire to return is His work within us, and an evidence of our election. Oh, the patience and tender grace of God toward us for Christ's sake! May we never ungratefully presume on it!

But to proceed; in the first half of this Book of Ezra (i.–vi.) there are *six steps* particularised in connection with the restoration of the Jews, and these six steps or stages correspond with the main factors in *spiritual* restoration.

1. *Back to the Land.*

The first step in Israel's restoration was *the return to the land* (i. 3). To the nation Israel, Canaan was in a special sense the place of blessing. It was their covenant inheritance, and their full enjoyment of the blessings of the Abrahamic covenant were associated with their occupation of it. Jehovah might preserve them distinct even amid dispersion, but there could be no fulfilment of the covenant promises and purposes while they were outside the land. So the first step in restoration was a return to the *place* of blessing.

And it is the same in the restoration of the *soul*. Is there, perchance, some reader of these lines who has lost the first joy, the early vision, the once-bright flame, through backsliding into the world? And is there a longing for restoration? Then let this be clearly grasped: the way of restoration is open, and the Lord waits to be gracious, but we must first get back to the

place where He can bless us. That is, we must turn our backs
on the Babylon of this world which has held us captive, we must
forsake that which has occasioned our declension, and get back
to the old ground of acceptance and blessing, namely, *God's
promise in the Gospel.* What Canaan was, with all its material
provisions, to the Israelite, the Gospel is, with all its spiritual
provisions, to the Christian. The first thing for any distressed
backslider is to get back to the clear word of God in the Gospel,
and to stand *there.* That is the ground on which alone God deals
with us in restoring grace. We must get back there, and take
up the old position of repentance toward God, and faith toward
our Lord Jesus, and obedience toward the written Word. We
must get back there on the old basis, that salvation is by grace
alone on God's part, and faith alone on our own part. Then,
when we are *there,* we may possess the promise, and begin to
rejoice in restoration.

But *which* promise? Well, take that very well-known promise
in 1 John i. 9. We cannot here start expounding it; but a few
minutes' reflection on it will show to any sorrowing backslider
what a wonderful provision it is. Often have we seen restored
backsliders weeping tears of joyous relief when once they have
had faith to count on it. Until we get our mind fixed on some
such word of God there is no relief; but when we firmly focus
our mind on some precious promise of the Word, the Holy Spirit
gets His opportunity to witness within us, on that basis, to the
reality of our restoration.

2. *The Altar Rebuilt.*

The second thing with the Jewish Remnant was *the rebuilding
of the altar* (iii. 1–6). It was built just where the former one had
been. Doubtless, the altar here, as in many other places, typically
anticipates the great altar of Calvary, as we ourselves, with our
fuller light, can now see. But what did it mean to those returned
Jews? Symbolically, that altar, with its various offerings, and
especially with its freewill offerings, spoke of *consecration to God;*
for the offerer symbolically offered up *himself* with his offering.

And that is precisely what we ourselves must do, if we would
be restored from our backslidings. We must rebuild in our hearts
the altar of dedication to Christ. There must be a complete

yielding of our lives to Him. You will notice that with the re-erection of the altar in Jerusalem, the old-time worship was re-established, that is, the old *fellowship* was restored. So is it with ourselves when the altar is re-erected and we are yielded again to our true Lord.

3. *The new Temple commenced.*

Those returned Jews were under a commission, not only from Cyrus, but from God himself, to build up, on the old site, a new temple to Him (i. 2, 3). After the altar had been rebuilt and the true worship restored, work on the new Temple was commenced. This speaks of *service* and *witness*. It was indeed their special purpose and service to raise up this new house of witness to Jehovah among the surrounding nations—"an house of prayer for all people" (Isa. lvi. 7).

Even so are *we* to erect a *spiritual* house of praise and witness to the Lord, in our own lives, in each local Christian church, in each community, and throughout all nations. Yes, there must be a restored service and witness to Christ in our lives; and in truth there *will* be, if we are back on the ground of Gospel promise, with the altar of consecration rebuilt, and the old fellowship restored.

4. *"Adversaries" encountered.*

Sometimes those of the Lord's people who have been restored from backsliding are so overjoyed at their sense of renewed acceptance and communion with God, that they tend to imagine, as many new converts do, that they have now reached a place where their difficulties are all at an end. But they soon find otherwise—as did the Jewish Remnant long ago when they started the rebuilding of the Temple. In all human history there has never been a true work for God without there being opposition from the devil. The opposition usually begins in a subtle way; then, if subtlety fails, it develops into open hindrance, and employs all sorts of crooked counter-measures.

That is just what happened in long-ago Palestine. There were "adversaries" (iv. 1), and they sought to hinder the rebuilding of the temple in three ways: (1) by trying to deceive the Jews into an unreal union—"Let us build with you"; (2) by open hindrance—"they weakened the hands of the people of Judah"; (3) by misrepresentation—"they hired counsellors against them." The first of these was the most dangerous; but it did not succeed. Yet here is one of those seeming enigmas which occur in work for God, namely, that although the Remnant stood firm, the "adversaries" were allowed to gain a victory for some time. They got the work suspended, and then the Remnant grew disheartened. We must be prepared for "adversaries," for strange and disappointing setbacks, even when we are faithfully working for God. Our motto throughout must be, "No compromise"; and we must also forearm our minds against disappointments, for somehow, under the present system of things on earth, testings are a necessary element in spiritual progress.

5. *Prophets raised up.*

New voices are now heard among the Remnant, exhorting and encouraging them with a special word from God. The prophets Haggai and Zechariah appear. Their words are like a strong breath from the hills. Zerubbabel and his helpers feel that God is among them again of a truth, and they resume the building with renewed resolution.

This carries a step still further the remarkable parallel between the story of the Remnant and the spiritual experience of Christian believers today. Let it be keenly realised that the Hebrew prophets were men under the constraint of a most definite supernatural inspiration (see our opening study on the prophets). They were the living voice of God to the covenant people, and it is noticeable how God raised up such men in times of accentuated need. The Old Testament prophets, like the New Testament apostles, are now passed from us, not only as individuals but as an *order* which we no longer need. We now have the completed canon of the Divinely inspired Scriptures by which we are "throughly furnished" for all exigencies of Christian life and service. These Scriptures are the living and vitalising word of God to us, and they have a prophetic ministry to our hearts akin to that of Haggai and Zechariah in those bygone days. In all our work for God, and especially in time of opposition, discouragement, or

apparent failure, we need to live close to the written Word.
That is one of the vital secrets of perseverance and final achievement. God help us to learn it!

6. *The work completed.*

If a work is truly of God it cannot know final defeat. This is
one of the inspirations of Christian service, and it finds illustration in the completed work of the long-ago temple rebuilders.
On the third day of the month Adar, in the sixth year of Darius,
"*this house was finished*" (verse 15). The dedication was an event
of great joy (verses 16, 22). Thereupon the Feast of the Passover
and of Unleavened Bread was held, which, as we saw in our
Leviticus studies, speaks typically of salvation and fellowship.
So then, despite opposition, in the end there is completion,
victory, joy, fellowship. Faith and work triumph in the name
of the Lord.

Yes, this is the sure outcome of work that is truly of God and
done for Him in the obedience of faith. We need have no doubt.
This sixth point in the parallel between those old-time temple
rebuilders and the experience of the Lord's people today is true
to fact. And thus we see in this six-fold development in the first
half of the Book of Ezra a striking historical object-lesson depict-
ing the laws and factors which operate, as we have said, in all
true spiritual restoration and Christian service. Note the points
of parallel once again—

1. Return to the land (i. and ii.)—back to right basis.
2. Altar re-erected (iii. 1–6)—dedication renewed.
3. New Temple begun (iii. 8–13)—service and witness.
4. "Adversaries" obstruct (iv.)—faith under testing.
5. Prophets exhort (v. 1–vi. 14)—need of God's word.
6. Temple finished (vi. 15–22)—faith wins through.

PART 2; EZRA (VII–X)

We have already spoken about the character of Ezra, and need
not cover the second half of the book again which tells of him
and his expedition. But here too we find rich spiritual values
which we ought just to jot down in skeleton form even though

we cannot give space to a fuller study of them. The four chapters
which tell of Ezra and his mission mark a fourfold progress. In
these chapters Ezra is a model of service and leadership.

1. EZRA'S PREPARATION FOR THE TASK (vii.).

True preparation: "Ezra had prepared his heart" (1) to
"seek"; (2) to "do"; (3) to "teach."

2. EZRA'S PROSECUTION OF THE TASK (viii.).

True dependence on God. See verses 21–3. "To seek a
right way." Also note Ezra's care of detail.

3. EZRA'S CONSTERNATION AT COMPROMISE (ix.).

See verses 2, 4, etc. "The holy seed have mingled." True
resort: "I spread out my hands to the Lord."

4. EZRA'S RESTORATION OF SEPARATION (x.).

The true course of action—put the wrong right. See
verses 6, 7, 10, "Make confession," "Separate."

THE GODWARD ASPECT

Up to this point we have been occupied with the *manward*
aspect of the spiritual teachings in this Book of Ezra ; but now let
us gather up into a few paragraphs its main *Godward* significance.
This is profound, yet full of rich comfort.

We go back to the first verse of the book—"Now in the first
year of Cyrus, king of Persia, *that the word of Jehovah by the mouth
of Jeremiah might be fulfilled . . .*" So the restoration of the
Jews was in fulfilment of prophecy made seventy years earlier.
This connects back to Jeremiah xxv. and xxix., from which take
the following excerpts:

*"And this whole land shall be a desolation and an astonishment;
and these nations shall serve the king of Babylon seventy years.
And it shall come to pass, when seventy years are accomplished,
that I will punish the king of Babylon and that nation, saith
Jehovah, for their iniquity, and the land of the Chaldeans, and
will make it perpetual desolations"* (xxv. 11–12).

"After seventy years be accomplished for Babylon, I will visit you and perform my good word toward you in causing you to return to this place. For I know the thoughts that I think toward you, saith Jehovah, thoughts of peace, and not of evil, to give you hope . . . and I will bring you again unto the place whence I caused you to be carried away captive" (xxix. 10–14, R.V.).

These prophecies were uttered before Jerusalem fell, and Jeremiah had a bad time of it for saying that the king of Babylon would be successful. But just as the restoration of the Jews by Cyrus must be read in the light of these prophecies, these prophecies themselves must be read in the light of another great pronouncement, in Jeremiah xviii. 1–6, concerning the *sovereignty* of Jehovah.

"The word which came to Jeremiah from the Lord, saying: Arise and go down to the potter's house, and there I will cause thee to hear My words. Then I went down to the potter's house, and behold, he wrought a work on the wheels. And the vessel that he made of clay was marred in the hand of the potter: so he made it again another vessel, as seemed good to the potter to make it. Then the word of Jehovah came to me, saying: O house of Israel, cannot I do with you as this potter? Behold, as the clay is in the potter's hand, so are ye in Mine hand, O house of Israel."

Get the tremendous facts here. God is the potter. Israel is the clay. History is the wheel. "The vessel was marred"—that is the Israel story right from the Exodus to the Exile. "He made it again another vessel"—that is the story in Ezra and Nehemiah. The time had come when God was shaping a new vessel, though out of the same clay.

"*He made it again*"—oh, lay hold of that! It is wonderful —wonderful because it tells us that which is the ultimate thing in the Divine sovereignty. The final fact is not that the vessel was "marred," but that it was "made again." *That* is the ultimate word in the Divine sovereignty. How it contrasts with the *human* idea and practice of sovereignty! Man's idea and exercise of sovereignty is that if you have had your chance, and have failed, sovereignty treads you down and rejects you. The last word in *God's* sovereignty is "He made it again."

What comfort there is in this—"He made it again"! Reflect, it is true about us as *individuals*. I am that marred vessel. I have failed to reach even my own ideal, let alone God's ideal for me. I have allowed this life of mine, which might have been a vessel of beauty, to become distorted, ugly, full of failure, "marred." The word of the Divine sovereignty is, "I will begin again." Does someone say, "Oh, it's too late now: I'm sixty. I cannot live my life again"? Well, if we were simply made for three score years and ten, that might be so; but "the grave is not our goal." There is a destiny of ages before us. The vital thing is to be willingly in God's hand. The dishonoured clay may be cleansed in the fountain of Calvary. The obstinate hardness may become pliableness through the renewing influence of the Pentecostal Spirit. If we are unreservedly in the master Potter's hand, he can make each of us a "vessel unto honour."

"He made it again"; this is also the final thing about *Israel*. Beginning with Abraham, God made a new vessel of the chosen *family*; but that vessel had to be broken in Egypt. Beginning again at Sinai, God made of the same clay another new vessel, the chosen *nation*; but that vessel had to be broken in the Assyrian and Babylonian exile. Beginning again at the Restoration under Zerubbabel and Ezra, God made of the same clay yet another new vessel, the returned *Remnant*; but that vessel had to be destroyed by the dispersal under the Romans in A.D. 70. The vessel is still broken: but the ultimate fact is that God will yet "make it again," and will fashion it into such a vessel of beauty and perfection as will occasion astonishment to men and glory to God. The Jew, who today is a vexation to all peoples, is to become the loveliest character on earth. The nation which today is crushed and broken beyond all others shall display the Divine ideal of nationhood in unsullied moral integrity and material prosperity.

THE BOOK OF NEHEMIAH (1)

Lesson Number 45

NOTE.—For this study read through the Book of Nehemiah twice.

The Babylonian Exile sounded the death-knell of the Hebrew language. The educated classes were deported to Babylon or fled to Egypt, and those who remained were not slow to adopt the language used by their conquerors. The old Hebrew became a literary and sacred tongue, the language of everyday life being probably Aramaic. Whatever may be the exact meaning of Nehemiah viii. 8, it proves that the people of that time had extreme difficulty in understanding classical Hebrew when it was read to them. Yet for the purpose of religion, the old language continued to be employed for several centuries.

—*T. H. Weir, in "International Standard Bible Encyclopaedia."*

THE BOOK OF NEHEMIAH (1)

NEHEMIAH is a gem of a book in the spiritual lessons which it teaches us. It tells how, under the new leadership of Nehemiah, the walls of Jerusalem were rebuilt by the returned Remnant, and how the people themselves were reinstructed in the Law which God had given to their nation, long before, through Moses. This rebuilding of the city wall is like a graphic object-lesson illustrating those truths which lie at the heart of all true service for God; and he who will give heed to the lessons here vividly pictured will be a wise and successful builder in spiritual things.

Although in this course of study we are more or less self-restricted to the leading ideas and significances of each book of Scripture, and do not wish to cumber ourselves with technical or scholastic questions, we are almost bound to take certain of these into consideration here and there. We shall find this more so when we come to books like Job, Isaiah, Daniel, and Jonah. Meanwhile, with each book we ought to know something, at least, about authorship, date, and background.

Who Wrote It?

As for this Book of Nehemiah, our remarks concerning authorship and date need only be few, for certain facts are patent even at a first reading. First, there can be no doubt that Nehemiah himself is the writer of the parts which are in the first person. These are chapters i. to vii., and xii. 27 to xiii. 31 where the book ends. Second, the intervening stretch (viii. 1–xii. 26) was probably incorporated by Nehemiah himself with his own record, even if, as scholars seem agreed, its style suggests a different author. Some suggest Ezra for this part. Third the genealogical list of the returned Remnant, which closes chapter vii., is evidently derived from an official list drawn up earlier; while the list in chapter xii. was probably commenced by Nehemiah himself, and added to at a later date (for the name, Jadua, in verses 11 and 22 takes us down to the time of Alexander the Great). We may say, then, that Nehemiah is *certainly* the actual *composer* of much of the book, and probably the *compiler* of the whole (allowing for supplementary touches as in xii. 11, 12, 23).

When was it Written?

The *date* at which Nehemiah completed the work would be about 430 B.C., that is, following upon his return to Jerusalem after his temporary recall to Babylon (xiii. 6, 7). The royal edict authorising Nehemiah's *first* coming to Jerusalem was "in the month Nisan, in the twentieth year of Artaxerxes" (ii. 1). The late Sir Robert Anderson, in his book, *The Coming Prince*, has shown, with the corroboration of the British Astronomer Royal, that this date was the 14th March, 445 B.C. Nehemiah's *second* coming to Jerusalem after his brief visit to Babylon was "in the two and thirtieth year of Artaxerxes" (xiii. 6), and was therefore twelve or thirteen years later, which brings us to 432 B.C. Then, allowing for the activities recorded in the closing paragraphs of the book, we find ourselves definitely at the conclusion that the book could not have been completed *before* 432 B.C., and was probably written *soon after* that date, for the events are still poignantly fresh in the writer's mind (xiii. 22, 29).

What is the Background?

As we have seen, Nehemiah came to Jerusalem in 445 B.C. The restored Jewish "Remnant" had then been back in Judæa over ninety years. Zerubbabel and his contemporaries were now passed away, and another generation filled their place. What had happened during those ninety years? The new temple had been built, much inferior to the original, of course; but although the actual building had taken only four years five months and ten days (Hag. i. 15 with Ezra vi. 15), the Remnant had been back twenty-one years when it was completed! Some sixty years after this, Ezra had come from Babylon to Jerusalem with his company of between two and three thousand (Ezra vii. gives 2,000, but this is males only). Moral and spiritual conditions in Judæa then were far from satisfactory. Princes, rulers, priests, Levites and people alike had largely intermarried with the surrounding idolatrous peoples, and although not themselves worshipping idols were thus conniving at idolatry and allowing its infiltration, to the jeopardising of the rising generation. Unchecked, such a fusion of the Remnant with the outnumbering Gentiles then in Palestine would have meant complete absorption and obliteration of them as a distinct people, and we can well understand Ezra's consternation at discovering it (Ezra ix. 3–15). Maybe the laxity came about during the interval of governmental debility between the death of Zerubbabel and the advent of Ezra. The default, however, had been drastically corrected by Ezra, whose timely measure was accompanied by widespread penitence (Ezra x.).

And now, when Nehemiah came to Jerusalem, another twelve years after Ezra, circumstances were far from consoling. The walls and gates of Jerusalem were still in ruins, a discouragement to eye and heart; and the people were in much "reproach" (Neh. i. 3). There was dearth (v. 3). Some of the poorer were mortgaged to their own better-off fellow-Jews (verse 5). There had been laxity about Sabbath observance and other obligations, as the covenant in chapter x. indicates. Such is the background of the book.

Subject and Structure

Nehemiah's special objective was the rebuilding of *the city walls*. We have seen how the Book of *Ezra* is in two main parts. In the first part, under the leadership of Zerubbabel, we are concerned with the rebuilding of the *temple*. In the second part, under the leadership of Ezra, we are concerned with the restoring of the *worship*. Similarly, this Book of Nehemiah, which is a natural sequel to the Book of Ezra, is in two main parts. In the first part we are occupied with the reconstructing of the *walls* (i.–vi.). In the second part we are occupied with the reinstructing of the *people* (vii.–xiii.). Thus, in Ezra and Nehemiah we have the restoring of the temple, the worship, the walls, the people. We have seen that Ezra is distinctively the book of the *restoration*. Nehemiah is distinctively the book of *RECONSTRUCTION*. When we come to the epic of Esther, we shall find that Esther is distinguishingly the book of preservation. Thus in this trio of books at the end of the seventeen historical books of the Old Testament, we have—

EZRA   RESTORATION
NEHEMIAH   RECONSTRUCTION
ESTHER   PRESERVATION

THE BOOK OF NEHEMIAH

THE BOOK OF RECONSTRUCTION

THE RECONSTRUCTING OF THE WALL (i.–vi.)

NEHEMIAH'S INTERCESSION (i. 1–11).
NEHEMIAH'S EXPEDITION (ii. 1–16).
NEHEMIAH'S EXHORTATION (ii. 17–20).
THE REBUILDING ATTEMPTED (iii. 1–32).
THE REBUILDING OBSTRUCTED (iv.–vi. 14).
THE REBUILDING COMPLETED (vi. 15–19).

THE REINSTRUCTING OF THE PEOPLE (vii.–xiii.)

RE-REGISTRATION OF THE REMNANT (vii.).
RE-INCULCATION OF THE LAW (viii.).
RE-CONSECRATION OF THE PEOPLE (ix.–x.).
RE-POPULATION OF THE CITY (xi.).
RE-DEDICATION OF THE WALLS (xii.).
RE-EXTIRPATION OF ABUSES (xiii.).

This undetailed skeleton will amply serve our purpose here. It gives the scope and shape of the contents at a glance. The book, however, lends itself to further analysis, and some of the sub-sections are pointedly instructive when analysed and given a spiritual application, as we shall show.

Spiritual Message

As we watch this strong, earnest, godly hero, Nehemiah, resolutely leading the rebuilding in the first part of the book, then resolutely resisting compromise and laxity and intrigue in the second part of the book, we find the spiritual message of it all coming home to us with great force. Let us heed its voice to us. There is no winning without working and warring. There is no opportunity without opposition. There is no "open door" set before us without there being many "adversaries" to obstruct our entering it (1 Cor. xvi. 9). Whenever the saints say, "Let us arise and build," the enemy says, "Let us arise and oppose."

There is no triumph without trouble. There is no victory without vigilance. There is a cross in the way to every crown that is worth wearing.

Lessons and analogies are everywhere in this book. There are the walls of a city of God to be built in every individual human heart. There are the walls of a city of God to be built among the nations of the earth. Nehemiah exemplifies the vital principles which are involved in all such building, if it is to be successful building in the true sense. And we must add that Nehemiah himself is a really first-rank character-study. He stands out conspicuously as a man of *prayer*, a man of *faith*, a man of *courage*, a man of *action*. Look up the verses and incidents which indicate these qualities. They are an inspiration to read and reflect on. The late Rev. Samuel Chadwick, beloved by all sound Methodists, once used the following words, or words very like them, in a prayer at a service which he was conducting in Manchester: "O Lord, make us intensely spiritual, but keep us perfectly natural and thoroughly practical." As we recall that prayer we cannot but think how Nehemiah illustrates those three expressions— intensely spiritual, perfectly natural, thoroughly practical. Both Nehemiah and Samuel Chadwick eminently fulfilled the terms of that prayer, and both were singularly owned of God as spiritual builders and soldiers. May God raise up a numerous succession to them among the needy churches of our day!

THE MAN AND THE STORY

In this Book of Nehemiah, the man and the story are inseparably wedded to each other. How different a story the rebuilding of Jerusalem might have been if that huge burden and *hazard* had fallen to a man of different calibre from Nehemiah! If ever a crisis-hour was matched by a man, it was so in that city-rebuilding episode.

Yet it is not only the man who makes the story. It is almost equally true that the story makes the man. The perils and problems of the undertaking bring out all that is finest in the man. How often that happens! How much we owe to the difficulties and setbacks, the obstructions and oppositions, which have been permitted to try us! The things which we have thought were breaking us were in reality *making* us—as we now see in retrospect.

So then, let us follow this man from the beginning of his story to the time when the walls of Jerusalem were rebuilt. In the little book which bears his name we see Nehemiah in three capacities—(1) the cupbearer; (2) the wall-builder; (3) the governor.

Nehemiah the Cupbearer (i. 1–ii. 10)

Nehemiah was "the son of Hachaliah" (i. 1), and apparently of the tribe of Judah (ii. 3). Evidently he was reared in exile, and in early manhood became attached to the Persian court, where he rose to the lucrative position of royal cupbearer before Artaxerxes Longimanus and queen Damaspia, in the royal residence at Shushan. "*I was the king's cupbearer,*" he says of himself (i. 11). To us western and modern readers, that may sound a rather unimportant position, not unlike that of a butler among our aristocracy; but we are wrong in so thinking. To quote Dr. Angus, it was "an office which was one of the most honourable and confidential at the court"; and to quote Dr. W. M. Taylor, it was an office "referred to by ancient writers as one of great influence." We know the great influence which Pharaoh's butler had on behalf of Joseph; and we see what high rank the foul-tongued "Rab-shakeh" (or chief cupbearer) had in the empire of Assyria (2 Kings xviii.).

One day, while Nehemiah was in attendance at the royal court, his brother, Hanani, and a group of Jews, brought him such a pitiful report concerning the condition of Jerusalem and the restored Jewish community in Judæa that he was quite overcome with grief. He learned that his countrymen away in the homeland were in dire straits because, among other things, the city walls were still in ruins, and the gates remained just as they had been burned and broken by the Babylonians a hundred and forty years earlier. Walls and gates mean nothing to cities nowadays, but long ago, in the east, they meant almost everything. Those torn-down walls and gates left the inhabitants always open to attack and plunder by vicious neighbours; and it is quite probable that Hanani's report to Nehemiah was made the more poignant by the fact that the citizens of Jerusalem had at that very time been suffering in this way from the deceitful and treacherous peoples who surrounded them.

Nehemiah, stricken with grief, thereupon gave himself to fasting and mourning and prayer (i. 2–11). During this process the conviction ripened in him that he himself should undertake the huge task of the rebuilding; but he was not his own master; and however difficult it might be to get *into* the Persian palace, when one *did* secure a position there it was even more difficult to get *out*. Nehemiah's grief and fasting, however, had so altered his appearance in four months that Artaxerxes asked what was wrong. The emperor's words seem to indicate that he had become really attached to his servant. None the less, as Dr. Kitto remarks, Nehemiah had reason enough to be *"very sore afraid"* (ii. 2), for it was considered a capital offence to appear sad in the royal presence (see also Esther iv. 2). Nehemiah answers with humble courtesy, not daring even now to make any request, but earnestly praying God to overrule; and the upshot is that Nehemiah is most generously commissioned to undertake the project which lies on his heart. Thus closes the first scene—Nehemiah the cup-bearer.

Note: *real godliness is not incompatible with earthly success*. Indeed it often happens that godliness is a first factor in promoting and furthering such success. One gets sick of hearing that to be a real Christian is impossible in the business world of today, and that to apply godly principles in modern commercial transactions is to invite bankruptcy. We could give many examples to the contrary. Certainly there is a price to pay, and there may be losses to incur; but observation convinces us that true Christian character and principle, allied to normal business ability, definitely contribute to success. If Nehemiah could keep his conscience unseared amid the cabals of that Persian court, so may we ourselves blend uprightness with success in modern business. Such present-day Nehemiahs are the salt of the commercial world. Better lose our job than sell our conscience! But in nine cases out of ten, keeping a good conscience will help us toward material as well as spiritual success, and will keep us steady when success actually comes.

THE BOOK OF NEHEMIAH (2)
Lesson Number 46

NOTE.—For this study read through chapters ii. to vi. again, marking those verses which reveal the special virtues or traits of Nehemiah's character.

Further Note.—For the benefit of any reader who may be interested in a fuller exposition and application of the spiritual lessons contained in Nehemiah's rebuilding of Jerusalem, we would add that the contents of the following study will be found, in considerably expanded form, in the last chapter of the author's book, *Mark These Men.*

—*J. S. B.*

It is not the arithmetic of our prayers, how many they are; nor the rhetoric of our prayers, how eloquent they are; nor the geometry of our prayers, how long they be; nor the music of our prayers, how sweet our voice may be; nor the logic of our prayers, how argumentative they may be; nor the method of our prayers, how orderly they may be—which God cares for. Fervency of spirit is that which availeth much.

—*William Law.*

THE BOOK OF NEHEMIAH (2)

THE MAN AND THE STORY—*continued*

Nehemiah the Wall-builder (ii. 11–vi. 19)

ARMED with royal authority, thrilled with a sense of Jehovah's overruling graciousness, and yet solemnised by keen appreciation of the hazards involved in his undertaking, Nehemiah sets off for Jerusalem, accompanied by an escort of Persian soldiers, and completes the journey in about three months. On his way he has to pass through the provinces of certain Persian satraps and governors. To those "beyond the river" (i.e., the Euphrates) he carries letters (ii. 7, 8) which he duly delivers (verse 9). Among such governors was a certain Sanballat, who, according to Josephus, was "satrap of Samaria." Also there was a certain "Tobiah the servant," who was either another petty governor or, more probably, a kind of secretary to Sanballat. These two, we are told, were greatly annoyed "that there was come a man to seek the welfare of the children of Israel" (verse 10). With these two, Nehemiah is now about to have much trouble.

Nehemiah safely reaches Jerusalem, and, after an interval of three days, makes a secret survey of the ruins by night, so as to escape observation by hostile spies from Samaria. Nor does he divulge his mission even to the leaders at Jerusalem until he has made plans to ensure that the whole work shall be started and finished within a few weeks (ii. 12–18).

His plan, so it turns out (for the account clearly implies it), was to *sectionise* the rebuilding among different work-parties, all acting simultaneously, and each responsible for its own section of the wall (iii.). The plan so succeeded that in spite of opposition the wall was completely rebuilt in just over seven weeks (vi. 15), after which solid folding-doors were placed at the gateways (vii. 1), guards were appointed, and regulations imposed concerning the closing of the gates at nightfall and their reopening in the morning (vii. 3). Thus Nehemiah's main objective was achieved —all within six months of his mandate from Artaxerxes!

See here also *the blending of practical organising with intense spiritual-mindedness*. The task is sectionised and systematically prosecuted. Nehemiah set each of the forty-two different work-groups to work on that part of the walls which was nearest to where its members themselves lived (iii. 10, 23, 29, 30). This gave them a special interest in the work. Our first obligation for Christ is always our own neighbourhood.

We find this blending of the practical with the spiritual all the way through the story of Nehemiah. In chapter iv. 9, for instance, we read: "We made our *prayer* unto God, and set a *watch* against them (the adversaries) day and night." Nehemiah never let presumption displace precaution. Organised Christianity is *over*-organised today, and we complicate our own progress by too elaborate machinery. Yet the real trouble is not so much the machinery itself as that the vital driving-force behind it all has largely failed. Organising has crowded out agonising. There is too much working before men and too little waiting before God. There is more and more motion, but less and less unction. It is the Nehemiahs whom God uses—the men and women who *blend* the practical and the spiritual.

Again and again, as we watch Nehemiah, we are reminded of Cromwell's famous words, "Trust in God, and keep your powder dry." Speaking generally of today, there is a brilliant but frustrating over-emphasis on the human, the energetic, in religious service. More than ever before we wrestle with social problems in committees and conferences, but less than ever do we wrestle on our knees against evil spirit-powers which lie behind the social evils of our day. Nearly everybody in committee has a fine programme, but few indeed seem to have a real spiritual burden. The practical has overridden the spiritual; and when that happens, the practical becomes utterly *un*practical.

But perhaps the most telling lessons of all in this story of Nehemiah occur in connection with the *obstructions and setbacks* which Nehemiah had to overcome in those months of rebuilding. There were three forms of opposition from *without*—scorn (iv. 1-6), force (iv. 7-23), craft (vi. 1-19). And there were three forms of hindrance from *within*—debris (iv. 10), fear (iv. 11-14), greed (v. 1-13). Each is a lesson, a study in itself, strikingly corresponding with what we are up against today in a spiritual sense.

OPPOSITION FROM WITHOUT

Scorn (iv. 1–6).

Take the opposition which Nehemiah encountered from outside. First it took the form of *scorn*. See chapter iv. 1–3.

Never was there more derisive sarcasm than in Sanballat's question—"What do these feeble Jews?" And that is exactly the first reaction of the worldly-wise today towards the spiritually-minded minority scattered through the churches. "What do these feeble folk?" they ask contemptuously. What are a few little prayer meetings compared with a European Pact or a revolutionary change-over to a Socialist Government or a United Conference of Nations? What is this paltry idea about converting people one by one compared with scientific, legislative, educational, economic and sociological programmes which can affect millions at a sweep?

Well, how did Nehemiah meet the scorn of Sanballat and Tobiah? Verses 4, 5 and 6 in that same fourth chapter tell us. He just kept on praying and kept on building. "Hear, O our God," he says; "for we are despised." And after his prayer he adds, "So built we the wall . . . for the people had a mind to work." That is the way to meet scorn—not by counter-scorn! The scorn of Sanballat and Tobiah soon began to look stupid as the walls of Jerusalem rose higher and higher. Always our best answer to the world's scorn is to keep on praying to God for Pentecostal blessing, and keep on striving to win souls for Christ. God always honours such earnest prayer and effort. It is always a big victory for the devil if he can laugh us out of some worthy work for Christ, and I fear he manages this far too often. We do well to learn a lesson from Nehemiah!

Force (vi. 7–23).

But look again at this opposition which Nehemiah encountered from outside. When taunts and sneers failed it took a more menacing form. Scorn gave place to *force*. Taunts became threats, and sneers became plots. Such enemies as Sanballat and Tobiah were not the sort to be content with venting their spleen in idle mockery. Their keenest shafts of sarcasm were lost on a devout soul like Nehemiah. So scorn now gives place to force. Read again in that fourth chapter, from verse 7 onwards.

Things certainly looked pretty serious. The opposition had now developed into a formidable alliance—Sanballat, Tobiah, Arabians, Ammonites, Ashdodites! It is remarkable (or is it?) how again and again mutual enemies will become mutual friends to make common cause against the people of God. Pilate and Herod patched up their quarrel and became "friends" in their joint condemnation and abuse of Jesus (Luke xxiii. 12). Romanism and paganism have joined hands before today against the true Protestant faith. Communist Russia and Nazi Germany once shook hands in common purpose against Christianity!

We must not be surprised even today if the Lord's enemies resort to force. And if this happens what are we to do? Well, what did Nehemiah and his company do? They did as before—kept on praying and kept on working; only now they had to join *watching* with praying, and *warring* with working. See verses 9 and 17.

"We made our prayer unto God, and set a watch against them, day and night" (verse 9).
"Every one with one of his hands wrought in the work, and with the other hand held a weapon" (verse 17).

Was not prayer alone enough, then? Why this setting of a watch and this arming with weapons if they trusted the Lord? It was because Nehemiah was not the fanatic to blunder into the delusion that faith is presumption.

Praying, watching, working, warring! How all this speaks to us today! We are not suggesting for a moment that when physical force is used against Christians they should resort to physical weapons, as Nehemiah was obliged to do; but there is a spiritual application. There is a proper place for resisting and attacking and exposing error, deception, falsehood, and sin, on the part of those who oppose the truth as it is in Christ Jesus. Nor must we shrink from such warring, whatever the risk or cost.

Craft (vi. 1-19).

But there was yet another kind of opposition from exterior foes which Nehemiah had to encounter. When scorn and force had failed, Sanballat and Tobiah and their confederates resorted to *craft*. This took four turns. First they tried *pretence* (vi. 1–4). "Come, let us meet together in one of the villages in the plain of Ono." This was an enticement to a pretendedly friendly conference on neutral ground, presumably with the suggestion that an alliance should now be made between Nehemiah and themselves. But Nehemiah saw through their hypocrisy (verse 2), and each time they repeated their request he repeated his reply—"I am doing a great work; I cannot come down" (verse 3). This is ever the one safe answer to such pretence—uncompromising separation.

Next they tried *bluff* (verses 5–9). They said that a charge was being lodged with the emperor against Nehemiah and the Jews, to the effect that they were planning rebellion, and that Nehemiah's only answer to this was to "take counsel with themselves." Nehemiah's reply is frank denial, renewed prayer, and a continued separation.

Next, and worst of all, they managed to intrigue some of Nehemiah's own kinsmen, and thus employed *treachery* against him (verses 10–14). Even some of the prophets were bribed. Nehemiah, however, refused to do the cowardly or shady thing even on the advice of a prophet. The perfidy of these Judases among his own followers was a cutting sorrow to Nehemiah, but he overcame by his courageous honesty and by prayer (verses 11, 14).

It seems an awful thing to say, yet it is true, that there are betrayers like Shemaiah and Noadiah (verses 10–14) in most Christian congregations today—men and women who have professed conversion to Christ, who share in the fellowship and labours of the saints, who nevertheless seem to find a cruel pleasure in the fall of a Christian leader. To his face they are friendly, fussy, saintly, but behind his back they are mischiefmakers. They profess loyalty and concern, yet if he slips or falls they love to gossip it among the brethren or talk it round the town. Oh, what heart-pangs such disloyal brethren give to Christian ministers, pastors, superintendents, and leaders! They are Tobiahs, Quislings, Satan's fifth-columnists. All that the Christian leader can do in his dealings with them is just to keep on building for God through "evil report and good report" (2 Cor. vi. 8), courageously refusing all shady expedients, and continually casting himself on God by prayer.

But Nehemiah's enemies did not cease their crafty activities even when this special bit of treachery had failed. They sought continually to unnerve and discourage Nehemiah through *cliques of compromised brethren* (verses 17–19). The artful Tobiah had become son-in-law to a leader in Israel with a large following. Then his son had taken a Jewish girl to wife; so that Tobiah was now both a son-in-law and an uncle to Israelite people; and there had grown up a clique in Jerusalem who let social and family ties with Tobiah override moral and spiritual duty. Oh, how compromise complicates things!

It must have been a sore problem to Nehemiah, to find that many of the leading men in Judah were hobnobbing by post with Tobiah, and that many, indeed, were "sworn unto him" because both he and his son had married into Israel.

And does not the same sort of thing curse Christian congregations today? How often it ties the hands and paralyses the lips and breaks the hearts of earnest Gospel ministers! Many a man in the ministry gives way, bit by bit, for reasonable comfort's sake; but he ceases to be a real Nehemiah. It is not easy to maintain the Nehemiah position; yet in the end it is the only one which wears the crown of Divine approbation and true success.

HINDRANCES FROM WITHIN

We have seen something of the opposition which came to Nehemiah from outside Jerusalem, but now look at the hindrances which he encountered from the *inside*. They were threefold—debris (iv. 10), fear (iv. 11–14), greed (v. 1–13).

Debris (iv. 10).

First, there was the problem of *debris*. "And Judah said: The strength of the bearers of burdens is decayed, and there is much rubbish, so that we are not able to build the wall." We can easily understand such discouragement. At the very beginning of the rebuilding Sanballat had sarcastically referred to the huge "heaps of the rubbish." It must have seemed a heartbreaking as well as a back-breaking job to get without all this before each part of the wall could be reconstructed; and now there had needed to be a reduction of workmen, owing to the appointing of a guard against attack from outside (verse 9), so that the remaining labourers removing the rubbish seemed near to exhaustion.

This has a pathetic counterpart in much Christian work today. There is many a devout servant of the Lord who cannot get on with the wall God has given him to build, because of the hindrance through "much rubbish." Oh, the "rubbish" in many of our churches today! I recently received a letter from a minister in the south of England asking advice whether to leave or stay on at a certain church. It is impossible, he says, to make any spiritual headway because of "much rubbish." The preceding ministers were Modernists. They have deposited all sorts of doubts and disbeliefs in the people's minds about the Bible, so that now his own references to the Scriptures are largely discredited and his messages thwarted.

But that is not the only sort of "rubbish." In a letter from another minister in England I read: "The people here have no ear for any spiritual challenge. They resent it. For years the place has been run on whist drives, social evenings including dancing, and so on." Yes, there is much rubbish!

Fear (iv. 11–14).

But there was another discouragement from within, namely, *fear*. Jews from outlying districts brought repeated warning that a surprise attack was being planned by Nehemiah's enemies (verses 11, 12). This spread fear among the workers. Nothing is more paralysing than fear; and how it often paralyses evangelical work today! It arises mainly from looking at circumstances and consequences instead of looking to God. Nehemiah's men were scared by the numerical superiority of Sanballat's forces. There is a parallel today. Never did the foes of evangelical Christianity seem bigger and deadlier than now. In Soviet Russia and Hitlerite Germany we have seen the State itself solidly against it—with Siberian exile or Nazi concentration camps as the penalty for faithfulness to Christ. Is it surprising that fear should have blanched many a cheek and stifled many a testimony?

It is instructive to see how Nehemiah turned the tables on this fear which had beset his men. First, they were to *look to*

God instead of at circumstances. "Remember the Lord, great and terrible!" cries Nehemiah (verse 14).

Second, they were to *reflect* on the issues. "Fight for your brethren, your sons and your daughters, your wives and your houses" (verse 14). Everything was at stake! No mercy could be expected from their spiteful foe.

Third, they were to be *armed in readiness* (verses 16–23). Henceforth they were to hold a tool in one hand and a weapon in the other. What wisdom there was in this union of sword and trowel! Even the nuisance diversion of anti-invasion preparation must not stop the building of the wall, for in the long run that rebuilt wall would itself be the supreme defence. Even battling must not exclude building!

How these three things come home to ourselves today! We must "*remember the Lord.*" There is no antidote to fear like a vivid God-consciousness.

Second, we must *keep the issues in mind*. If the distinctive doctrines of the evangelical faith are really true concerning the Bible and the person of Christ and the shed blood of Calvary and the message of the Gospel, then the distinctive doctrines of the Modernists and the Romanists are wrong. And the issues are measurelessly graver than were those in the Nehemiah episode. Souls are at stake! Eternal destinies hang in the balance!

And third, we must not forget our need of being *armed to fight*. Our weapons are: (1) the Bible, which is "the sword of the Spirit"; (2) prayer, which can avail to thwart error just as much as to save souls; (3) the continually-renewed infilling of the Holy Spirit.

Greed (v. 1–13).

Alas, there was a third hindrance from within, a plague of *greed*. This came nearer to wrecking Nehemiah's project than all the stratagems of Sanballat and Tobiah, for it threatened internecine strife among Nehemiah's own men. The circumstances were most disturbing. Many of the people, in order to raise money with which to buy corn (verse 3) or to pay tribute (verse 4), had been obliged to mortgage land holdings, and in some cases even to pledge their sons and daughters; and the richer

Jews, instead of sinking private interests in the critical public need, had selfishly exploited it until a point was reached where there was an outcry.

If Satan cannot ruin a work for Christ today by "much rubbish" or by "fear" of one sort or another, he will try to do so through self-seeking and other wrong motives between Christian and Christian. He will seize on every possible circumstance to provoke this; and his heart-rending success is known in earth and heaven! How disheartened Nehemiah must have been! And how disheartened many a godly minister is today when he finds that even among his keenest and ablest workers there are wrong motives and feelings which thwart blessing and frustrate revival despite all the praying and working.

See now how Nehemiah dealt with this trouble. First, he challenged the offenders by prompt, even drastic action (verse 7). Second, he appealed to them by his own example (verses 8–11). Third, the offending party admitted their blame and made restitution (verses 12, 13). Oh, what a good thing is promptness, frankness, boldness, in such matters! Nehemiah is a robust example to all leaders in Christian work.

The trouble in Nehemiah's day was put right because the offenders, being frankly charged with wrong, admitted their blameworthiness, and repented, and put the wrong right. No wonder that "all the congregation said, Amen, and praised the Lord" (verse 13)! Would that ills and grudges and animosities among Christian groups today might be as fearlessly and faithfully dealt with. It would bring spiritual revival much nearer.

Thus the setback through greed, like the other troubles, was overcome, and the building of the wall went on. Look back, once more, over the difficulties which brave Nehemiah encountered and surmounted—from *without* scorn (iv. 1–6), force (iv. 7–23), craft (vi. 1–19); from *within*, debris (iv. 10), fear (iv. 11–14), greed (v. 1–13). In each case the difficulty becomes more acute and deadly, but in each case the victory becomes more telling, until, stone by stone, and day by day, despite all opposition from without and all hindrance from within, *the wall is completed*!

These, then, are some of the lessons which come home to us from Nehemiah's rebuilding of that city wall. May we read, mark, learn, and act accordingly! The days in which we live have an intensity and complexity such as eclipses that of all former times. The need is vast. The issues are tremendous. The time is short. The wall must be built, even "in troublous times." God help us to keep at it, warring and working, watching and waiting, battling and building! Let us mark this man, Nehemiah, the man who rebuilt Jerusalem, and keep him in mind as we work for God today under difficult conditions. He will be an inspiration to us. God is building with us; and at last we too shall certainly see the walls of God's "New Jerusalem" completely built up on the earth, and "the nations shall walk in the light of it."

> We are builders of a city
>   In the minds and lives of men,
> And we work with love and pity,
>   Using voice and deed and pen;
> It shall certainly be finished,
>   Tho' as yet we know not when,
> This fair city of true worship
>   To the one true God again.
>
> And this city, we must build it
>   In the nation's social life,
> For if but the many willed it,
>   It would end our social strife.
> And this city we are building
>   Must encompass every land,
> Tho' it has no outward gilding,
>   Yet the wise ones understand.
>
> Though Sanballats and Tobiahs
>   In their thousands may oppose,
> God has still His Nehemiahs
>   Who at last repulse all foes;
> Oft resisted, ne'er defeated,
>   With our trowels on we plod,
> Till that city is completed
>   By the reigning Christ of God!

THE BOOK OF NEHEMIAH (3)

Lesson Number 47

NOTE.—For this final study in Nehemiah read chapters vii. to xiii. again, picking out those verses which reveal the special virtues of Nehemiah's character.

The Theory of Evolution has dominated the critical mind in complete disregard of historical facts. Whatever may be said for the evolution of the material universe, there is little that can be said for the evolution of Man, as a dogma. Thus history teaches us that while civilization is progressive it is also retrogressive. When its moral and spiritual factors decline, civilization destroys itself. But the evolution conception, being based upon the idea of steady consistent progress, from barbarism to the present day, underestimated the knowledge and culture of Old Testament times, and postulated something far too primitive. Thus, for example, the Israelites should have been illiterate; but it will now be seen (i.e. in the evidence of recent archaeological findings) that they possessed facilities for literary expression, from the days of Moses onwards, that were actually superior to those of their contemporaries.

Sir Charles Marston.

THE BOOK OF NEHEMIAH (3)

Nehemiah the Governor (vii.—xiii.)

FINALLY, in our rapid review of this man and his story, we see Nehemiah as the *governor*, that is, as governor of the rebuilt Jerusalem and the province of Judæa, under the Persians. We see him in this capacity in the second half of the book, chapters vii. to xiii.

Many a man who is a genius in ruling a crisis is a failure in the follow-up process. Not so Nehemiah, as these chapters show. There is much here to catch the eye and hold the mind, but our comments must be limited simply to pointing out the main lines and lessons.

There is a downrightness and forthrightness about Nehemiah which strikes us throughout the story, and which now comes out most of all in these later chapters telling of his governorship. Whether we approve or not his *method* of handling this or that irregularity, his *motive* is always clear as noon and sound as a bell. There is not a fleck of camouflage anywhere in his character or conduct. Mark his four outstanding qualities here—

1. Clear-seeing.
2. Plain-speaking.
3. Firm-dealing.
4. God-honouring.

And now let us just glance through the chapters.

Security precautions (vii. 1–3).

First, in chapter vii. 1–3, we see Nehemiah making the necessary regulations for the security of what had now become a first-class fortress. His assigning the guarding of the gates to Levites (verse 1) may seem strange, but we need to remember that just then the priests formed nearly half the scanty population (compare xi. with 1 Chron. ix. 10–19). Then he appoints two

municipal officers to have general charge over all such matters
—his own brother, Hanani, and a certain Hananiah who was
already "commandant of the fort" or temple tower (verse 2,
see R.V.).

Population problem (vii. 4–73 with xi.).

Next Nehemiah tackles the problem of the too scant population
(verse 4), and decides on a census as a first step (verse 5). In this
connection he looks up the genealogy of "them which came up
at the first" (i.e. ninety years earlier with Zerubbabel); and the
rest of this seventh chapter reproduces that register (which we
have seen before, in Ezra ii.).

The lack of population is rectified by the casting of lots, to
bring one in every ten from the Judæan population *outside*
Jerusalem to live *inside* the now rebuilt capital (see xi., which
connects back to this seventh chapter).

Note in verse 5, that the keeping of these careful birth-registers
in Israel was *according to the mind of God*. It was important to
determine who were the true seed of Israel, especially so as
Israel looked for the coming of One who should give an imperish-
able glory to her genealogies, even David's greater Son who
should spring from this very line of Zerubbabel and finally "turn
again the captivity" of Judah; the supreme Zerubbabel, who
should consummatingly restore the temple; the supreme Ezra,
who should write the Law in the very hearts of the chosen people;
the supreme Nehemiah, who should build up the walls of Zion
for ever (Isa. liv. 11, 12; Zech. vi. 12, 13; Jer. xxxi. 33; Ps. xlviii.
12, 13; Isa. lx.).

"Back to the Bible" movement (viii.–x.).

Chapter viii. should really begin with the last clause of chapter
vii., thus: "And when the seventh month came (i.e. the specially
sacred month), the children of Israel were in their cities; and all
the people gathered themselves together as one man into the
street that was before the water gate; and they spake unto Ezra
the scribe to bring the book of the law of Moses, which the Lord
had commanded to Israel."

Then follows the remarkable account in chapters viii., ix., and x., of what we should call today a great "back to the Bible" movement. There was held a most remarkable religious convention. The people themselves ask for the Scriptures to be expounded to them (viii. 1). Ezra and his helpers explain afresh the Law. The observance of the Feast of Tabernacles is revived. A great day of humiliation is observed in which the people confess their sad failures and acknowledge the wonderful mercy of their long-suffering God (ix.). Then they enter into a self-imposed covenant, with deep moral purpose to order their ways in future according to the revealed will of God in the Scriptures (x.).

The new census (xi.).

Chapter xi. gives the main results of the new census taken by Nehemiah. Verses 3 to 19 tell us of the dwellers at Jerusalem. Verses 20 to 36 tell us of the "residue" in the other Judæan cities. Note in verse 2 that "the people blessed all the men that willingly offered themselves to dwell at Jerusalem." These were the men, one in every ten, on whom the "lot" fell that they should come and dwell in the capital. The words indicate that they accepted the fall of the "lot" gladly, and patriotically submitted, even though apparently no compensation was made to them. It is not surprising that the people applauded them, for the transfer would mean, in many cases, the quitting of possessions, exchange of riches for poverty, leaving a comfortable house for one half in ruins, giving up the life of a small, landed proprietor for that of an artisan or hired labourer. (We may mention, incidentally, that forced enlargements of capital by transfers of this kind were not uncommon in the ancient world, where the strength of states was considered to depend greatly on the size and predominance of the capital.) The city census in this eleventh chapter is that of the now *augmented* population.

The dedication of the walls (xii. 27–47).

So far the chapters have been quite straightforward reading, and detailed comment has scarcely been needed; but an explanatory word is certainly called for when we come to the passage narrating the dedication of the walls. To the unwary reader it would seem as though this passage (xii. 27–47) follows immediately and without any interruption upon what goes before, whereas the fact is that there is *a break of some twelve years* between the end of chapter xi. and this dedication of the walls.

There are three circumstances which indicate this. (First) if the *dedication* of the walls had taken place immediately after the *rebuilding* it is unlikely that the narrator would have separated the two events by five and a half chapters. (Second,) between the end of chapter xi. and xii. 27 there is inserted (presumably by another hand than Nehemiah's) a descent of the *high priests* right from Jeshua (ninety years *before* Nehemiah) down to Jaddua (about ninety years *after* Nehemiah), so that there is definitely a break here in the narrative.

But (third) Nehemiah himself gives us certain time-marks which conclusively settle it. In chapter xiii. 7 he says that when Eliashib the priest treacherously gave Tobiah an apartment in the Temple courts, he himself (Nehemiah) was "*not* at Jerusalem," but away on recall to the Persian emperor. Now Eliashib's treachery during Nehemiah's absence is introduced by the words, "And *before this . . .*" (xiii. 4), which means that it was before the incident recorded in verses 1–3, in which the people rediscovered what the Law of Moses had said about the Ammonite and the Moabite (Tobiah was an Ammonite, remember: see ii. 10). But then *this* incident itself begins with the words, "*On that day . . .*" (xiii. 1), which means that it coincided with the restoration of the temple services, described just before it (xii. 44–7); and we know from chapter xii. 44 that this *coincided with the dedication of the walls*. This means that Nehemiah's absence and Eliashib's treachery *preceded* the three incidents which are related before them, *including the dedication of the wall*; and as Nehemiah's brief absence occurred twelve years after his first coming to Jerusalem as wall-builder (compare ii. 1 with xiii. 6), it means that *the dedication of the wall was about twelve years after the completion of the rebuilding*.

What struggles Nehemiah had known before he saw those walls rebuilt! And what struggles he afterwards had before he gained the reward of seeing a spiritually revived people gratefully dedicating those walls to God! Truly, there is no triumph without travail. The only service which really tells is that which really costs. There seems to be a cross in the way to every crown worth wearing!

The dedication of the walls was performed with all due pomp and circumstance, with full religious ceremony and solemnity; and the people seem to have entered into it with zest and reverence. The ceremony took a three-fold course: first there were two processions of singers who chanted praises to God; second, the reading of the Law; and thirdly the separation of the mixed multitude from the true Israel. It must have been a heart-gladdening day indeed for Nehemiah and Ezra. As the dedication (xii. 27–47) really *followed* in point of time, the happenings recorded in chapter xiii., it is really the climax of the book. It is a lovely climax too: "That day they offered great sacrifices, and rejoiced; *so that the joy of Jerusalem was heard even afar off*" (xii. 43).

Last glimpses of Nehemiah (xiii.).

Glance again at chapter xiii. See how quickly evil compromises had devoloped during Nehemiah's short absence from Jerusalem; and see how firmly he attacked these on his return. (By the way, there is further corroboration that this thirteenth chapter really precedes chapter xii. in point of time, inasmuch as the treacherous high priest Eliashib, who here consorts with Tobiah, is never once mentioned in chapter xii., in the account of the dedication of the walls. Understandably he was in disfavour.)

In this thirteenth chapter we see Nehemiah's zeal for God enduring strong to the end. He returns to Jerusalem, and immediately fights the new outbreak of evils. He will not tolerate for one minute longer the intrusion of Tobiah's "household stuff" where the sacred vessels belong (verses 4–9). He will not tolerate self-indulgence at the expense of the service of God (verses 10–14). He will not tolerate dishonour to the Sabbath day, business being put before religion (verses 15–22). He will not tolerate the breaking down of Israel's separatedness through intermarriage (verses 23–8).

There are touches of grim humour in some of the drastic measures taken by this man of flashing eye and godly indignation. He never lets time slip away while he ponders whether a course of action is "usual" or dignified. He has the firm hand and confident stride of one whose purpose and conscience are absolutely honest before God. Such men never hesitate in dealing with sin.

Promptness and firmness are more than diplomacy! We cannot resist a smile as we see Nehemiah actually throwing Tobiah's household furniture out-of-doors (verse 8), or "smiting" and "plucking off the hair" of those Jews who had married wives outside of Israel (verse 25), or, "chasing" the young Jew who had become son-in-law to Sanballat (verse 28). Yet all this must have cost Nehemiah much. Indeed his ejaculatory prayers, three of which occur in these paragraphs, show us plainly enough how keenly he felt all these things in his own spirit.

Summary of Nehemiah as governor.

See how really great this man was. Cast the eye back over these chapters, and gather out the various reforms effected by him They make an impressive aggregate.

1. Augmentation of population of Jerusalem (xi. 1).
2. Redemption of Jews sold into slavery among heathen (v. 8).
3. Abolition of borrowing on mortgage and of money-raising by selling children (v.).
4. Strict Sabbath observance restored, also the Sabbatical year (x. 31; xiii. 15–22).
5. Annual levy of one-third shekel instituted toward temple services and fabric (x. 32).
6. System of wood-supply introduced for temple sacrifices (x. 34).
7. Profanations of temple rectified and interdicted (xiii. 4–9).
8. Re-enforcement of tithe payment (x. 37; xiii. 10–13).
9. Divorce of all foreign wives and re-effecting of national separation (xiii. 1–3; 23–8).
10. Various others such as regulations regarding city gates, etc. (xiii. 19–22).

Oh, Nehemiah is a grand example to us all, but especially to all public Christian workers and leaders. His clear-seeing and plain-speaking and brave-dealing, and his God-honouring motive throughout, are both a challenge and an inspiration. For we cannot forget that all his efforts to effect the various reforms just mentioned were resisted by an influential group among the

priests and nobles who were bent on secularism, were addicted
to inter-marriage with the surrounding Gentile peoples, and in
fact were quite willing for fusion with those other peoples. Any
ordinary man might have quailed at opposing the will of such a
strong party, upheld as it was by the high priest himself, and
supported by neighbouring princes. Yet Nehemiah resolutely
set himself to "contend with the rulers" (xiii. 11) and "the nobles"
(verse 17) on these urgent and sensitive issues; and he adorns
with an abiding lustre the great truth that one consecrated man
and God are more than a match for all the powers and subterfuges
of evil.

There are many lessons running through this Book of Nehemiah,
which we cannot stay to point out here; but we would call special
attention to *Nehemiah's ejaculatory prayers*. There are eight of
them (ii. 4; iv. 4, 5; iv. 9; v. 19; vi. 14; xiii. 14; xiii. 22; xiii. 29).
Undoubtedly, in this habit of ejaculatory prayer we have a
principal key to the fine temper and sanctified drive and God-
glorifying exploits of one of Israel's greatest figures. Nehemiah's
ejaculatory prayers presuppose three things—first that God is
sovereign every minute; second that God is *present* in every place;
third that God *really hears and answers each sudden call*.

Oh, it is a great thing to cultivate the habit of ejaculatory prayer
to this wonderful "God of heaven" (ii. 4) whose will is sovereign
over emperors and kingdoms, whose presence is ever with us in
every place, and who hears instantaneously every SOS of the
soul, every whisper of adoration, every sigh for holiness, every
cry for help, every appeal for strength, every prayer for guidance,
every secret utterance of the heart! Every day we ought to be
in touch with Him again and again by this wonderful "communic-
ation-cord" of ejaculatory prayer. It will keep us calm and steady.
It will keep us patient and cheerful. It will keep our minds on
a high level. It will enrich and sanctify us. It will bring a thousand
streams of blessing into our lives from the hills of God.

Just a parting word. We have shown that this Book of Nehemiah is in two parts—

> The rebuilding of the wall (i.–vi.).
> The reforming of the people (vii.–xiii.).

There is a climax to each part. The climax in part one is the
completion of the wall—"So the wall was finished." The climax

in part two is the *dedication* of the wall—at which "the joy of Jerusalem was heard even afar off." The signs of our times are that the return of Nehemiah's heavenly Antitype is rapidly nearing. Then will be the climax of all climaxes. The walls of Zion shall be built up for ever, and "the joy of Jerusalem" shall again be "heard even afar off"!

THE BOOK OF ESTHER (1)
Lesson Number 48

NOTE.—For this study read the whole Book of Esther through twice or three times.

There is no situation in human life or experience for which a message of God cannot be found through the Book. I do not care whether it be a personal, social, national, or international situation. And about the future, this Book has no hesitation. There is much it does not reveal, but the reality of it is insisted upon from beginning to end. The great fundamental things that we need to know in this preparatory life are all here in this Book.

—*G. Campbell Morgan.*

THE BOOK OF ESTHER (1)

THE THREE little books of Ezra, Nehemiah and Esther record God's dealings with the Jews after their going through the predicted seventy years of their servitude to Babylon: but while Ezra and Nehemiah deal with the remnant of the people which returned to Judæa, the book of Esther is concerned with those— the far greater number—who stayed on in the land of their captivity.

Esther is a *crisis* book. It is a drama—not of fiction, however, but of genuine fact. It is set on the stage of real history, and gathers round actual personages. Five figures move before us— Ahasuerus, the Persian monarch; Vashti, the deposed queen; Haman, the Jew-hater; Mordecai, the Jewish leader; and Esther, the Jewish girl who became queen. In the background are the royal palace, the Persian capital, and the several millions of Jews scattered throughout the emperor's domains.

Esther is the *crucial* figure in the drama inasmuch as everything turns upon her elevation to the throne and her influence as queen. The book, therefore, is fittingly called after the name of Esther. It describes events which took place at Susa, the principal Persian capital, and covers a period of some twelve years.

A Drama of Providence

The *purpose* of the book is to demonstrate the providential care of God over His people. It is vital to see this, for herein lies the living significance and permanent value of the book. The great thing here is the fact of *providential preservation*—"providential" as distinct from what we call the "miraculous." We are meant to see providential *overruling* as distinct from supernatural *intervening*.

That word "providence" comes from the Latin *provideo*, which means that I see a thing beforehand (*pro* = before; *video* = I see); so that the root meaning of providence is foresight. Inasmuch, however, as foresight always occasions *activity* in relation to that which is foreseen, providence comes to have the acquired meaning

of *activity arising from foresight*. Strictly speaking, there is only
One who has foresight, and He alone, therefore, is able to act
on the basis of foreknowledge. Providence, then, in its one absolute
sense, is the Divine foreknowledge and the Divine activity which
arises therefrom; and such providence implies that God wields
absolute power over all the works of His hands.

Providence Demonstrated

It is this which we see demonstrated in the Book of Esther.
The crisis about which the book is written is providentially anticipated and then providentially overruled just at the crucial
moment. No miraculous intervention is resorted to. All the
happenings recorded are the outworking of circumstances in their
natural sequence. Yet while there is no miracle recorded, the
whole thing, in its ultimate meaning, is a mighty miracle—the
mighty miracle whereby a sovereign Deity so manipulates all
non-miraculous events as to bring about a predetermined outcome; and this miracle is all the more miraculous just because
it achieves the predetermined outcome without the *need* for using
miracles! Truly, this mysterious reality which we call providence, this sovereign manipulation of all the ordinary, non-miraculous doings which make up the ordinary ongoing of human
affairs, so as to bring about, by natural processes, those results
which are Divinely predetermined, is the mightiest of all miracles;
and it is this, we repeat, which is strikingly demonstrated in this
Book of Esther.

The non-mention of God

It is this which explains why the name of God does not occur
in the Book of Esther. This non-mention of God in the story
has been a problem to many. Martin Luther, in one of his
occasional lapses of self-restraint, went so far as to say that he
wished the book did not exist! Others have contested its right
to a place in the canon. Yet surely to find a problem in this
non-mention of God is to miss that which above all else we are
intended to see! We say it reverently, yet none the less unhesi-
tatingly, that if God had been specifically mentioned in the story,
or, still more, if the story had specifically *explained*, in so many
words, that it was God who was bringing about all those happenings which are recorded, the dramatic force and moral impact of
the story would have been reduced; for, above all, we are meant

to see, in the natural outworking of events, how, without violating human free will, and without interrupting the ordinary ongoing of human affairs, a hidden Power unsuspectedly but infallibly controls all things. There may have been other reasons why the anonymous author omitted any direct reference to God, as, for instance, that the book was intended for Persians as well as Jews; and there may also be, as some have suggested, the deeper reason that inasmuch as the Jews were away from their own land, following the rupture in their special relationship with God, the name of Jehovah is avoided as being in keeping with this broken relationship: but we believe one main reason to be that which we have given, namely, the emphasising of God's invisible activity in providence.

As a matter of fact the name of God *does* occur in this Book of Esther, in a most remarkable way. The name "Jehovah" is secretly hidden four times in an acrostic form, and the name Ehyeh ("I am that I am") once. In several ancient manuscripts the acrostic consonants which represent the name are written larger, to make them stand out, as though we might write it in English thus—*JeHoVaH*. There are no other acrostics in the book, so that the intentionalness of these five is clear. The five places where the acrostics occur are i. 20; v. 4; v. 13; vii. 7; vii. 5.

In the four acrostics which form the name of Jehovah, the four words forming the J H V H are in each case consecutive. Each of the four is spoken by a different person. In the first two cases the acrostic is formed by the *initial* letters of the words. In the other two it is formed by the *final* letters of the words. In the first and third acrostics, the letters spell the name *backwards* and the speakers are *Gentiles*. In the second and fourth, the letters spell the name *forwards* and the speakers are *Hebrews*. There are other points of interest, also, which we need not stay to mention here. The point we now make is that the name of Jehovah is actually here, in the Book of Esther, in this secret form—as though the anonymous author would anticipate any who might stumble at his non-mention of God in the story. The writer says to us, in effect: "Lest you should think that God is left out of consideration, see the recognition of Him in these five acrostics, which, being themselves secretly hidden in the writing, are symbolic of God's secret working throughout the story." Yes, God *is* in this Book of Esther, not in so many syllables, but in events; not in miraculous interventions, but as guiding the wheels of providence; not in open communication, but as the unseen Power overruling all.

Who was Ahasuerus?

Who was this king Ahasuerus? We ought to ask this before we go further. Can we regard him as a real historical figure? In the opening verse of the book he is said to have reigned over an empire of a hundred and twenty-seven provinces stretching from India to Ethiopia. Until quite recent times his identity has remained puzzlingly obscure; but now, thanks to diggers and decipherers, the mystery is cleared up, and Ahasuerus is definitely identified. He is known to us in history outside the Bible as Xerxes, which is the Greek form of his Persian name. This Xerxes reigned over the Persian empire from 485 to 465 B.C.

The laurel for the first identifying of Ahasuerus as Xerxes goes to Georg Friedrich Grotefend, who, when he was a young student at the University of Göttingen, set himself patiently to decipher the curious, wedge-shaped Persian characters which had been found on inscriptions among the ruins of the ancient Persian city of Persepolis. The name of the son of Darius was deciphered as *Khshayarsha*, which, when translated into Greek, is *Xerxes*, and which, when translated into Hebrew, is, practically letter for letter, *Akhashverosh*, that is, in English, *Ahasuerus*. As soon as the name was read in Persian, the identity of Ahasuerus was settled; and later findings have corroborated Grotefend.

What then of Xerxes? This is the king who ordered a bridge to be built over the Hellespont, and who, on learning that the bridge had been destroyed by a tempest, just after its completion, was so blindly enraged that he commanded three hundred strokes of the scourge to be inflicted on the sea, and a pair of fetters to be thrown into it at the Hellespont, and then had the unhappy builders of the bridge beheaded. This is the king who, on being offered a sum equivalent to five and a half millions sterling by Pythius, the Lydian, towards the expenses of a military expedition, was so enraptured at such loyalty that he returned the money, accompanied by a handsome present; and then, on being requested by this same Pythius, shortly afterwards, to spare him just one of his sons—the eldest—from the expedition, as the sole support of his declining years, furiously ordered the son to be cut into two pieces, and the army to march between them. This is the king who dishonoured the remains of the heroic Spartan, Leonidas. This is the king who drowned the humiliation of his inglorious defeat in such a plunge of sensuality that he publicly offered a prize for the invention of some new indulgence. This is the king who cut a canal through the Isthmus of Athos for his fleet—a prodigious undertaking. This is the king whose vast resources, and gigantic notions and imperious temper made the name of Persia to awe the ancient world. Herodotus tells us that among the myriads gathered for the expedition against Greece, Ahasuerus was the fairest in personal beauty and stately bearing. But morally he was a mixture of passionate extremes. He is just the despot to dethrone queen Vashti for refusing to expose herself before his tipsy guests. He is just the one to consign a people like the Jews to be massacred, and then to swing over to the opposite extreme of sanctioning Jewish vengeance on thousands of his other subjects.

Two Main Movements

Look now at the story itself. In our English Version it is given in ten short chapters. As we read through these chapters we cannot fail to see that in the first five chapters everything is leading up to the crisis-point in the drama. Events move quickly toward the threatened disaster, until, at the end of chapter v., the very gallows are prepared for Mordecai, and it seems as though nothing can avert the impending tragedy. Then, with chapter vi., there comes a sudden turn in the story. The crisis has been providentially anticipated, and is now overruled. The tables are turned. God's people are both saved and avenged. Threatened tragedy gives place to triumph and blessing. The black clouds break apart; the sun bursts through; the earth is green again; and there is a song of prosperity.

We note, then, that this drama of providential preservation is in two main movements. In chapters i. to v. we have *crisis anticipated*, while in chapters vi. to x. we have *crisis overruled*. Thus we see, in this historic episode, that union of Divine *pre*-vision and *pro*vision which constitutes providence. We see, also, that this Book of Esther fills a unique and necessary place in the canon of the inspired Scriptures, as being distinctively *the book of providential preservation*. We see, still further, the central spiritual message of the book, namely, that amid the shadows God stands, keeping watch upon His own. He sees and knows and cares for His own. He may be out of their sight: but *they* are never out of *His* sight. "He that keepeth Israel shall neither slumber nor sleep." He may be invisible, but He is infallible. He may seem strangely silent, but He remains actively sovereign. He may be unsuspected; yet omnisciently, omnipresently, omnipotently, He guides and guards. Evil may be temporarily permitted, but ultimately it is frustrated. Behind a frowning providence God hides a smiling face. We may now set all this out in the following analysis.

THE BOOK OF ESTHER
THE BOOK OF PROVIDENTIAL PRESERVATION

GOD IN THE SHADOWS WATCHES HIS OWN	
CRISIS ANTICIPATED (i.–v.)	CRISIS OVERRULED (vi.–x.)
QUEEN VASHTI DEPOSED (i.)	MORDECAI IS HONOURED (vi.)
ESTHER BECOMES QUEEN (ii.)	HAMAN IS EXECUTED (vii.)
HAMAN PLOTS MASSACRE (iii.)	THE JEWS ARE AVENGED (viii.)
MORDECAI PLEADS HELP (iv.)	PURIM IS INSTITUTED (ix.)
ESTHER CONTRIVES AID (v.)	MORDECAI MADE PREMIER (x.)

Whatever else we may see in chapters i. to v., we miss their supreme significance if we fail to see in them a most remarkable providential predisposing of all contributory factors in anticipation of a foreseen crisis. The feast of Ahasuerus to his lords and satraps, his inebriate jollity and indecent request, Vashti's valorous refusal and her dethronement—these things seemed far from having any connection whatever with the as-yet-undreamed-of peril to the Jews which was to head up through the anti-Jewish hatred of Haman, who at this time had not even risen to public eminence. Yet these things were being so overruled as to subserve the unsuspected Divine preparation for that which was to come later. Indeed, the crisis had been anticipated years before ever Ahasuerus's feast-making took place, in the bestowment of an extraordinary feminine beauty upon Mordecai's cousin; and now, as a result of the vacancy created by Vashti's deposal, the matchless Esther is elected to be queen, so that she is in the place of influence when the critical moment comes, to avert the seemingly inescapable disaster, and to turn the tables on Israel's wicked enemies.

Oh, this wonderful fore-planning of providence! It is here brought vividly out to view so that through our seeing it thus clearly demonstrated in this one notable episode we may believe in the fact of its operation through *all* the vicissitudes of our life, and through all the history of the human race, and especially in those trying times when rampant evil seems to have snatched the reins of government from higher control.

THE BOOK OF ESTHER (2)

Lesson Number 49

NOTE.—For this further study in the Book of Esther read again chapters vi to x.

Higher criticism is not an evil thing in itself. It is the discussion of dates and authorship. Of course, when the method adopted is that of rationalism and naturalism, it becomes destructive and pernicious. When Jesus attributed the 110th Psalm to David, He was in the realm of higher criticism. It is perfectly proper to discuss dates and authors, but one may spend one's whole life trying to find out how many men wrote Isaiah, who was the author of the Pentateuch, or who wrote the letter to the Hebrews, without ever studying the Bible.

—*G. Campbell Morgan.*

THE BOOK OF ESTHER (2)

NOTES ON THE STORY

LONG-CONTINUING royal banquets on an enormous scale like that which is described in this first chapter of Esther were not uncommon among the Persians. References in ancient Greek authors leave us in no doubt about this. Royal state seems to have reached its highest splendours in the great Persian empire; and sumptuous banquets were a prominent feature in the life of the Persian court. Such a lavish feast and display as here described would be much to the taste of the vainglorious and ostentatious Ahasuerus.

The occasion of this huge festal gathering is now known, almost with certainty, to have been the summoning together of all the chief men of the kingdom, and especially of the satraps, or "princes of the provinces," to deliberate upon the contemplated expedition against Greece.

The king's order that Vashti (Vashti means "beautiful woman") should come and immodestly display herself before a vast company of half-intoxicated revellers was not only a gross breach of Persian etiquette, but a cruel outrage which would have disgraced for life the one whom, above all other, the king should have protected. Vashti's refusal was courageous and fully justified: though we can well understand that such a public rebuff to one who was an absolute monarch, and vainglorious in the extreme, must have been as humiliating and exasperating as it was richly deserved.

Without doubt, it would have a suddenly sobering effect upon the emperor and the high lords of the realm. Nor is it surprising that when the king's high council of wise men came to consider the matter, they concluded that Vashti must forfeit her royal diadem.

About four years slip away (compare i. 3, 4, with ii. 12 and 16) between the end of chapter i. and Esther's being elected queen —which is the principal happening recorded in the second chapter. During this time Ahasuerus has undertaken his expedition against Greece, and has returned ingloriously frustrated. Maybe he is the more disposed through this to turn his mind from uneasy war thoughts to the pleasures of the seraglio.

Esther, the Jewish orphan girl, daughter of the deceased Abihail, and cousin of Mordecai, is now selected to become queen. Verses 7, 9, 15, leave us in no doubt that Esther must have been a most beautiful young woman. Verses 9 and 15 also suggest a winsome nature. The process by which choice was made was in full accord with Persian and Oriental custom. Esther's Hebrew name was Hadassah, which means *myrtle*, while the Persian name Esther, which was given to her, means a *star*. Jewish, tradition says that Mordecai tried to hide Esther so that she should not be taken by the royal agents. Mordecai also instructed her not to make her Jewish parentage known (ii. 10), presumably lest it should occasion prejudice or intrigue against her. That such prejudice could have been aroused by her Jewish parentage is shown by chapter iii. 4.

Mordecai himself was evidently employed in the service of the royal court, for in chapter ii. 5, where he is first mentioned, we are told that he was resident in "Shushan the Palace" (not just in the city, which was quite separate from the palace, as archæologists have now clearly shown). No one who was not connected with the royal service would have been permitted to reside within those jealously guarded precincts. In chapter ii. 19, 21 we see him fulfilling a regular duty at "the king's gate," and in chapter iii. 2 we see him counted among "the king's servants" which served at the gate. In chapter vi. 10 we see that the king himself knew him as "Mordecai the Jew, that sitteth at the king's gate." Had not Mordecai been there on royal service, the palace guards would have summarily dispatched him on his refusing to obey the decree regarding Haman.

Haman

Another five years have passed by the time we reach the middle of the third chapter (see verse 7). A new character, Haman, appears on the scene. This man, Haman, has so risen in the king's favour as to have become grand vizier of the realm. The king has even commanded that every knee shall bow to him. But while others bow the knee there is one who refuses, even "Mordecai the Jew." Unlike the Persians, who, according to Plutarch, regarded their king as the very image of God, Mordecai will not yield to any man the reverence which belongs alone to the one true God in whom he believes, any more than Daniel would pay Divine homage to king Darius. Haman's fury at this results in the decree for the slaughtering of all the Jews in the Persian empire, on the thirteenth day of the twelfth month.

From the fact that Haman is actually designated "*The enemy of the Jews*" (viii. 1; ix. 10, 24), and from his words to the king about the Jews as a *race*, and from the fact that it was when he had learned Mordecai's Jewish nationality that he decided to make his revenge the occasion for a general anti-Jewish massacre, we infer that Haman was a hater of the Jews before ever Mordecai's refusal of homage had stung his pride.

The light and careless way in which Ahasuerus handed away to Haman the lives of tens of thousands of his industrious and useful subjects is deservedly branded as "perhaps the most shocking example of oriental despotism on record." It ranks with the recent callous announcement of Nazi Hitler, that he was prepared to sacrifice the lives of a million Germans to invade England. Conscience and common sense alike protest the wrongness of such wide power being in the hands of any one man. A really sound and good man will refuse to bear such a responsibility singly. A bad man can only abuse it. Democracy may be beset with many complex difficulties, but it is immeasurably preferable to despotism or dictatorship. Such was the fatuous conceit of Ahasuerus that besides heartlessly handing over an unknown number of men, women and children to cold-blooded murder, he actually made a present to Haman of the ten thousand talents of silver which Haman had offered to pay into the royal treasury, to compensate the emperor financially for the destruction of the Jews (iii. 11)! Even when Haman's real motives were later exposed by Esther, and the king's anger burned against his guilty favourite, the anger was not because Haman had been deceiving him into the committing of a savage crime, but because the crime concerned the people *to which the queen belonged*! (vii. 5).

The awful decree for the annihilation of the Jews was duly promulgated (iii. 12–15). Chapter iv. records the grief and mourning of Mordecai and the Jews, Mordecai's appeal to Esther, by Hatach, one of the king's chamberlains, and Esther's courageous decision to risk her life in an appeal to the king. The risk arose from the awing Persian law that whoever entered unbidden into the king's inner court paid the death penalty (iv. 11). At the time, Esther had not been called in for a whole month (iv. 11), which possibly indicated a cooled regard towards her; so that the risk which she would run in intruding was a very real one. But she resolved to take the risk, saying: "If I perish, I perish" (iv. 16).

At this point in the story the implicit recognition of God is unmistakable. Mordecai's urgent words: "Who knoweth whether thou art come to the kingdom for such a time as this?" are really the key to the whole episode, and reveal his sudden perception of the providential anticipation underlying Esther's strange exaltation to the throne. Moreover, his words, "If thou altogether holdest thy peace at this time, then shall there enlargement and deliverance arise to the Jews from another place," reveal his unshakable faith in Jehovah, and in the indestructibility of His people. Esther's appeal to Mordecai for a three days' fast for her among the Jews is really a plea for prayer, and a casting of herself on the mercy of God in the matter; for, in the Old Testament, fasting is a symbolic form of prayer.

On the third day Esther enters the inner court, and stands opposite the gate of the king's throne-room so as to attract his notice. The king is sitting on his throne at the time, looking down the pillared vista and through the open door, where he beholds, with some surprise, the graceful figure of his young and beautiful wife. His immediately extended sceptre assures Esther that any breach of etiquette is excused. Then the king, realising that only some grave concern could have brought Esther thus, generously reassures her with the words: "What wilt thou, queen Esther? It shall be even given thee to the half of the kingdom." Esther asks that the king and Haman should come to a banquet for them later that day.

By such a banquet as she knew the king loved, she would make the more sure of his favour, and at the same time ensure the presence of Haman himself when she exposed his wicked plot. Haman would thus be tongue-tied. He would not be able to deny the truth of the accusation, nor would he dare to contradict the queen in the very presence of the king, nor would he get any opportunity of misrepresenting the matter to the king in the queen's absence. When the feast took place, however, Esther apparently did not think the most advantageous moment had

come, but she promised to make her request certainly known at
a further banquet on the following day.

There was a higher Mind than Esther's at work in this post-
ponement, however. During that day the gloating Haman caused
the gallows to be prepared for Mordecai; and during that night
the sleepless king determined that the same Mordecai should be
exalted before all the people! The crucial moment had been
prepared for Esther to speak.

The Turning Point

With the opening of the sixth chapter comes the sudden new
turn of events. The crisis which has been providentially anticipated is now amazingly overruled. With consummate skill, He
that sitteth in the heavens turns the tables on the wicked, and
delivers His own people. A few master strokes, and the whole
situation is revolutionised. The dramatic irony of the new
developments which now rapidly succeed each other leaves us
exclaiming, "Truth is stranger than fiction!"

The king cannot sleep. The night drags. He calls for the
chronicles to be read to him. He hears how a plot against his
own life was foiled through the timely action of Mordecai, and is
surprised to find that Mordecai has not been rewarded. He
resolves that Mordecai shall be rewarded without delay. The night
is now wearing into early morning. He asks who is in the court,
and learns that Haman is there (for Haman had come for the
earliest possible interview with the king, to obtain sanction for
the hanging of Mordecai). The king asks Haman: "What shall
be done unto the man whom the king delighteth to honour?"
Haman, headily presuming that he himself is the man in the king's
mind, and that he is the prospective candidate for still further
preferments, swells with self-congratulation, and then makes
the following glamorous proposal: "Let the royal apparel be
brought which the king useth to wear, and the horse that the
king rideth upon, and the crown royal which is set upon his head;
and let this apparel and horse be delivered to the hand of one of
the king's most noble princes, that they may array the man withal
whom the king delighteth to honour, and bring him on horseback
through the street of the city, and proclaim before him: Thus
shall it be done to the man whom the king delighteth to honour!"
Haman's proposal lays bear his unbounded conceit, his sickly

thirst for the praise of men, and his paltry idea of greatness. His pulse throbs the more quickly as he imagines himself being thus publicly borne aloft amid the adulations of his fellows. Then he hears the king say: "Make haste, and take the apparel and the horse, as thou hast said, and do even so—*to Mordecai the Jew*"! What!—do this to Mordecai the Jew! Are Haman's ears mocking him? No; it is real enough: the king has spoken, and must be obeyed! The subtle gleam pales from Haman's eyes. The swollen bubble of his pride suddenly bursts. A sickening pall turns his heart cold. For a few age-long seconds he stands, dumbfounded, before his royal master; then he slowly withdraws, with leaden footsteps, to exalt Mordecai in the very way which he, Haman himself, had so stupidly proposed. "He that sitteth in the heavens shall laugh. The Lord shall have them in derision." The utter irony of it! Haman, through his own stupid conceit, has tripped himself into publicly exalting and parading the very man for whose death-warrant he had come to apply, and for whom he had already presumed to prepare the gallows!

Haman's Doom

Chapter vii. tells of Esther's second banquet to the king and Haman. It is a much changed Haman who now sits uneasily at the royal board. His mind is the more disturbed because his "wise men" and his wife Zeresh have said to him: "If Mordecai be of the seed of the Jews, before whom thou hast begun to fall, thou shalt not prevail against him, but shalt surely fall before him" (vi. 13). Yet Haman little guesses how suddenly he is now to be precipitated to his miserable end. In the king's sleepless night, and the exaltation of Mordecai, and the chagrin of Haman, and the now obvious good will of the king, Esther recognises the control of a higher Power, and knows that the moment to speak has come. The king again asks what her special request is, and is amazed to learn that it is a plea *for her life to be spared*—"O king, if it please the king, let my life be given me at my petition, and my people at my request: for we are sold, I and my people, to be destroyed, to be slain, and to perish." The astonished Ahasuerus looks on the lovely face and form of his wife, who is now deeply wrought with emotion, and exclaims: "Who is he, and where is he, that durst presume in his heart to do so?"— to which Esther replies: "The adversary and enemy is this wicked

Haman." Then, in a flash the king sees through Haman's hypocrisy. Rising from the banquet, the king strides agitatedly into
the palace garden. Haman, in a frenzy of cowardly terror, over-
steps the bounds of etiquette, and falls upon Esther's couch,
pleading with her to spare his life. The king re-enters to find him
thus; and, either in reality or in sarcastic pretence, misconstruing
Haman's action as implying immoral motive, speaks words which
immediately cause the attendants to remove Haman, with his
face covered—the covering of the face being a Persian custom
to indicate that a person was no longer fit to see the light. Without
delay, Haman is sent to his doom. Before another sunrise sheds
its light over Shushan, the corpse of Haman dangles fifty cubits
aloft, on the very gallows which he himself had caused to be made
for Mordecai.

Lest it should be thought incredible that the gallows would
be so high ("fifty cubits"—about seventy-five feet), we would
mention that the Hebrew word translated as "gallows" means
a tree. The tree which Haman had selected was in the grounds
of his own house (vii. 9); and it was here that, with awful irony,
he was made to swing before the horrified gaze of his own family!

THE BOOK OF ESTHER (3)
Lesson Number 50

NOTE.—For this final study in this Book of Esther read again right through the whole book, asking: "Do the figures and incidents in this story suggest or seem to parallel with spiritual or prophetic truths elsewhere enunciated in Scripture?"

I was never out of my Bible.—*John Bunyan.*

I am a man of one Book.—*John Wesley.*

That Bible on the table is a book to you. It is far more than a book to me. It speaks to me; it is as it were a person.

—*Napoleon Bonaparte.*

If we abide by the principles taught in the Bible, our country will go on prospering; but if we and our posterity neglect its instructions and authority, no man can tell how sudden a catastrophe may overwhelm us and bury all our glory in profound obscurity.

—*Daniel Webster.*

THE BOOK OF ESTHER (3)

LATENT TYPE-TEACHING

THIS Book of Esther, besides being of high interest historically, seems to contain latent *type-teachings* which ought not to escape our notice.

The Persian Jews

First of all, and without doubt, *the Persion Jews as a whole* are here used as a type of *the worldly among the Lord's people.*

We have already referred to the non-mention of God in the story. The more we ponder it, the more remarkable does this resolute non-reference to God or to anything religious become; and the more definitely do we see it to have been *intentional* on the part of the writer, for some special reason.

Can we really believe that in a crisis which threatened death to every Jew in the Persian empire there was no agonised calling upon the God of their fathers? Can we believe, too, that after the amazing deliverance which came to them there was absolutely no voice of thanksgiving to God?

No; never could there have been more heart-wrung prayer. Never could there have been more fervent praise. Why then is there absolutely no word of this? Is it due to the author's spiritual blindness or to an unpardonable forgetfulness? If so, how shall we account for the fact that such a stupid, blameworthy book should have been given a revered place in the Hebrew canon? If, on the other hand, the non-mention of God was *not* due to spiritual blindness or godless forgetfulness, there is only one possible inference—*the silence was intentional.*

Why, then, this intentional silence? I think we are not left in doubt. More than fifty years before this Esther episode, the Persian emperor, Cyrus, had made the proclamation which permitted and exhorted all Jews to return to Judæa, as reported in the Book of Ezra (i. 2–4).

Now Ezra is careful to say that this proclamation of Cyrus was in fulfilment of Jeremiah's prophecy which had been made

before ever the captivity of the Jews had begun. The seventy
years of captivity had been forefixed (Jer. xxix. 10, etc. See also
xxv. 11, 12). Moreover, the prophet Isaiah had actually spoken
of Cyrus by name, as the coming restorer of Jerusalem, before
ever Cyrus was born (Isa. xliv. 28, etc.).

Here, then, was the voice of Jehovah to His people throughout
the Persian empire. Here was the Divine recall of the Jews to
Jerusalem and Judæa. There could be no mistaking it. It bore
a supernatural seal. First the release had been predicted; and now
it had been effected. Not a Jew ought to have remained in
Persia. The people, without exception, should have flocked to
Zion with thanksgiving. Yet the unhappy truth is that only a
remnant returned. The rest were content to stay on in Persia.
Of course they were ready to applaud those who were returning,
and to say how splendid it was of them to undertake the rebuilding of Judah's ruined cities and Jehovah's temple; but they
themselves did not find it convenient at the time to break away
from their Persian connections. In truth, they were selfishly
indisposed to leave the plenty of Persia for the leanness of desolated
Judæa, even though that was the place of covenant blessing.
They believed in Jehovah, and acknowledged Him as the one true
God; but their hearts were set on the things of this world.

Undoubtedly these Jews are types of the worldly among the
Lord's people today. They are the figures of those who profess
faith in Christ but who love the world and the flesh too well to
make renunciation for Christ's sake. They want to be numbered
with the redeemed of the Lord; but they also want to enjoy the
pleasures of the world for a season.

And what of these worldly believers, these modern correspon-
dents of the old-time Jews who stayed on in Persia? Well, just
this—God will not allow His name to be bound up with them
any more than He allowed His name to be associated with the
Jews who stayed on in Persia. God watched over those Persia-
loving Jews, and remained faithful to them even though they
had slighted Him. In their trouble they cried to Him, and He
delivered them; but He would not allow His name to be bound
up with them. His deliverance of them, in the Esther episode,
was so recorded that the striking circumstances unmistakably
demonstrated His providential care over them; *yet His name
must not be once mentioned in the account.*

Let the absence of God's name from the Book of Esther burn this truth into our minds: God will not associate His name with the worldly among His professing people today, any more than He would associate it with those old-time Jews in Persia. Through the centuries, God is developing His purpose for the earth's salvation; and, in the end, those who have "come out" from the Babylon of this world, to "be separate" unto Him, will shine as stars in the eternal kingdom: but those who have said "Lord, Lord," without renouncing the world, will not be known in that day. Their record will not shine on high. They may be saved, as by fire, but they will never hear the King of kings say to them: "Come, ye blessed of my Father; inherit the kingdom." Our Lord's promise to the overcomer is: "I will give him a white stone, and in the stone a new name written, which no man knoweth saving him that receiveth it"; but there will be no such "secret of the Lord" for the worldly disciple. The final description of the glorified saints says that the very name of God shall be "written on their foreheads"; but God's name will never be imprinted on those who have loved self and the world in preference to sanctification. It is possible to be saved from Gehenna, the final doom of the lost (as the Jews in Esther's day were saved from massacre) and yet to miss that "eternal weight of glory" which God has prepared for them that love Him with all their heart.

But we may go further. These Persian Jews of Esther's time were also types in a dispensational and prophetic sense. They typically portrayed the history of *the Jewish race as a whole*, right on to the end of the present dispensation, in which fact we see a still more meaningful reason why the name of God is omitted from the book of Esther. This cannot be better expressed than in the following quotation. "These Persian Jews are the types of their fellow-countrymen who were afterwards to reject God's salvation in Christ, and who, scattered among the nations, were again and again to be threatened with destruction. God's name and theirs have not been bound together for nineteen hundred years. God has been working marvellously in these centuries; but those rebellious Jews and He have not been found together. God's temple has been reared, and it is being reared now; but the work is done by other hands than theirs. God's battles have been fought and won; but *their* names have not been inscribed in the glorious story." Yet, on the other hand, "He has watched over His rebellious people, and He watches over them still. Haman may plot their destruction; but he plots against his own life and the lives of all that are dear to him. Let every foe of that apparently God-forsaken people take heed to it: God will avenge the wrong done to His people even though they have despised their heritage." Their unbelief cannot make God forget His word: "I will bless them that bless thee, and curse him that curseth thee" (Gen. xii. 3). Never have the Jews suffered more than they have recently suffered in Nazi Germany and Rumania and other European countries. Germany already curses the day she followed Hitler in his anti-Jewish atrocities; and Hitler himself, like Haman of old, has perished forever on gallows of his own making.

Haman

The wicked *Haman* prefigures "the man of sin" who is predicted to appear, toward the end of the present age, as the last and worst enemy of God's people on earth. Haman is a type of the "man of sin" in six ways.

First, mark his *name*. In chapter vii. 6 Esther brands him as "Haman the wicked"; and it is a singular fact that the numerical value of the Hebrew letters which make up his title is 666, the number of Antichrist (Rev. xiii. 18).

Second, see Haman's *power*. With meteoric rise he outranks all his fellows. The opening verses of chapter iii. tell us that his place was set up above all the princes of the realm, and a royal decree was issued that every knee should bow to him. Thus does he foreshadow the fearsome "beast" of Revelation xiii., which receives its power and eminence from the dragon, and the "little horn" of Daniel vii. 8, which has "the eyes of a man and a mouth speaking great things."

Third, observe Haman's *pride*. Hear him boast his glory and riches to Zeresh, and to his friends (v. 11). See his conceited exasperation when Mordecai withholds obeisance (v. 13). Hear him planning to ride the king's own horse, clad in the royal apparel, wearing the crown royal, and being borne ostentatiously aloft amid the adulations of the people (vi. 7–9). Thus does Haman forepicture that coming "man of sin" who, as Paul says,

"opposeth, and exalteth himself above all that is called God"
(2 Thess. ii. 4).

Fourth, mark Haman's *hate*. Four times over he is designated
as "the enemy of the Jews" (iii. 10; viii. 1; ix. 10, 24). Five
times, also, he is called an "Agagite" (iii. 1, 10; viii. 3, 5; ix. 24).
Modern discovery has shown that Agag was a territory adjacent
to Media; but symbolically interpreted this word "Agagite"
connects Haman with the Agagites mentioned earlier in the
Scriptures. Agag was king of the Amalekites (1 Sam. xv. 8), who
were descended from Esau (Gen. xxxvi. 12). Amalek is always
Israel's enemy (Exod. xvii. 16; Deut. xxv. 17–19). But there
was to come a Star out of Jacob and a Sceptre out of Israel
which should bring destruction to Amalek (Num. xxiv. 17–20);
even as the New Testament says that Christ shall yet smite the
Antichrist (2 Thess. ii. 8). The coming "man of sin" will be the
latter-day Haman. He will be history's supreme Jew-hater.

Fifth, note Haman's *plot*. He makes Mordecai's conscientious
resistance the occasion for a contemplated annihilation of the
whole Jewish race. With specious guile he works toward this
through his political power, so that the Jews are plunged into
great sorrow and suffering (chapters iii. and iv.). So yet will
the coming Antichrist, the evil "prince" of Daniel ix., plunge
the Jews into the "great tribulation" by a political betrayal
(Dan. ix. 26, 27).

Sixth, see Haman's *doom*. While he is in power he is terrible;
but he lasts only a few years (compare ii. 16 with iii. 7); and his
end is as sudden as it is ironic. One day he vaunts himself: the
next day he hangs by his own rope. Moreover, all his progeny
perish with him; for in chapter ix. 7–14, we find that Haman
had ten sons who were hanged along with him.

Just as suddenly and ironically will the coming Antichrist
perish. Weymouth's translation of 2 Thessalonians ii. 8 is: "The
lawless one will be revealed, whom the Lord Jesus will slay with
the breath of His mouth, and overwhelm by the splendour of
His coming." Thus suddenly will the "man of sin" meet his
doom. He who has overcome men by supernatural wonders will
himself be overcome by a bigger wonder still! Moreover, as
Haman had ten sons who perished with him, so the final form
of Gentile government, at the end of the present age, is to be

that of "ten kings" who reign for "one hour" through whom Antichrist works, and who perish along with him (Dan. vii.; Rev. xvii.). Haman, then, is a grimly significant figure!

Esther

We have left ourselves little space to trace out the type meaning of Esther and Mordecai. Esther may be taken as a type of the Church.

First, she is so *in her Jewish antecedents*. She was the daughter of Jewish parents; but her parents were dead. Even so, the Church, considered historically, emerged from Jewish antecedents. The Saviour Himself was a Jew. The Scriptures which prepared the way for the Christian Church were Jewish. The first Christian community was Jewish. Yet, in its very emergence from Judaism, the Church carried with it the sign that its Jewish antecedents were now passed away. The Law was done away in Christ. The Mosaic economy was now dead. As Esther's parents were passed away, so were those Jewish antecedents from which the Church had emerged.

Second, Esther is a type of the Church *in her womanly beauty*. God had given her a beauty which surpassed that of all others. Even so has God given a surpassing beauty to the Church of Christ—even the very beauty of Christ Himself. We become "the righteousness of God in Him." We are "accepted in the Beloved." We are yet to be presented as Christ's bride, "a glorious Church, not having spot or wrinkle, or any such thing" (Eph. v. 27).

Third, Esther typifies the Church *in her exaltation*. She becomes married to one whose title was "King of kings"—and although Ahasuerus, in his personal character, is far from typifying Christ, yet, in his being a "king of kings," he may fitly speak to us of the Church's royal Bridegroom who, indeed, is "*The* King of kings, and Lord of lords."

Fourth, Esther typifies the Church *in her intercession*. Esther went in to the king "on the third day," which speaks symbolically of resurrection, and of interceding in resurrection power. It was against the "law" for Esther thus to go in before the king. The law excluded her; yet she was accepted on the ground of pure grace; for the king beheld her wearing the royal apparel which he himself had given her (v. 1). Even so, we ourselves are excluded by the Law; but we are fully accepted on the ground of free grace when we appear in the royal robes which Christ Himself has given us. It was through Esther's intercession that deliverance came to the Jews. Will it not be through the intercession of the Church's believer-priests that deliverance comes to the Jews in their *final* tribulation? Are not the "golden vials full of incense" said to be "the prayers of the saints"? (Rev. v. 8).

Mordecai

As for *Mordecai*, he may fitly represent to us the faithful Jewish remnant which will be preserved through the great tribulation, to enter the millennial kingdom. We see this in four ways.

First, *in his refusal to bow to Haman*. When the king's servants asked Mordecai: "Why transgressest thou the king's commandment?" he "told them he was a Jew" (iii. 4); so that his refusal was clearly because of his Jewish faith. He would not yield to man that which is due to God alone; even as the faithful Jewish remnant in the final tribulation will not bow to the beast nor receive his mark upon them.

Second, Mordecai typified the Jews of the tribulation period *in his bitter mourning and fasting and weeping*, which becomes shared by thousands of other Jews, and which forepictures that preparation of penitence which will finally lead the Jews to "look upon Him whom they pierced," and own Him as their King.

Third, he typifies the Jewish remnant *in his marvellous deliverance*. As he was delivered so will his brethren of the future be. The seventh chapter of Revelation shows us the sealing of the Jewish remnant before "the wrath of God" is poured upon the earth. They are sealed and saved.

Fourth, Mordecai typifies these *in his wonderful exaltation*. The closing chapter of Esther shows him exalted above all his fellows, made the grand vizier of Persia, and next to the king and queen! Even so, through the faithful remnant will the Jews and Jerusalem take the supreme place among the nations in the coming kingdom of David's greater Son.

This brings us to the end of the seventeen historical books of the Old Testament, and to the end of volume 2 in our course of study.